EMPLOYMENT AND WORK RELATIONS IN CONTEXT SERIES

Series Editors

Tony Elger and Peter Fairbrother

Centre for Comparative Labour Studies

Department of Sociology

University of Warwick

The aim of the *Employment and Work Relations in Context Series* is to address questions relating to the evolving patterns and politics of work, employment, management, and industrial relations. There is a concern to trace out the ways in which wider policy-making, especially by national governments and transnational corporations, impinge upon specific workplaces, occupations, labour markets, localities and regions. This invites attention to developments at an international level, marking out patterns of globalization, state policy and practice in the context of globalization and the impact of these processes on labour. A particular feature of the series is the consideration of forms of worker and citizen organization and mobilization in these circumstances. Thus the studies address major analytical and policy issues through case study and comparative research.

THE GLOBAL ECONOMY, NATIONAL STATES AND THE REGULATION OF LABOUR

Edited by Paul Edwards and Tony Elger

MANSELL

London and New York

First published 1999 by
Mansell Publishing, *A Cassell imprint*
Wellington House, 125 Strand, London WC2R 0BB, England
370 Lexington Avenue, New York, NY 10017–6550, USA

British Library Cataloguing in Publication Data
A catalogue record for this book is available from the British Library.

ISBN 0–7201–2370–4

Library of Congress Cataloging-in-Publication Data
The global economy, national states, and the regulation of labour/edited by
Paul Edwards and Tony Elger.
    p. cm.—(Employment and work relations in context)
    Papers originally presented at a conference. University of Warwick, 1996.
    Includes bibliographical references and index.
    ISBN 0–7201–2370–4
    1. Labor policy—Congresses. 2. Industrial relations—Congresses. 3.
Labor laws and legislation—Congresses. 4. Comparative law—
Congresses. 5. Comparative industrial relations—Congresses. 6.
International trade—Congresses. 7. Foreign trade and employment—
Congresses. I. Edwards, P. K. (Paul K.) II. Elger, Tony. III. Series.
  HD4813.G55 1999
  331—dc21   99–13913
                                                     CIP

Typeset by York House Typographic Ltd
Printed and bound in Great Britain by
Biddles Ltd, Guildford and King's Lynn

CONTENTS

NOTES ON CONTRIBUTORS

Robert Castle, D. P. Chaudhri, Chris Nyland and Trang Nguyen are at the University of Wollongong, New South Wales, Australia. Castle's research interests are in labour and international economics. He is currently studying child labour in Asia, with particular reference to Vietnam. Chaudhri is author of *Dynamic Profile of Child Labour in India 1951–1991* (1996). Nguyen has carried out research on the World Trade Organization.

Chas Critcher, Dave Parry and Dave Waddington have worked together on studies of the British coal industry and its restructuring. This includes joint articles in the *British Journal of Industrial Relations* (June 1997) and *Work, Employment and Society* (June 1998). Critcher is Professor of Cultural Studies at Sheffield Hallam University and was formerly at the Centre for Contemporary Cultural Studies at the University of Birmingham where he co-edited *Working Class Culture* (1979) and other volumes. Parry is Research Officer for the Coalfields Community Campaign. Waddington is Reader in Cultural Studies at Sheffield Hallam University and is author, with Maggie Wykes and Chas Critcher, of *Split at the Seams? Community, Continuity and Change after the 1984–5 Coal Dispute* (1991) and *Trouble Brewing? A Social Psychological Analysis of the Ansells Brewery Dispute* (1987).

Peter Burnham is a Senior Lecturer in the Department of Politics and International Studies at the University of Warwick. His research focuses on the changing role of Britain in the global political economy since 1945 and his main publications include *The Political Economy of Postwar Reconstruction* (1990) and *A Major Crisis? The Politics of Economic Policy in Britain in the 1990s* (with W. Bonefeld and A. Brown) (1995).

Julia O'Connell Davidson is Reader in Sociology at the University of Leicester. She has published widely on contemporary changes in work and employment and on gender and sexuality. She has been involved in research on prostitution and sex tourism since 1993 and recently published *Prostitution, Power and Freedom* (1998). **Jacqueline Sanchez Taylor** is Research Associate in the Department of Sociology, University of Leicester. She has researched and published on sex tourism in Latin America and the Caribbean and is currently working on an ESRC-funded project investigating tourist-related prostitution in Jamaica and the Dominican Republic.

Paul Edwards is Director of the Industrial Relations Research Unit, University of Warwick. Recent research is on new forms of work organization, including teamworking and total quality management. He is editor of *Industrial Relations* (1995) and co-author of *Managers in the Making: Careers, Development and Control in Corporate Britain and Japan* (1997).

Tony Elger works in the Department of Sociology and the Centre for Comparative Labour Studies at the University of Warwick. He has written on labour process theory and work reorganization in manufacturing and is currently involved in research on Japanese manufacturing firms in Britain and Europe. He edited *Global Japanization? The Transnational Transformation of the Labour Process* (with Chris Smith) (1994).

Ian Hampson lectures at the School of Industrial Relations and Organisational Behaviour, University of New South Wales. He has published on post-Fordism, work organization and corporatism. Recent research includes critical management studies and management education policy.

Jamie Peck is Professor of Geography and Director of the International Centre for Labour Studies at Manchester University. He is currently researching the comparative political economy of welfare reform and 'workfare' in Britain, Canada and the United States, and also has research interests in labour-market restructuring, urban politics and regional economic development. Recent publications include *Work-Place: The Social Regulation of Labor Markets* (1996) and *Workfare States* (1999).

Pauli Kettunen is Senior Fellow of the Academy of Finland, Renvall Institute for Area and Cultural Studies at the University of Helsinki. He has published widely in labour history and the history and sociology of industrial relations, including books on the history of social democracy and trade unions, and on labour protection in Finland. He has edited collections in English on *Strikes and Social Change* (1993) and *Models, Modernity and the Myrdals* (1997). His current research concerns the changing meanings of internationality in national working-life institutions in Finland and in the wider Nordic context.

Gillian Whitehouse is a Senior Lecturer in the Department of Government at the University of Queensland, where she teaches industrial relations and political economy. One of her main areas of research and publication concerns the impact of industrial relations systems on employment equity, especially cross-nationally comparative work on this issue, and she is currently extending this work to include analysis of the South East Asian region. **Di Zetlin** is a Lecturer in the Department of Government at the University of Queensland, where she teaches political theory, industrial relations and women's studies. Her research and publications have focused on concepts of citizenship and women's rights, including work on women in parliament and in paid employment, and her current research concerns women in the Australian parliament and employment equity issues in the Asia-Pacific region.

TABLES

ABBREVIATIONS

ACIRRT	Australian Centre for Industrial Relations Research and Training
ACTU	Australian Council of Trade Unions
AGPS	Australian Government Publications Service
ALP	Australian Labor Party
AMWU	Australian Metal Workers' Union
ASEAN	Association of South East Asian Nations
ASF	Australian Standards Framework
AWIRS	Australian Workplace Industrial Relations Survey
AWOTE	Average Weekly Ordinary Time Earnings
BCA	Business Council of Australia
BCE	British Coal Enterprise
CAI	Confederation of Australian Industry
CCLS	Centre for Comparative Labour Studies
CSEC	commercial sexual exploitation of children
DPSS	Department of Public Social Services
DVP	Dearne Valley Partnership
EC	European Community
ECPAT	End Child Prostitution in Asian Tourism
ECSC	European Coal and Steel Community
EEA	European Economic Area
EEC	European Economic Community
EMU	European Monetary Union or Economic and Monetary Union
ENISA	Empresa Nacional de Innovación (Spanish national state-owned innovation company)
EPAC	(Australian) Economic Planning and Advisory Council
ERM	(European) Exchange Rate Mechanism
EU	European Union
FVIU	(Australian) Federation of Vehicle Industry Unions
GAIN	Greater Avenues to Independence program, California
GATT	General Agreement on Tariffs and Trade
GDP	Gross Domestic Product
GLS	Generalised Least Squares

HF-B	Hovedorganisasjonenes Fellestiltak–Debriftsutvikling (Norway's social partners' joint action programme for enterprise development)
HREOC	(Australian) Human Rights and Equal Opportunities Commission
HRM	human resource management
HUNOSA	Hulleras del Norte Sociedad Anónima (Spanish state-owned coal mining enterprise)
IBRD	International Bank for Reconstruction and Development (the official name of the World Bank)
ICFTU	International Confederation of Free Trade Unions
IFR	Instituto de Fomento Regional (Institute for Regional Development, Spain)
IG	Industriegewerkschaft (German Industrial Union)
IIRA	International Industrial Relations Association
ILO	International Labour Office, renamed International Labour Organization (1945)
IMF	International Monetary Fund
INSAF	Indian National Social Action Forum
IPE	international political economy (theoretical approach)
IPEC	ILO's International Programme on the Elimination of Child Labour
IR	industrial relations; international relations (interdisciplinary areas of academic research)
LO	Landsorganisationen i Sverige (Swedish Confederation of Trade Unions); Landsorganisasjonen i Norge (Norwegian Confederation of Trade Unions)
LSDV	Least Squares with Dummy Variables (model)
MDRC	Manpower Demonstration Research Corporation
MITI	(Japan) Ministry of International Trade and Industry
NAECL	(Indian) National Authority on the Elimination of Child Labour
NAFTA	North American Free Trade Area
NBPI	(UK) National Board for Prices and Incomes
NGO	non-governmental organization
NHO	Næringslivets Hovedorganisasjon (Confederation of Norwegian Business and Industry)
NLI	(Indian) National Labour Institute
NTB	(Australian) National Training Board
NUM	(British) National Union of Mineworkers
OECD	Organization for Economic Co-operation and Development

OLS	Ordinary Least Squares
PRO	Public Record Office
PSOE	Partido Socialista Obrero Español (Spanish Socialist Workers' Party)
R&D	research and development
RPL	Recognition of Prior Learning
SAF	Svenska Arbetsgivareföreningen (Swedish Employers' Confederation)
SAYE	El Servicio de Asesoramiento y Promoción Empresarial (Business Assessment and Promotional Service, Spain)
SEP	Structural Efficiency Principle
SERC	(Australian) Senate Economic References Committee
SME	small and medium enterprises
SOU	Statens offentliga utredningar (series of official committee reports in Sweden)
TDC	(Australian) Trade Development Council
TEC	(UK) Training and Enterprise Council
TNC	transnational corporation
TUC	(UK) Trades Union Congress
UNCTAD	United Nations Commission on Trade and Development
UNESCO	United Nations Educational, Scientific and Cultural Organization
UNICEF	United Nations Children's Fund
WTO	World Trade Organization
ZAK	*Zukunftsaktion Kohlgebiete* (German Campaign for the Future of Coal-Mining Areas)

PREFACE

This world to me is like a lasting storm
Whirring me from my friends.
(Shakespeare, *Pericles*, IV, i, 19)

This book and its companion volume *Globalization and Patterns of Labour Resistance*, edited by Jeremy Waddington, intervene in several hotly debated topics. Each has an introductory chapter spelling out in detail its contribution, but some common overall themes should be highlighted. They are best introduced by reference to Burawoy's 'arrow' (Burawoy, 1983). Burawoy argued that debates on the role of the state in economic management and on the regulation of labour at the point of production had become disconnected. Theories of the state were over-politicized in the sense that the state was treated as separate from the underlying political economy and analysed in terms of its largely autonomous politics. Accounts of labour regulation were under-politicized by neglecting the active role of the state in shaping workplace regimes. The concept of the politics of production was the arrow which was pointed at each target and which then integrated the two issues.

In the fifteen years since 1983, research in the politics of production has advanced significantly, with ideas of national regimes of accumulation and even regime shopping becoming commonplace. It has also been greatly extended with the rise, over much the same period, of the concept of globalization. In addition to relationships within nation states, researchers have had to address issues at an international level. Among these issues are the following. First, there is change at the level of the world economy, where some authors detect a move towards a genuinely global and borderless world while others prefer the more limited concept of internationalization. The second is the effect of any such changes on the behaviour of nation states. Third, there is the role of supra-national regulatory bodies. Fourth, what has been the effect of any global or international trend on existing national structures of regulation? Finally, how far are employers, trade unions and workers the hapless subjects of impersonal forces (as illustrated by the motto at the head of this preface) and how far can they resist or at least shape the forces to which they are subject? How far, indeed, are at least some actors, particularly nation states and multinational companies, the active agents of international developments?

The purpose of these two volumes is to bring together some recent theoretical and empirical contributions within the overall objective of the politics of production, that is, to develop connections between international forces, nation states and the regulation of work. These matters are often discussed in separate debates. Changes at the level of the state are debated by political scientists. Students of management have addressed such concepts as lean production and its allegedly global reach. Industrial relations research has addressed the responses of trade unions and the concrete workplace effects of lean production and other models of work organization. And so on. These volumes contribute to the project of linking together such varied themes.

They originated in a conference on 'the globalization of production and the regulation of labour' held at the University of Warwick in 1996. The conference, organized jointly by the Centre for Comparative Labour Studies (CCLS) and the Industrial Relations Research Unit (IRRU), attracted over 150 participants from 24 countries. The organizing committee comprised, in addition to the three editors of these volumes, Peter Fairbrother and Carol Wolkowitz of the CCLS and Judy Wajcman, then on a research secondment to IRRU and now at the Australian National University. We are extremely grateful to our colleagues for their hard work in organizing what proved to be a successful co-operative endeavour, and also to other colleagues, in particular Lesley Williams (IRRU) and Karen Prescott (CCLS) who bore much of the administrative burden. We should also like to thank participants at the conference, in particular our plenary speakers Mitsuo Ishida, Walther Müller-Jentsch, Ruth Milkman and E. A. Ramaswamy.

The themes of the conference were broad, including the management of labour in multinational companies and the effects of 'globalization' on the gender division of labour. Several papers that were presented have been published in journals and other books. The chapters in the present volumes, which have been extensively revised and where relevant updated, draw on papers which best go together to address some themes which are both coherent and relatively under-researched.

Paul Edwards
Tony Elger
Jeremy Waddington

October 1998

1 NATIONAL STATES AND THE REGULATION OF LABOUR IN THE GLOBAL ECONOMY: AN INTRODUCTION

Tony Elger and Paul Edwards

The social regulation of the labour market and industrial relations in capitalist societies has characteristically been organized through the nation state. Now, however, globalization appears to be eroding the power of the state, limiting its capacity to regulate labour relations and in turn reducing the potential leverage of organized labour to influence such regulation. Indeed, some interpretations of contemporary developments, especially those which stress the growing importance of transnational corporations and the integration of world financial markets, suggest that the era of the nation state is ending. In such views, corporations are indeed transnational and global rather than simply being collections of operations in different countries, or multinationals. In common with many contributions to the globalization debate we use the term transnational corporation (TNC) rather than multinational corporation to signal these developments, though we will later register disagreements as to whether the TNC is truly stateless.

The argument of the more radical theorists of globalization is that this is reducing the nation state to an empty shell, hollowed out both from the outside and within. State agencies face constraints on policy options from beyond their borders which flow from the leverage and sanctions exercised by both corporate decision-makers and financial markets, which can thus impose their priorities on the state. Meanwhile central state power is also eroded from within by the growing importance of regional and local initiatives designed to attract and retain investment: if the national state is unresponsive to global pressures, localities are likely to be more responsive. At the same time supra-state forms of regulation are seen as incapable of filling the gap left by the nation state, especially in regard to labour regulation, as they primarily reflect employers' preferences for limited constraints upon their freedom of action, not least in hiring and deploying employees.

The character and implications of 'globalization' are, though, controversial. In particular the extent to which the internationalization of production has been translated into the decoupling of TNCs from their home states has been questioned; the active rather than passive role of at least some states as actors in the reconstruction of the global economy has been emphasized; and the continuing importance of distinctive patterns of national and even regional labour regulation has been documented. This suggests that the scope, character and implications of 'globalization' remain open and contested, and that this is reflected in the practical remaking of regulatory regimes at a national, regional and global level. It is the purpose of this collection to develop a reassessment of key features of this interplay between globalization and national and supra-national forms of labour regulation, and thus to contribute to a growing body of recent work which seeks to grasp the significance of contemporary transformations without resorting to the hyperbole which projects the demise of the state and related forms of labour regulation in the face of stateless global capital.

As explained in the preface, this set of essays and the companion volume complement one another. *Globalization and Labour Resistance*, edited by Jeremy Waddington, examines one feature of the relationship between globalization and labour regulation in particular detail, by exploring both the impact of globalization on organized labour and labour's influence on the dynamic of globalization, primarily from the perspective of the enterprise and the workplace. This tightly focused analysis of a key but under-studied area forms an important counterpoint to the broader range of the present volume, where the implications of globalization for labour's experience of, and activity in relation to, state and supra-state forms of regulation become the central concern.

Academic debate on these latter issues has not only been characterized by persistent contrasts of interpretation between those who emphasize the forward march of globalization and those who are sceptical about the novelty of current developments, but these contrasts can be seen as having distinctive disciplinary roots. Thus on the one hand it is students of international business and analysts of international political economy who have tended to be the most vigorous exponents of globalization as a process which transcends existing regulatory norms, while on the other hand students of industrial relations and economic sociology have tended to emphasize the path-dependent distinctiveness and continuing salience of national and regional forms of labour regulation. Nevertheless current debate is characterized by a growing and fertile interdisciplinarity, and our purpose is to contribute to this. In particular, while most of the contributors to this collection come from disciplines traditionally associated with the analysis and comparison of national forms of regulation they are all seeking to reappraise the interplay between changes in the international economy and the contemporary crises and reconstruction of forms of state and supra-state regulation of labour. At the same time our focus on the significance of employment relations and labour regulation seeks to probe a set of pivotal social relations which are often neglected, or at best hypostasized in the forms of Fordism and post-Fordism, in the usual emphasis of 'international political economy' on the interplay between states, corporations and markets.

In this introduction we will locate the later chapters in relation to key features of the current debate, not by providing potted summaries of the different contributions but rather by identifying key issues and common themes. We will start by commenting on the concept of the regulation of labour and exploring the ways in which different national regimes of labour regulation have been conceptualized in recent years. This provides a baseline for considering the ways in which international social and economic processes impinge upon such national regimes. We then turn to a reappraisal of the notion of globalization itself, with particular attention to the role of transnational corporations as key actors within the global economy.

We then bring these two lines of discussion together by assessing contemporary debates about 'regime shopping' by TNCs and the evolving character of state strategies in the face of 'regime competition'. In this discussion we first stress the continuing role of states in actively managing the relationship between internal forms of labour regulation and the dynamics of the global economy, while secondly underlining the contradictory and often contested features of the resulting national state policies and forms of class relations. Finally we turn to the changing role of supra-state forms of labour regulation, such as those developed around the promulgation of international labour standards through the ILO and those associated with the more recent consolidation of regional common markets such as the EU and NAFTA. Here we seek to identify key aspects of the scope and limits of such forms of international labour regulation, and the ways in which they relate to the evolving politics of labour regulation within national states.

Conceptualizing Regulation: Themes and Variants

Our starting point in discussing variations and changes in the social regulation of labour is a conception of such regulation in terms of 'the rules and expectations governing employment which develop from the interaction between states, employers, unions and workers' (Edwards *et al.*, 1994, p. 3), and a recognition that historically such systems have often developed in distinctive ways on different national terrains. Underlying this conception are a series of analytical arguments which have been spelt out more fully elsewhere (Edwards, 1986) but can be summarily indicated here. First, the capitalist employment relation is structured as an antagonistic relationship with a persistent potential to generate conflict. Secondly, capitalist development is premised on the more or less successful management of this antagonism, through a combination of domination and accommodation, that is through the social regulation of labour. Thirdly, such regulation most directly involves the institutional structuring of the work process, the labour market, collective representation within and beyond the enterprise and the political representation of labour – in this view 'market relations' are only ever one crucial aspect of such regulative forms. Fourthly, the forms taken by such regulation have developed and varied over time and space. Fifthly, the state is implicated in such forms of regulation, not as a neutral agency or the successful agent of the 'needs' of capitalism but as a more or less adequate manager of the process of capitalist development. The state remains a capitalist state because it has developed in active relation to, and remains constrained by the character of, a capitalist productive system, a point which is made explicitly by some of our contributors and implicitly by others. Finally, such regulation remains persistently incomplete and recurrently contested.

It may be evident that this perspective borrows from, but is distinctly less elaborate than, the French 'regulationist' approach (Aglietta, 1979; Boyer, 1994) to the analysis of distinct phases and national variants of capitalist development, and it is therefore appropriate to seek to clarify our position in regard to this school. We would certainly acknowledge that the regulationist approach represents the most sophisticated contemporary research programme for investigating the evolving relationship between national regulatory regimes and the development of capitalism on a global scale, involving an extensive and systematic analysis of the interlocking character of the social forms of organization of production, consumption, investment and credit in recent phases of capitalist development. The pivotal insight which they signal through the concept of regulation is that the process of capitalist development is not simply a smooth outcome of market mechanisms but is characterized by recurrent instabilities, rooted in antagonistic features of the employment relationship and also expressed in imbalances between investment, production and consumption. Thus the relative stability of specific phases of capitalist development is only secured through the interplay of a whole series of regulatory mechanisms including state policies, management strategies, bargaining processes and consumption norms.

However, we have not sought to impose a regulationist vocabulary upon the contributors to this volume because of several important limitations of this approach. The first of these is that the analysis of the interlocking features of phases of capitalist accumulation has generally been developed at the cost of a schematic and over-coherent representation of major phases of successful capitalist regulation and accumulation, albeit punctuated by phases of conflict and crisis. As several critics (Clarke, 1988a; 1992; Brenner and Glick, 1991) have noted, this tends to overstate the functional integration of regulatory apparatus and accumulation in periods of growth and to relegate conflict to moments of transition between regimes of accumulation. Second, although this approach pays some attention to the distinctive forms taken by such regulation within specific national states, it also tends to assimilate these national variants to a broader succession of modes of regulation (for some of the analytical challenges this poses see Peck and Miyamachi, 1994).[1] We have therefore chosen to retain a more open-ended conceptualization of the evolving character of class relations and the regulation of labour in this introduction.

While regulation theory has focused primarily upon the temporal evolution of regulatory forms, by developing a stylized account of the consolidation and crisis of a Fordist regime of accumulation, many other analysts have focused on the distinctiveness of co-existing forms of national regulation, either seeking to explain the experience of specific countries or grouping them into distinctive clusters. In the 1970s and into the 1980s much attention was given to corporatism as a form of intermediation between organized capital and labour, with Sweden as the key exemplar. From the late 1980s attention switched to the 'developmental' model, exemplified by Japan and other South East Asian states, which was seen as promoting capital accumulation whereas corporatism had ostensibly focused primarily upon issues of redistribution between capital and labour (Weiss, 1998a). We consider such analyses below, arguing that they tend to be too stark and to present each model as a successful intervention rather than as conflict-prone and uncertain.

These arguments about the significance of distinctive institutional matrices in generating variant forms of contemporary capitalism were developed in studies of work organization, industrial relations, welfare arrangements and business organization (Gourevitch et al., 1984; Maurice et al., 1986; Lane, 1989; Esping Andersen, 1990; Whitley, 1992a). Confidence in such neo-institutionalist analyses of the specificity of different national social formations was strengthened by the apparent persistence and resilience of such variation. This prompted a range of sophisticated theorizing about the historical roots of these differences and the path-dependent trajectories of change which they have sustained, and the development of increasingly complex discussions of the diversity of national patterns of state, business and labour relations. For example, Ferner and Hyman (1992b) recognize the persistent heterogeneity of European industrial relations systems, while Whitley (1992b) has emphasized that there are substantial differences between the East Asian 'business systems' of Japan, Korea, Taiwan and Hong Kong.

However, such theorizing also evinced important weaknesses. First, the internally contested character of these national institutional complexes could easily be overlooked in characterizations of their internal coherence and persistence. Secondly, there was often considerable ambiguity about the external conditions of sustainability of these national forms. This latter weakness is highlighted by the very different emphasis of international political economy and some versions of the sociology of the global system, for they, by contrast, start their analyses from a conceptualization of a global system and seek to trace the ways in which the activities of states are inserted into and conditioned by such a system (Sklair, 1995; Strange, 1997). In our view, however, these approaches are vulnerable to the contrasting risk of simply reading off the fate of distinctive national institutional arrangements from the dominant features of the global system. What is required, therefore, is more detailed attention to both the constraints impinging upon national patterns and the active ways in which the state and other national actors seek to manage and modify those constraints. This is an important theme in several of the contributions to this volume, and a central concern of the chapters by Burnham, Hampson and Kettunen.

Having recognized the salience of differences between national configurations of labour regulation, a prime analytical concern has been to distinguish major variants among these forms of capitalism, not in terms of specific institutional details but more in terms of their broad dynamics and trajectories. This endeavour has, for example, informed the long debate over the strengths and weaknesses of neo-corporatist regimes. The simplest among such underlying typologies are those which contrast organized and market capitalisms, or in Albert's (1991) terms the Rhine model and the neo-American model. The Rhine model is characterized by interest intermediation between the state, employers and unions, each highly organized and disciplined actors, in a way which sustains long-term calculations of the shared benefits of concertation in regard to investments, productivity, jobs, wages and growth. The neo-American model, by contrast, is characterized by arm's-length relations between the state and economic actors and market transactions between the latter, which sustains short-term economic calculations. As Goldthorpe's (1984) earlier discussion of the contrast between dualist and corporatist forms of labour regulation suggests, these models have quite distinctive distributional implications, for the former moderates inequalities among employees while the latter amplifies divisions between the secure and the insecure and marginalized.

In the late 1970s and early 1980s such contrasts were buttressed by the arguments that economic performance, measured by inflation and rates of growth, was greatest at the two ends of the spectrum (Calmfors and Driffill, 1988; Crouch, 1993, pp. 12–17). Highly inclusive forms of organized capitalism achieved wage moderation through political exchange while market-led systems used the free market to attain the same end. Countries in the middle of the range had worse performance. This neat U-curve relationship has not, however, been sustained during the 1990s, prompting a reappraisal of the simple contrast between organized and disorganized capitalisms.

Furthermore, there are good analytical reasons for moving from this binary account to a tripartite model, in particular because of the need to distinguish between those forms of organized capitalism which have been characterized by a strong and inclusively organized labour movement and those forms which have been characterized by a weaker and more fragmented labour movement (Crouch, 1995; Coates, 1998). Such three-way comparisons are attractive on three counts. First, the more complex and contradictory patterns of economic performance of the advanced capitalist economies in the late 1980s and early 1990s highlighted the importance of this internal contrast within 'organized capitalisms' (Crouch, 1993, p. 17). Secondly, tripartite models can be seen to approximate to the dominant social relations in the three regional poles of metropolitan global capitalism – North America, East Asia and Europe – the importance of which we will highlight below. And finally, as Coates (1998) has recently emphasized, such a tripolar model can be developed out of a logical analysis of the alternative forms of relation between the fundamental actors in each national system, namely the state, capital and labour.

In his version of such a tripolar model Coates (1998) proposes to simplify the multitude of typologies of forms of capitalist regulation by highlighting the varied relations between capital, labour and the state in this process. He suggests that within market capitalisms both labour and the state play a secondary and subordinate role in the orchestration of the process of accumulation, but that while in some forms of organized capitalism the state plays a more central role in concerting industrial strategy and organizing the relations among capitals, in other forms of organized capitalism organized labour is able to entrench substantial worker rights which at least close off certain options for capital accumulation. In mapping particular capitalist states onto the terrain defined by these three extreme analytical possibilities, he identifies the USA as a close approximation to the first, market-led form, Japan as closest to the second, developmental state form and Northern Europe as closest to the third form, of negotiated corporatism – though he also envisages movements across this terrain as state policies evolve in the face of challenges and contradictions.

As this implies (and in keeping with the sorts of premises we outlined earlier) Coates emphasizes that each of these variants faces distinctive problems. In very summary terms the market-led or neo-liberal variant faces problems of corporate short-termism and incremental deindustrialization (and probably of disorganized dissatisfaction); the statist model faces problems of inflexible investment, scandals over state-corporate corruption (and possibly of worker disillusionment); and the neo-corporatist model faces problems with reconciling concessions to workers with profitable accumulation (and the overt politicization of distributive issues). Such a characterization clearly opens up questions about the relative viability of different national regulatory regimes and how this may change with the reconfiguration of the international economy. At the same time its explicit recognition of important sources of tension and contestation within each form of labour regulation is a valuable counter to simple characterizations of the dominance of any one form over the others. For these reasons it provides a valuable conceptual backdrop to the more substantive discussions of specific national experiences provided by many of our contributors.

Coates's mapping in terms of a triangular field also stresses that different states will change their positions, a key illustration being the UK's move towards the market-led pole between 1979 and 1997. National systems are not timeless, and trajectories will change in response to external pressures and internal processes. This is reflected in the analyses developed by our various contributors to this volume in ways which we will discuss in more detail below, once we have developed our critical characterization of the dynamics of globalization more fully in the next section.

Finally in this introductory section, it is important to make explicit a more general point about economic organization which underlies our broader methodological stance. Much of the debate about evolving modes of social regulation seems to have a truncated view of history which results from an inadequate theoretical perspective. This view of history often contrasts the current period with a past in which firms enjoyed a bargained compromise with their workers and in which states operated Keynesian economic management to maintain a reasonably stable macro-economic environment. Yet the period of Fordist compromise between 1945 and 1970 was short and a reflection of a particular combination of circumstances. As Matthews (1968) argued very foresightfully, what seems odd in historical perspective is not a sustained high level of unemployment but the very low levels of unemployment that marked the post-1945 capital–labour accord. As Matthews put it, high levels of demand were due to growing export markets and an unprecedentedly high level of investment. The latter may have reflected not a secular shift but 'a conjunction of circumstances similar to those which have caused past booms of a cyclical character' (p. 563). The period did not resolve the uncertainties of capitalism but allowed a temporary respite from boom and recession. The 1980s and 1990s saw the return of persistently high unemployment as the conditions of the postwar hiatus unravelled.

The inadequacy of conventional explanation lies in the assumption that stability is the normal pattern and that capitalism moves from one stable social settlement to another. Yet capitalism is about the striving for new markets and accumulating surplus. At times, particular conjunctures of forces generate stability. The 1945–70 period was unusual in two respects: the establishment of a reasonably standard production system ('Fordism') at the same time that states created the Bretton Woods structure of fixed exchange rates. We should not, then, see regime competition as a challenge to a previously stable world order. Rather, it is part of the continuing development of an economic system.

The Debate about the Dynamics of Globalization and the Role of TNCs

The history of capitalism has been a history of international trade and widening markets, and the social settlements characteristic of specific national states have always been conditioned by the mode of insertion of such states within the wider international economy. The proponents of globalization nevertheless suggest that these features have assumed a new importance in recent years, with a qualitative change in the speed of operation of transnational social agencies and the depth of penetration of global economic processes. Such changes embrace the technological enhancement of international communication through travel and telecommunications and the spread of a shared cultural repertoire of commodified consumerism, but the pivotal actors in this process are the TNCs and the financial markets.

The TNC is commonly seen as one of the main engines of globalization. Extreme versions of the thesis speak of the end of the nation state as a result of the combined effects of growing TNC influence, the rise of supranational institutions and the importance of new local centres of excellence, often called industrial districts (Ohmae, 1995). According to Schmidt (1995, pp. 76, 79), TNCs are 'less tied to nations and national interests' and are growing increasingly stateless, as indicated by a 'dispersion of operations; the loss of loyalty to home or host country when it comes to jobs and operations; and the ability to avoid burdensome taxes'. More modest accounts similarly stress the role of industrial districts and global-local connections; for example, Kanter (1995) identifies several distinct local economies in the USA, such as the Spartanburg-Greenville area of South Carolina, with the networks to generate global competitive advantage (including attracting overseas investment, in this case the likes of BMW). Other writers identify new systems of production that operate at the global level. The most famous (indeed, now notorious) example is the claim by Womack *et al.* (1990) that what they termed lean production has benefits that allow it to out-compete all others. The result is said to be a spread of this system throughout the world, with the transmission mechanism being TNCs which either transplant the new system to different countries directly or copy each other. The nation state, and indeed other actors, notably labour organizations, are left as observers.

This book does not make the analysis of the organization and activity of TNCs a central focus, for these features have been extensively debated elsewhere. For example, it is well established that TNCs are not truly stateless, that their impact through foreign direct investment remains relatively small, and that international trade is in some ways less open than in the past (Hirst and Thompson, 1996; Weiss, 1998a). Instead we are concerned with the implications of the activities of TNCs for the capacities of nation states and their evolving forms of labour regulation.

We do not deny the central importance of TNCs, and would reject the extreme views of those like Hirst and Thompson (1996), who, on the basis of reasonable individual pieces of evidence – such as that global trading is not a new phenomenon – reject any idea of globalization led by TNCs (for a critique see Radice, 1997). On any one indicator, the idea that the global power of TNCs has increased can be questioned. But the combination of increased international trade (in Britain, for example, manufactured imports were worth only 4 per cent of domestic spending on manufactures in 1950, a figure which had risen to 38 per cent by 1992: Brown and Rea, 1995, p. 369), rising foreign direct investment, improved communications and the conscious copying of concepts like lean production is surely distinctive.

What we question is not the power of the TNCs but ideas that they have thereby become stateless, or converged on one model, or grown immune to governmental pressures. The statelessness thesis has been well criticized by Hu (1992), who shows that firms depend on national bases for many of their operations and that most TNCs retain distinct national characters (think of IBM, Toyota, or FIAT). As for universal models of operation, the car industry is the best test case for it is here that the lean production thesis was first developed. Yet in this sector an international survey concludes that, though lean production may be a benchmark, its implementation has been shaped by many forces that are specific to individual countries, firms and even plants (Kochan *et al.*, 1997, pp. 305–7). Pressures which continue to be exerted on TNCs at the level of nation states include environmental legislation (for example in Canada the requirement that aluminium firms phase out their outdated carcinogenic technologies, even though these firms are crucial to the economies of some provinces, notably Quebec) and strong expectations that firms will produce locally (e.g. direct pressure on defence firms to produce in the USA if they want government contracts, or indirect pressures on pharmaceutical firms for which the USA is the largest market and where Food and Drug Administration authorization of new products is eased if a firm produces locally).

A good illustration of linkages between states and TNCs is provided by Snell's (1997) study of the world beef industry and in particular Australia's insertion in the world economy. The fact that Australia became a major beef producer stemmed initially from British imperial preference, stimulated in the 1950s by an agreement between the two governments. Later exports to America reflected a US ban on imports from Brazil because of health concerns. It is true that global TNCs now control the supply chain much more directly than in the past but this control is mediated by government regulations on food standards as well as by the tastes of consumers in different countries.

From this perspective, then, states continue to play a central role, both in the regulation of social relations within their jurisdictions and in the regulation of the global capitalist economy, but in both of these arenas the capacities of states to sustain the conditions for a smooth trajectory of capital accumulation remain uncertain and contested. Changes in the organization and operation of TNCs, not only in manufacturing but also in trade and financial services, have significantly altered the terrain upon which these states operate, but nation states (though with very varied capacities) remain important actors on the global stage. To characterize the changing relations between TNCs and national forms of labour regulation more precisely we will now focus on the changing dynamics of 'regime competition'.

Regime Shopping by TNCs and the Dynamics of Regime Competition

It is useful to distinguish three major phases in the debate about the manner in which TNCs may play off different states and regions through their decisions about location and investment.

New International Division of Labour

The first phase, epitomized by the work of Fröbel *et al.* (1980), focused on the discussion of the 'new international division of labour' being generated by the relocation of low-wage labour-intensive production from developed capitalist economies to developing industrializing countries and enclaves. This dramatized the possibility that TNCs could systematically shift their major operations away from countries characterized by high wages, social costs and labour standards, inducing a competitive 'race to the bottom' (a phrase coined by Justice Brandeis in the USA in 1933, see Stone, 1996, p. 448) as newly industrializing countries eager to attract investment set the standards for wages, conditions and worker rights. However, as we have seen, a general application of this model is misleading, first because productivity gains can compensate for the direct and indirect costs integral to the regimes of labour regulation which have characterized some of the advanced capitalisms, and secondly because issues such as market access also play a significant role in corporate calculations (Jenkins, 1984; Ruigrok and van Tulder, 1995; Harman, 1996). Such criticisms of the 'new international division of labour' scenario are buttressed by the extent to which TNCs invest within the advanced capitalisms of the triad, with substantial though uneven cross-penetration of American, but also more recently European and Japanese, capital in the other major regions.

The 'High Road'

Of course, such inter-penetration of home territories does not mean that TNCs have ignored the possibilities of relocating certain of their operations, or the activities of the supplier chains which they orchestrate, in areas of cheaper labour, sometimes in newly developed industrializing economies and sometimes in lower wage states or districts within the advanced economies. However, it suggests that other cross-cutting dynamics are also at work, and it is these which were emphasized in the next phase of the debate, which highlighted the scope to attract or retain high-skill, high-wage, high-productivity (in the American summary terminology 'high-road') investment in advanced capitalist economies. This approach was exemplified in celebrations of the German model of diversified quality production (Streeck, 1992a; Lane, 1995), which sought to draw out the manner in which a dense institutional framework of skill formation, regulated bargaining and worker voice could sustain such 'high-road' investment. Furthermore, in the 1980s this analysis could be allied with those which identified the virtues of neo-corporatist bargaining between the labour market partners, to map out a distinctive global niche and growth trajectory for the Northern European economies, and indeed to contrast this with the limitations of a less skill-intensive and more adversarial trajectory of restructuring characteristic of Anglo-American deindustrialization.

One version of this optimistic scenario for the generation of a 'high-road' growth trajectory from the interplay of private corporate calculations and state policies hinges upon the development of a new information age. A crucial feature of the argument here is that individual firms are unable to provide the infrastructural support for the high levels of R&D activity and a skilled and innovative workforce which are required for commercial success in high-technology informational production and services. Thus the state is necessarily implicated in the provision or co-ordination of such resources, in part through the education and training systems and in part through the focusing of R&D activities through research funding, 'national champions' and 'strategic alliances'. In turn the state and its citizens benefit from the enhanced productivity and prosperity which results: 'the payoff to national governments from such investments is that the local economy can become internationally competitive while maintaining national autonomy and – more important – that such investments lead to higher levels of local productivity, providing greater political space for any government' (Carnoy, 1993, p. 89).

As this argument implies, such a 'high-road' trajectory based on the confluence of interests between high-technology TNCs and governments with sophisticated national human resource policies may only be available to a minority of states. Indeed, the extent to which this may be so depends heavily upon underlying assumptions about, first, the knowledge-intensive character of emerging forms of production and servicing, and secondly, the resources available to states to sustain such a sophisticated infrastructure. Furthermore, Carnoy himself acknowledges that such a virtuous circle may characterize only one segment of a national labour market, and be accompanied by increasing inequality between beneficiaries and those excluded from knowledge-intensive production. In these respects the experience of the USA, for example, provides cause for scepticism, both in terms of the real extent of such knowledge-intensive operations and in terms of the ramifications for labour market inequalities.

Regime Shopping

In the 1990s, however, such perspectives based upon a virtuous circle of high-quality, skill-intensive production, capable of yielding joint benefits for capital and labour, were increasingly challenged by a reappraisal of the calculations and leverage which inform the strategic choices of TNCs. Streeck (1992b), for example, developed his comparison between Northern European and Anglo-American corporate strategies, to emphasize that managements were unlikely to prefer a high-involvement, high-wage approach on the grounds of its strength as a production and accumulation strategy alone. Rather, they were only likely to opt for this line of action if easier alternatives – including the imposition of quality programmes within standardized mass production – were closed off by institutional, and particularly labour movement, constraints. However, in contemporary conditions, increasingly sophisticated TNCs were in a position where they could more and more challenge such constraints, in part by shifting production between different sites but also by making future streams of investment conditional on concessions in the more densely regulated regimes (Mueller, 1996; Mueller and Loveridge, 1997).

Thus Streeck argues that market incentives and technological imperatives are not in themselves sufficient to prompt employers to develop labour-inclusive high-trust work regimes or to sustain a dense infrastructure and strongly regulated labour markets. Rather they will support an optional involvement in 'high-skill, high-trust' production, in which managements will first pick and choose so that labour market inequalities and instabilities will grow and secondly seek to implement qualified forms which compromise the transferability of skills and the independence of unions. Thus a high-road model is not impossible, but it will not be built out of the enlightened self-interest of employer calculations unless these are substantially constrained by the power of states and, ultimately, labour movements to generate substantial institutional limits to such erosion. Such arguments do not return the discussion to a simple emphasis on capital flight to areas of low-cost production, but rather highlight the manner in which employers are likely to engineer the incremental erosion and recasting of terms and conditions, initially at plant level and through the compliance of workers fearful for their jobs but potentially with much wider ramifications in changing the terms of labour regulation across whole national economies (Edwards *et al.*, 1996; Smith and Elger, 1997). This underlines the continuing importance of the responses of states and labour movements while underlining the more difficult terrain on which those responses must operate.

Furthermore, once we appreciate both the range of priorities sought by TNCs and the contradictory character of many of these priorities, it is easier to understand that their calculations do not result in any simple process of homogenization, but in significant ways operate upon and serve to reproduce unevenness across operations based in different countries and plants (Harman, 1996; Dicken, 1998).[2] The extent to which global trade and investment is concentrated between the advanced capitalist states highlights the critical importance of access to the major mass markets which these economies represent. In turn this suggests that the national states in such regions retain some leverage over both inward investors, who seek access to their markets, and their own domestically based TNCs, who are likely to seek state support as national champions in the 'national economic interest'. In this triadic perspective states are strongly implicated in the competitive strategies of both domestic and foreign TNCs, but this implies active regulation and support rather than a withering away of regulatory activity. Furthermore, this perspective does not simply cast national states as the sponsors of 'their' national corporate champions, in a competition between national state capitals. Rather, states persistently confront contradictory pressures from different TNCs (Carnoy, 1993).

State Policies and Regime Competition

With these considerations in mind we can return to an examination of the range of national forms of capital–labour relations and state policies mapped out by Coates, to explore how these features have been understood in the context of the increasing power of TNCs and the intensified forms of regime competition which this engenders. We first review the long-standing debate about neo-corporatism and then turn to briefer discussions of the dynamics of state policies and class relations in statist and neo-liberal regimes.

The Scope and Limits of Corporatism

There are several reasons for taking the debate about postwar corporatism as a starting point. The first is that in recent years such corporatist regimes have been seen as especially vulnerable to the pressures of regime competition, both through the decisions of mobile manufacturing and finance capital and through the direct borrowing of neo-liberal recipes for the restructuring of national states. Thus a whole series of commentaries have focused upon the 'crisis', 'erosion' or even 'collapse' of the Swedish and more recently the German models of corporatism (Lash, 1985; Martin, 1987, 1995; Kjellberg, 1992, 1998; Streeck, 1984, 1997). Secondly, one line of argument about corporatism which we will discuss suggests that such regimes are capable only of dealing with issues of distribution as opposed to those securing effective accumulation, underlining the problematical relationship between internal patterns of class conflict and accommodation and the positioning of such national economies within the international economy. Thirdly, several of the chapters in this volume have a direct relevance for these debates, partly through a reappraisal of the experience of the classic Northern European exemplars of corporatism (see Critcher *et al.* on the experience of industrial restructuring in Germany in the 1980s, and more particularly Kettunen on the repositioning of the Nordic model in recent years) and partly through an assessment of more recent adaptations of neo-corporatist forms in other capitalist states (see Critcher *et al.* on the Spanish experience of restructuring, Whitehouse and Zetlin's discussion of the distributional ramifications of state policies in Australia, and most particularly Hampson's direct interrogation of the significance of the recent Australian experience of the implementation of the 'Accord' for the corporatism debate). It is our view that, while the promise of the initial corporatism debate to offer clear-cut results in this respect has faded, and the literature no longer provides simple categories into which to place individual countries, the residue of the debate nevertheless permits the construction of more sensitive and indeed more sociological accounts of these relationships.

From the 1970s political scientists and sociologists resurrected the term corporatism (for a good brief historiography, see Crouch, 1993, pp. x, 11–20). The core idea was that a corporatist state was one in which the state recognized and bargained with institutions which aggregated the interests of, especially, capital and labour. Corporatist systems, then, were those in which each grouping had a powerful peak association that engaged in bargaining with its counterpart and with the state. Such corporatism was seen as an alternative to, and indeed the successor of, market-driven systems. The concept was seen as important because, as noted above, corporatism was claimed to produce low levels of unemployment, inflation and strikes, and thereby to contribute to economic performance and social welfare. In particular, the cohesion of organized labour and the involvement of left-wing parties in government were seen as bases of 'political exchange', whereby gains in the labour market and social welfare were bargained in exchange for industrial moderation and the avoidance of strikes.

During the 1970s and 1980s numerous efforts were made to measure corporatism by assigning scores to countries according to such criteria as labour movement unity and the presence of left-wing parties in government, and to test its links with such outcomes. In retrospect, however, these attempts were unsatisfactory. This was partly for technical reasons, associated with the arbitrary aggregation of different indices of corporatism, such as those measuring the horizontal unity and the vertical cohesion of labour movements. The exercise was also rather static, placing a country at a given level of corporatism for a lengthy period. More importantly, however, such measures threw up too many anomalies. A key example was Germany, which failed to score very highly on measures of corporatism, largely because its Social Democrat Party was out of office for long periods, but long enjoyed the supposed fruits of corporatism such as low inflation. Furthermore, several countries, including Switzerland and Japan, did not rank as corporatist but enjoyed many of the claimed benefits. Finally, some countries which manifested some of the characteristics of corporatism during the 1970s showed few of the benefits, the UK being one obvious case.

Such anomalies prompted considerable conceptual refinement, focused particularly upon probing the distinctive roles of capital, labour and the state (or if this seems a reification, 'state managers' – key decision-makers within the state – to use the phrase popularised by Block, 1980) and on distinguishing different levels at which corporatist relations might operate, from the macro level of the economy, through the meso level of regions and sectors, to the micro level of the enterprise. Soskice (1990) argued that, in place of a unilinear measure of corporatism, it was important to distinguish between 'co-ordinated market economies' according to the strength of their labour movements. Only where labour was strong, as in the Nordic countries, was corporatist exchange necessary. Elsewhere, as in Japan, such concessions were not required. Such arguments helped to refine the idea of negotiations between capital, labour and the state, though other developments, for example that which dealt with the anomaly of Japan by describing it as micro-corporatist, arguably engaged in re-labelling rather than constructive analysis.

The main problem with such analytical refinements was that they added so many qualifiers to the idea of corporatism that it appeared increasingly vague. The original definition seemed to identify neither necessary nor sufficient conditions for the claimed economic results. Furthermore, even this qualified mapping of possibilities was thrown into further question by developments from the mid-1980s, when on the one hand apparently stable corporatist systems, notably the Swedish, seemed to decay, while on the other hand market-led economies, notably those of the USA and the UK, revived economically and in the process enjoyed reduced inflation and much reduced strike rates (in the case of the UK, a fall in strikes to levels not seen for a century). In our view, however, two core ideas captured by the corporatism debate remain salient to our present concerns. The first was outlined by Panitch (1981) early in the debate, when he defined corporatism not as a set of structures, but as a political activity designed to manage the 'labour problem' in a particular phase of capitalism. Corporatism was not something to be measured on a scale but a political strategy which grew out of particular historical circumstances and which might work for a time and then break down. The second idea was also signalled by Panitch but underlined in Therborn's (1992) later overview of the debate. He concluded that the basic thrust of the corporatist writers was correct, in that they sought an explanation of the differing ways in which the state can intervene in the capital–labour relation. The error was to move towards static indices and correlations with possible outcomes, with a resulting loss of sensitivity to the uncertainties, tensions and dynamics of the relationships that were involved.

On this basis we can see the pivotal case of Sweden as illustrative of a set of key themes. It was characterized by a particular historical trajectory of interest mobilization which gave a distinctive inflection to its corporatist politics, but we can also identify a process of the remaking of the Swedish 'model' in response to recurrent tensions and a shifting balance of social forces. In this context changing external pressures are a crucial part of the account, but these are continually mediated through the organized actions and ideological mobilizations of capital, labour and the state. Thus the basic conditions of Sweden's corporatism were laid through the reciprocal development of highly organized federations of capital and labour, the former dominated by the export manufacturing sector and the latter by the manual union federation (despite the co-existence of white-collar and professional confederations), and through the political dominance of social democracy, albeit initially in coalition (Fulcher, 1991). Through the 1950s and 1960s this sustained the celebrated Swedish model which involved bipartite central bargaining between capital and labour which was increasingly built around a trade-off between solidary wages policy and corporate rationalization. This was underpinned by Keynesian state policies and tripartite active labour market policies rather than any direct state intervention in bargaining, though there was the implied threat that in the event of major disputes the state would step in

(Jackson and Sisson, 1976). By the late 1960s and early 1970s this model came under increasing pressure, both because of the costs of rationalization experienced by workers and because of the tensions between union federations and between export, domestic and public-sector workers and employers (Lash, 1985). In this context the state became increasingly directly involved in bargaining while both manual and white-collar federations developed more radical demands which challenged the entrenched prerogatives of management (Martin, 1987).

Here we would emphasize that corporatism's role in accumulation has been neglected, but was actually critical. The core idea of a virtuous circle of low inflation and low unemployment was that it would promote economic growth. Mechanisms could include Sweden's celebrated manpower policy, with its goal of moving labour from low- to high-productivity sectors. Another mechanism was labour's acceptance of technical change, where surveys routinely showed greater acceptance in a country like Germany, where inclusive unions took an industry-wide perspective, than in Britain, where unions tended to pursue short-term sectional interests. Hampson's chapter in this volume also stresses how Australia's various experiments were driven by concerns about the economy's productive capacity. Corporatism was not merely about distribution.

The terms of the corporatist bargaining became more fraught and contested through the 1970s and the 1980s. Against this background export-oriented manufacturing capital, which had been a dominant force in the construction of the Swedish model, increasingly sought to dismantle the model, initially through a systematic drive to decentralize bargaining and later by withdrawal of political support from tripartite arrangements. This strategy arose both from their opposition to the new demands of labour and the competitive pressures they faced as exporters, and was facilitated by their increasing involvement in internationalization, the pace of which accelerated sharply in the 1990s (Wilks, 1996). Nevertheless, the Swedish model has not simply collapsed but continues to be remade, in a form which involves a mix of deregulatory and interventionist state policies and the persistence of substantial co-ordinated sector bargaining alongside pressures for the fragmentation of employment arrangements (Kjellberg, 1992). Indeed the future fate of the model continues to be hotly contested, not only by the powerful agencies of internationalizing capital but also through the renewal of union policies and mobilization (coupled with persistently high union densities) even in these difficult conditions (Mahon, 1991). Thus Pontusson (1997) argues that Sweden has moved somewhat towards a German model of 'diversified quality production' in recent years, but primarily as a product of a compromise or even stalemate between marketizing preferences of capital and labour's defence of elements of the earlier settlement, rather than as a strategic shift.

Even within Western Europe, and more so beyond those confines, capitalist states have clearly followed rather different trajectories in these respects, as commentators such as Crouch (1993, 1995), Streeck (1992b) and Ferner and Hyman (1992b) have emphasized. Nevertheless we can gain valuable analytical leverage over those cases which involve some variant of centralized bargaining between state, labour and capital, and can thus be regarded as genuinely corporatist, by tracing the salience of differences in such key features as the articulation of central and local bargaining and the relationship between public sector and export sector employment for the manner in which they have responded to both internal tensions and external pressures. This not only provides a basis for analysing similarities and differences in the experiences of such countries as Sweden, Germany and Australia, but also for considering developments in some of the Southern European states which have pursued more recent and fragile essays in neo-corporatism. Thus Regini (1997) discusses recent developments in Italy in terms of the emergence of a neo-corporatist policy which involves political exchange focused upon national competitiveness and accumulation rather than egalitarianism. In this account the state continues to play an active role in promoting particular routes of economic development; firms have an incentive to participate because it helps them to deal with two fundamental issues, controlling costs and securing workforce co-operation; and new forms of interest articulation have emerged – themes which Regini argues are pertinent to an understanding of both the German and the Italian experience. Yet he also notes the uncertain basis on which such co-operation may rest, thus underlining the way in which corporatism is a way of balancing tensions and not a self-contained structure. Visser (1998) similarly argues that, where unions have political and institutional legitimacy, they can play a role in wage moderation; using the example of the Netherlands he offers 'two cheers for corporatism' and one for the market.

As we noted earlier, several chapters in this volume engage directly with these issues. First, Critcher, Parry and Waddington use the specific case of the recent restructuring of regionally concentrated coal sectors in Germany, Britain and Spain in the face of reorganization and intensified competition in the global fuel market to underline the continuing salience of state policies in mediating such global pressures. They demonstrate that in Germany a neo-corporatist political culture and relatively decentralized institutional structures have mitigated the damaging effects of sectoral rationalization and facilitated regional regeneration. But they also show that not only the strong-state neo-liberal imposition of market disciplines pursued in Britain but the institutionally shallow and adversarial version of corporatism pursued in Spain are resulting in devastated local economies and imposing heavy social costs on their erstwhile mining regions. As a final twist they register that the comparative capability of German neo-corporatism in this regard nevertheless remains vulnerable and contested by fresh pressures, both from wider problems facing the contemporary German political economy and from the deregulationist imperatives of EU policy. This illuminates the interplay between the changing parameters within which states may pursue neo-corporatist restructuring policies and the specific forms of labour regulation (with distinctive costs and gains for labour) which they sustain.

Kettunen's chapter on the recent fate of the Nordic exemplar of neo-corporatism adds another important dimension to these debates. He emphasizes the significance of shifts in the ideologies which inform the contemporary reworking of labour market and industrial relations institutions in these societies, and especially the ways in which discourses of national and enterprise competitiveness have helped reconstitute the identities and interests of the labour market partners and thus the terms upon which institutional reforms and compromises are likely to occur. In this context he suggests that revised versions of Nordic neo-corporatism should be understood in terms of the reworking of influential discourses and agendas as much as in terms of the remaking of institutional configurations. In particular he argues that there has been a substantial realignment of the relationship between dominant understandings of equity, solidarity, competences and competitiveness as the roles of the state and the 'labour market partners' have been recast, even where neo-corporatist strategies remain central. At the same time he registers both subtle differences among national variants in the recasting of the 'Nordic model' and the extent to which such ideological realignments have remained problematical and open to challenge.

Hampson's discussion of the trajectory of Australia's more recent experience of neo-corporatism also highlights the changing relationship between competing conceptions of industrial restructuring, as an initial vocabulary of centrally regulated, skill-based, bargained reform gave way to a decentralized and market-led enterprise restructuring in the name of a new industrial competitiveness. However, he builds more directly on neo-Marxist analyses of the dynamics of corporatism by emphasizing the capacity of organized capital to influence the reshaping of the corporatist agenda; the key role of labour movement institutions, especially the Australian Labor Party (ALP) in government and trade union leaderships involved in centralized political deals, in negotiating and justifying this shift; and the manner in which this evolution effectively eroded both the legitimacy of these policies within the wider labour movement and the institutional cohesion of that movement. Thus the Australian experiment with corporatism played a pivotal role in seeking to reposition Australian capital in the global economy, but in ways which appear to have profoundly changed the political and institutional terrain of both future state and labour movement strategies. In this context Hampson also discusses the implications of efforts to develop an alternative labour movement agenda to that pursued by the ALP during this period.

Finally, Whitehouse and Zetlin address another aspect of the Australian experience of revised corporatism, the implications of changes in the organization of collective bargaining for gendered inequality. Their discussion complements Hampson's, as each analyses key features of the active role of state policy in mediating global pressures and their distinctive effects on employees. Whitehouse and Zetlin use comparative data to show that gendered pay inequality was most limited in countries where centralized pay fixing was in place. They then trace how the decentralization of bargaining in Australia had weakened the institutional leverage of demands for equality and opened the way for a more inegalitarian labour market. Finally they also note that this has not gone unchallenged – indeed trade unions and politicians have sought to use international labour standards as a brake on such developments, though so far with limited effect. Together, then, the two chapters on Australia also identify sources of incipient contestation surrounding the remaking of state and employer policies under the rubric of global competitiveness, in a way which connects with the analysis of worker and union responses in our companion volume (Waddington, 1999).

Statist Regimes

As we have seen, several chapters in this volume address corporatism. None looks directly at developmental states, but here we wish to argue that the perspective which we have been developing also applies to them.

In non-corporatist states the virtual exclusion of organized labour from any formal process of economic and political exchange means that the corporatist debate can at best pose questions by analogy rather than providing a directly applicable analytical framework. In Europe France provides a particularly tantalizing case, as a strong state which on the one hand has sought to orchestrate the modernization of national capitals and on the other has pursued interventionist policies of national labour regulation, including from time to time that favourite corporatist device, incomes policy (Howell, 1992).

But workers have played a role in this process only through spasmodic mass mobilization by politically divided union federations rather than via more institutionalized forms of interest representation (Van Ruysseveldt and Visser, 1996b). Thus such policies, and indeed the state's ambitious pursuit of a proactive decentralizing strategy of industrial relations reform during the 1980s, have primarily been negotiated between employers and the state, further weakening institutionalized union representation, particularly in the private sector (Gallie, 1985). In this context the state and employers have been free to experiment with the dilution of labour market regulation in such areas as 'non-standard employment', despite significant resistance especially within the public sector, but have struggled to translate a policy of supporting 'national champions' onto a wider European plane, prompting Boyer (1997) to emphasize that these actors currently face a particularly acute crisis of choice between a range of alternative but problematical accumulation and growth strategies.

More pertinent for our purposes, however, is the case of Japan, often seen as the prototype of the developmental state. In recent years the deepening of economic crises in Japan's East Asian periphery and the economic downturn in Japan itself have fuelled a rapid neo-liberal dismissal of the relevance of developmental state strategies in the contemporary global economy (discussed in Wade, 1996). In turn this has provoked an impressive critique of this neo-liberal orthodoxy, arguing in a more measured fashion for the continuing importance of developmental state capacities, while also seeking to specify the scope and limits of these capacities as these arise from different institutional configurations, social settlements and policy perspectives (see in particular Weiss, 1998a, 1998b). Building in part upon such critiques, we would suggest that an appropriate analytical response to the crises experienced by the leading developmental state should be based upon both a more critical account than has often been offered of the earlier trajectory of the Japanese 'economic miracle' and a more measured assessment of the limits and possibilities of the current Japanese institutional configuration.

First, then, Japan's postwar growth trajectory was based on a 'class settlement' which included not only lifetime employment and training for core workers, but also the defeat of militant trade unionism, entrenched managerial prerogatives in the work process, long working hours and an extensive periphery of low-paid and insecure workers (Elger and Smith, 1994). Furthermore, this settlement continued to be contested and modified at its margins even as it framed the development of new variants of intensive teamworking which became celebrated in the literature on Toyotaism (Price, 1997). Meanwhile the strong co-ordination of industrial policy through MITI has been marked by important limitations as well as evident successes, for example in the failure of Japanese electronics companies to develop a competitive advantage in the personal computer market (Fransman, 1995).

Secondly, not only broader competitive pressures but the internationalization of Japanese capital itself has placed considerable stresses upon this institutional configuration, forcing a significant dilution of some of its key features such as the lifetime employment system (Sako and Sato, 1997; Benson, 1998). Meanwhile workers in relatively tight labour markets have become increasingly reluctant to embrace intensive production regimes, forcing some modifications in the labour process (Gronning, 1995; Benders, 1996). Finally, while the recent consolidation of a moderate union federation dominated by private-sector unions has reinforced management–union co-operation in the core enterprises, the impact of restructuring is also stimulating new radical currents in the labour movement, and in conjunction with new challenges for state crisis-management and a new fluidity of political party alignments this may be opening new possibilities for neo-corporatist bargaining over economic and industrial policy between the union confederation and the state (Suzuki, 1998). All this suggests the continuing relevance of an institutionalist analysis of the responses of both Japanese capital and the Japanese state apparatus to the current crises, just as to the earlier oil shocks of the 1970s. It also suggests that, as elsewhere, labour cannot be seen as a merely passive recipient of reformulated patterns of labour regulation in Japan, though as yet conditions do not justify any direct application of a corporatism analysis to relations between the state, capital and labour.

In short, France's economic development was evidently both punctuated and punctured by crises in which labour was a key actor despite its political divisions and organizational weakness. Japan's developmental state more effectively subordinated labour, but was not thereby free of constraints and contradictions. Thus our argument is not simply that these states remain active agencies in such developments rather than passive recipients of global pressures, but also that their responses to such pressures confront distinctive opportunities and constraints arising from existing forms of national labour regulation, with their characteristic contours of subordination and conflict. Furthermore, the extent to which such developmental states may continue to pursue a distinctive pathway as 'transformative' states (to use the strong terminology proposed by Weiss, 1998b), or move towards a competition-oriented neo-corporatism, or shift towards deregulation and even neo-liberalism, remains uncertain and indeed contested.

Neo-liberal Regimes

Two chapters in our collection look specifically at the reconstitution of labour regulation in what can be broadly termed neo-liberal state regimes, namely Burnham's discussion of the elaboration of an ostensibly depoliticized form of market regulation in the UK and Peck's analysis of the development of new forms of labour market discipline in the USA, while Critcher *et al.* also assess neo-liberal state policy in their comparative treatment of the restructuring of the European coal industry. Here we want to underline two of the key features of such forms of labour regulation which are demonstrated by these contributions and which extend the arguments which we have sketched out above. The first point is that these forms of market regulation do not represent an absence of state policy, for such 'deregulation' is better conceptualized as an active process of re-regulation. The second is that such state policies are no more contradiction-free in managing processes of labour regulation and capital accumulation than those which have been discussed under the rubric of corporatism.

In broad terms neo-liberalism as a form of labour regulation can be conceptualized as an attempt to depoliticize class relations by utilizing the anonymous play of the market, but one which in turn involves strong state regulation of the supply side of the economy – both in the form of legal constraints on collective action and in the form of the organized reinforcement of the rigours of labour market discipline through such initiatives as 'welfare to work' (Clarke, 1987; Gamble, 1988). These features of the neo-liberal reconstruction of market capitalism are graphically illustrated and analysed by our contributors. Burnham traces the roots of contemporary neo-liberal policies in Britain to the contentious, politicized and unstable character of efforts to pursue neo-corporatist policies of wage restraint and industrial restructuring during the 1960s and 1970s, though he also notes that this orientation is echoed in earlier arguments about policy options within the state. His key argument is that at this juncture the British state is not simply bowing to the external pressures of a global economy, but is actively embracing 'rules-based' monetary policies, reinforced by reconstituted financial markets and enhanced central bank independence, because they constitute a relatively depoliticized discipline upon domestic class relations and especially inflationary wage pressures. This brings invocations of the apparently inevitable exigencies of global competitiveness and financial rectitude to centre stage in the contemporary reconstruction of national class relations, presenting distinctive challenges to a weakened and fragmented labour movement in Britain. At the same time Burnham notes not only that the implementation of 'rules-based' fiscal discipline remains subject to 'technical' disputes and uncertainties, but also that the extent to which this process will remain effectively depoliticized or uncontested remains unresolved.

Peck's chapter complements Burnham's by analysing a key state initiative in reconstituting internal class relations in contemporary neo-liberal regimes, namely the reconstitution of the nexus between welfare provisions and labour market discipline through the development of 'workfare' programmes. First, he shows that the pioneer US programmes replace any notion of income support with that of the compulsory pursuit of poor-quality paid work, driving people into the expanding cluster of low-wage, insecure jobs at the bottom of the US labour market. Secondly he argues that the national state remains a crucial orchestrator of such policies, but also shows how the devolution of responsibility for implementation to local state and private agencies promotes experimentation and limits scrutiny, facilitating a policy bandwagon which erodes existing entitlements. Thirdly he registers the growing international popularity of workfare as a state policy, while also noting the ways in which different national and local labour markets are likely to influence its implementation. Finally, however, he suggests that workfare may have contradictory effects even on its original terrain, because it is likely to further destabilize the low-paid 'contingent' labour market.

Thus these authors not only draw out the active and central role of national states in the reconstitution of neo-liberal state regimes, but also register significant ways in which such broad strategies take distinctive forms in different national states and even localities as they articulate with specific institutional legacies and are conditioned by existing forms of organization and disorganization of capital and labour. Thus, as with the debate surrounding corporatism, neo-liberalism should be seen as a broad strategic repertoire for labour regulation which is played out in active processes of contestation and follows different trajectories in response to particular internal and external pressures on national states. Indeed one critical feature which emerges from the recasting of both neo-corporatist and neo-liberal regimes is the scope for the combination of important elements of both, for example by blending a depoliticization of financial and labour market discipline with increasingly devolved forms of bargaining between organized labour market partners.

Furthermore, the shifting fortunes of such neo-liberal regimes within the international political economy remind us of the limits and contradictions of these policies. On the one hand the increasing reliance upon private capital for the provision of the infrastructure for capital accumulation tends to reinforce the short-term calculations of individual capitals at the expense of a longer term investment in collective goods, resulting, for example, in persistent skill shortages and inflationary pressures within an increasingly inegalitarian labour market (Peck and Tickell, 1992; Hollingsworth, 1997). As Weiss (1997, 1998a, p. 22) argues, such states can be strong in their capacity to impose market solutions but weak in their capacity to transform a nation's productive capabilities, so that deindustrialization is reinforced, a feature illustrated by Critcher *et al.* in their discussion of the virtual destruction of Britain's coal industry coupled with the absence of any effective regeneration strategy. On the other hand, the supposed depoliticization of labour regulation in such regimes remains problematical. In part this arises from the disaffection engendered by deepened inequalities and insecurities in the labour market. In part it arises from the incompleteness in practice of market rule, as illustrated by the continuing role of overt state/capital co-ordination in key sectors, such as agriculture or those associated with military production.

States and Labour: Conclusion

The approach underlying this volume, then, is that states remain important actors in the regulation of labour. This is not just through the passive provision of support and infrastructure to firms or industrial districts that is envisaged in the 'end of the nation state' literature. It also entails active choices regarding the way in which labour is regulated. These occur in three areas. First, there is the direct regulation of the employment contract, for example through legislation. Second, there is the indirect shaping of the contract through social welfare and other provisions which affect the overall social wage. Third, there is wider economic policy, both macro- and micro-economic, with the former affecting unemployment and investment levels and the latter shaping such things as industrial development and the encouragement of overseas investment. Having outlined some features of the dynamics of labour regulation in what we have broadly designated corporatist, statist and neo-liberal variants of industrial capitalism, we wish to register three important directions in which this agenda deserves further development.

First, the above discussion has important implications for debates about the terrain upon which labour, and especially organized labour, responds to the growing leverage of TNCs and global financial markets. On the one hand there have been significant efforts to renew and extend forms of international labour solidarity which seek to challenge the developing strategies of transnational capital (most recently addressed in e.g. Moody, 1997 and Waterman, 1998). On the other hand, however, our argument suggests that labour movements must also continue to address themselves to the specific patterns of labour regulation which characterize different capitalist states. Thus analyses of the dilemmas, contradictions, strengths and weaknesses which characterize contemporary labour movements cannot simply invoke the end of the nation state, but must recognize the complex interplay between the national and global terrains upon which capital–labour relations are currently being recomposed (Panitch, 1994; Moran, 1998). In this regard the contributions in this collection complement those in the companion volume (Waddington, 1999), which focuses specifically upon the strengths and limitations of labour organization and activity in the context of contrasting production regimes and forms of national labour regulation.

Secondly, the forms of differentiation of employment experience within the different regimes of labour regulation we have discussed deserve a much fuller analysis than we have been able to provide above. While we have registered significant quantitative differences in patterns of inequality among workers – as in the contrasts between the effects of the solidarity wages policy in Sweden and the deepening inequalities in the labour markets of neo-liberal regimes – a more extended treatment would clearly need to address the distinctive ways in which labour markets and employment forms are segmented within specific nation states, and the ways in which this is organized in terms of gender, ethnicity and the scope and limits of collective organization. For example these varied forms of labour regulation are not simply constituted as distinctive class settlements but in important respects as distinctive gender settlements as well, as the ways in which the gendered division of labour is structured also differ in significant respects across the advanced capitalisms of the triad as well as more broadly across the global economy (see, for example, Jenson et al. 1988; Lewis and Åström, 1992; Rubery and Fagan, 1995). The character and implications of such forms of differentiation are addressed by several of our contributors, but especially by Whitehouse and Zetlin in their discussion of the distributional consequences of the reorientation of Australian state policies and by O'Connell Davidson and Taylor in their discussion of the gendered and sexualized forms of inequality which have developed under the impact of global tourism in the developing world.

Finally, our focus on the industrialized capitalist societies of the so-called 'triad' follows from the concentration of transnational trade and investment within these regions, but we also recognize the importance of developing equivalent analyses of the character of state policies, internal social settlements and changing modes of insertion in the international economy in relation to those states and societies which occupy a much more subordinate place within the global system (see particularly Sklair, 1995 and Dicken, 1998). In this regard two of our chapters, by Castle et al. and by Davidson and Taylor, serve as valuable counterpoints to those already discussed, as they are both concerned with the forms taken by the state regulation of labour in developing countries, India and the Dominican Republic respectively. However, though they are each concerned with the interplay between national forms of state regulation and supra-state interventions in fundamental aspects of the social organization of labour (child labour and sexual exploitation respectively), they also point to the differentiated character of state capacities in the developing world. Thus Castle *et al.* suggest that *some* states in India have been relatively successful in using a combination of welfare and legal controls to combat damaging forms of child labour, but Davidson and Taylor argue that states like Dominica, both closely implicated in an inegalitarian gender order and heavily dependent on the tourist industry, have done little to inhibit the commercialized sexual exploitation of children.

The Role of Supra-State Forms of Social Regulation

While we have emphasized the continuing importance of national states in constructing and reconstructing forms of labour regulation, supra-state institutions have also played a significant role in labour regulation over a long period, and the limits and contradictions of national regulatory regimes have continued to prompt not only states but also employers, unions and other social movements to push for a variety of changes in international regulatory regimes. Analyses of the origins, scope and limitations of such supra-state forms of social regulation have been the focal concern of students of 'international organization' within the intellectual framework of studies of 'international relations', so to address these issues in relation to labour regulation it is necessary to briefly outline the terrain of debate within this distinctive literature; to bring the IR of 'industrial relations' into some relation with the IR of 'international relations'.

International Relations and Regulatory Hegemony

International relations has long been characterized by a well-entrenched debate between 'neo-realists' and 'liberal institutionalists'. Although both approaches are heavily state-centred, the former are prone to emphasize the incomplete and contested character of international regulatory regimes founded on power relations between rival states while the latter stress the scope for more robust international institution building guided by the convergent interests of states in sustaining a liberal economic order (Murphy, 1994; Bayliss and Smith, 1997). Recently, however, this debate has been cross-cut and qualified by a body of work which emphasizes the necessary interconnectedness of the economic and the political aspects of the 'international system' and thus challenges such heavily state-centred arguments under the banner of 'international political economy' (Strange, 1994; Tooze, 1997). This reorientation towards the analysis of international political economy (IPE) returns us directly to our earlier discussion of the changing relations between states, markets and transnational firms, but with a fresh focus on the scope, limits and contradictions of *international* regulatory regimes.[3]

One direction in which this analysis of IPE can be developed is by embracing the radical globalization thesis which portrays states as terminally incapable of playing any role in the international regulation of market relations, but more often this literature has continued to address the often fraught and contradictory dynamics of such regulation. In this context a particularly important, though contentious, strand of theorizing has utilized Gramscian concepts of hegemony and the formation of historic social blocs to embed an understanding of international regulatory regimes within a wider analysis of changing patterns of capitalist development and class relations at national, regional and global levels, in a way which addresses the shifting mixes of consent and coercion, and stabilization and crisis, which characterize these phenomena (Cox, 1977; Burnham, 1991; Murphy, 1994; Panitch, 1994). Much of this literature actually has little explicit to say about labour standards, but the founder of this analytical tradition, Robert Cox, worked for many years as a senior official of the ILO, and actually developed his approach through a critical assessment of the role of the ILO in the international regulation of labour relations (Cox with Sinclair, 1996).

We can draw on some of the work within this neo-Gramscian school to help frame our discussion of contemporary debates about the international regulation of work and employment relations, albeit in the light of critiques (Burnham, 1991; Panitch, 1994) which have highlighted an over-emphasis on ideological hegemony in these accounts, both in terms of their characterizations of the bases and extent of working class integration into corporatist bargaining structures within specific national and regional social settlements, and in a related under-emphasis on the contradictory and contested character of both national and international forms of labour regulation. Like French regulationist conceptualizations of the national political economy, these neo-Gramscian conceptualizations of the international political economy tend to operate with rather too neatly demarcated phases of stable regulation and accumulation punctuated by phases of crisis, underpinned by strong claims about the coherence and cohesion of an emergent transnational capitalist class.[4]

Here we can take Murphy's (1994) analysis of successive waves of development of international organization and supra-state regulation, which seeks to synthesize neo-Gramscian and regulationist approaches, as an example of the strengths and weaknesses of this school. Murphy argues that there have been several distinct waves of development of international regulatory regimes associated with successive social structures of capital accumulation. In each case he traces a dynamic of initial intellectual and administrative advocacy by influential individuals, the involvement of powerful states and ruling classes as sponsors of institutionalization, but also the consolidation of a wider legitimacy through alliances with other social forces within and across national states. And in each case he argues that the initial focus was on the establishment of regimes for the regulation of transport and communications, which laid the basis for the international regulation of a period of trade liberalization which was in turn followed by initiatives in the management of social conflict and in the area of human rights.

The ILO and the Regulation of Labour

In relation to the regulation of employment, the social origins of supra-state regulation mirror those which fuelled the development of state regulation of working hours and conditions within states in the late nineteenth century, namely a concern to subdue labour unrest combined with a preoccupation with taking any necessary concessions to labour out of inter-state and inter-enterprise competition. In particular, the formation of the ILO after the First World War represented a concertation between metropolitan capitalist nation states against the background of widespread working-class unrest (Alcock, 1971; Murphy, 1994; Haworth and Hughes, 1997), informed by the argument that the 'failure of any nation to adopt humane conditions of labour is an obstacle in the way of other nations which desire to improve the conditions of their own countries' (Preamble to ILO Constitution, 1919). Thus pressured by, but also in part incorporating, working-class demands, the efforts of the ILO participants sought to go beyond an earlier round of bilateral agreements between national states on such matters as age minima and maximum working hours for young workers, but at the same time faced the critical constraints of national sovereignties.

Key debates during the formation of the ILO revolved around the prerogatives of member states, which states would be participants, what principles might be embodied in the charter and finally the form of representation of employers and workers. In each case the contrasting industrial relations traditions and labour movement orientations of different countries, and especially of the USA on one side and continental Europe on the other, informed the resulting controversies and compromises. On the one hand the scope of membership of the organization in terms of states was drawn fairly broadly; a tripartite form of representation gave some voice to organized labour within a 'co-operative' framework; and the list of principles agreed by at least two-thirds of delegates covered such key issues as the right of association, a forty-eight-hour week, equal pay for equal work, and an end to child labour. On the other hand, however, the formulation of these principles fell well short of the demands of organized labour; their implementation was also sig-nificantly qualified in practice; 'economic' as against labour issues remained excluded from the competence of the ILO; the prerogatives of individual states remained intact as governments were simply required to put regulatory proposals to their legislatures; and 'the penalties for non-observance of ratified Conventions were highly theoretical' (Alcock, 1971, p. 36).

The strengths and weaknesses of the resulting pattern of international regulation have continued to reflect these conditions of the formation of the ILO system, though Murphy emphasizes that the transition from the Inter-national Labour Office to the International Labour Organization after 1945 involved the insertion of the ILO into a distinctive phase of international regulation characterized by the consolidation of Fordist production, Key-nesian demand management and the dominance of US state power (Murphy, 1994). Certainly, in the postwar decades cold war politics heavily shaped the role of the ILO. On the one hand the tripartite structure was made to cover very different forms of organization and representation from diverse national states, and cold war competition encouraged Western states to seek some accommodation with organized labour, both nationally and internationally. On the other hand, however, the dominant ideology of the organization became a strong version of 'free collective bargaining' which both qualified this inclusiveness and delimited the scope for active international regulation. Furthermore, this agenda was reinforced both by the sanction of withholding funds and by the active role of the AFL-CIO as an instrument of US foreign policy in Europe and the third world. In the light of such features, Murphy, following Cox, emphasizes that the forms of regulation pursued by the ILO through the cold war period contributed to a consolidation of US hegemony and a regime of capital accumulation in which organized labour in the metropolitan capitalist states was a subordinate but substantial beneficiary.

Cox links this to a strong version of the thesis of the emergence of a

corporatist state form, not only in Europe but especially in the USA, characterized as 'an increasingly visible and effective corporative state in which
organized labor forms an integrated whole with corporate management and
government for the control of the American economy' (Cox, 1977, reprinted
in Cox with Sinclair, 1996, p. 423). A virtue of this perspective is that it
underlines the limits of the ILO's capacity to address the problems facing
unorganized producers and marginalized masses in the third world, where
corporatism may be extended only to small minorities of employees and then
often in highly repressive forms. These authors also use the language of
primary and secondary labour markets to recognize that some workers within
the capitalist core remained outside such a corporatist embrace. However,
even in more recent versions of this analysis there is little recognition of the
internal tensions and limits of the forms of labour regulation which characterized the metropolitan capitalist states across this period, arising in
substantial part from forms of organized and unorganized labour resistance,
or of the very varied character of labour regulation in different national
settings. From the vantage point of our earlier discussion of the corporatism
debate this lack of differentiation is evident in the ready use of the term
corporatism to characterize class relations in the USA as well as Europe
through much of the postwar period; and it is also reflected in the way this
school later sought to analyse what Cox characterizes as the 'emerging promi-
nence of hyperliberalism' as a new hegemonic project (Cox with Sinclair,
1996, p. 457) in the 1980s.

   If we look beneath the veneer of generalized corporatist hegemony, however, the manner in which ILO-sponsored forms of transnational regulation
continued to be contested and negotiated between different metropolitan
states and capitals becomes clearer. For example, Vosko (1998a) uses an
analysis of the regulation of temporary employment/help service agencies to
compare the manner in which the supra-state regional regulation of pre-
carious forms of labour has developed in North America and Europe. She
traces the orientation of ILO policy towards the sponsorship of free public
employment services, initially (in the 1930s) through proposals to prohibit
private employment agencies and later (in 1949) by seeking either abolition or
regulation. She then shows how in practice this latter policy stimulated three
divergent state policies, those of prohibition, regulation and non-regulation.
In particular the growing sector of private temporary placement agencies in
the USA lobbied for 'employer status', remained unregulated at either state or
federal level and prompted non-ratification of the relevant ILO convention,
while in Europe regulation was the dominant policy response, though both
prohibition (mainly in Southern Europe) and non-regulation (in Ireland and

the UK) were also in evidence. More generally it should be noted that even by the 1990s the ratification of ILO conventions was very uneven across national states (OECD, 1994, p. 141; Haworth and Hughes, 1997, p. 185), while the USA had 'signed only one of the five core labour standards conventions issued by the ILO, and ratified only 12 of the total 176 ILO conventions' (*Financial Times*, 20 June 1996, quoted in Dicken, 1998, p. 464), underlining the manner in which the ILO framework has operated as a rather limited and flexible constraint upon the regulatory frameworks of national states in this period.

Trade Liberalization and Labour Standards

In this context a critical issue has been the relationship between processes of trade liberalization and the enforcement of internationally agreed labour standards. This has been an important issue ever since 1945, as the GATT regime of tariff reduction was developed as an alternative to the tariff wars of the inter-war period, but it has become pivotal in the context of the rapid reduction of tariffs since the 1960s, which culminated in the formation of the WTO in 1995. Of course, it is important to recognize that this process of trade liberalization has not created an open market of the sort envisaged in some neo-classical economic models. As Ruigrok and van Tulder (1995, chapter 9) emphasize, most of the key corporate actors in the current international economy grew in conditions which involved substantial state protection or support and this legacy continues to colour the character of their contemporary oligopolistic rivalry. Furthermore, with the decline in tariff barriers a whole range of non-tariff barriers (such as local content and anti-dumping regulations and import quotas) have become increasingly important as instruments for regulating trade between nation states (Dicken, 1998, pp. 91–6). Nevertheless, the evident limitations of the ILO processes of international labour regulation have sharpened controversy about a more direct linkage of trade and labour standards.

Such a linkage had been debated in the early postwar years, but the USA, the hegemonic state of the postwar order, refused to ratify such a linkage when it was proposed by the UN Conference on Trade and Employment in 1948, and as we have seen initiatives on labour standards remained separate and subordinate to the international trade and tariff agreements which have been negotiated since (Sengenberger and Wilkinson, 1995, p. 115). Now, however, these arguments have re-emerged, first in the context of GATT and the WTO and secondly in the context of the construction of more developed regional free trade zones, in particular NAFTA and the EU.

Significantly, in the final GATT rounds of the 1990s the US government, in the context of intensified international competition and significant national deindustrialization, was at least rhetorically championing the linkage of trade and labour standards as a basis for a level playing field. Meanwhile the local elites of many developing countries were fiercely critical of such proposals, primarily because they were seen as a covert form of protectionism exercised by the advanced capitalist states through the erosion of the competitive advantages of less developed societies. However, as both Haworth and Hughes (1996, 1997) and Castle *et al.* in their chapter suggest, the array of protagonists in play remained more complex than this. The labour movements of many advanced capitalist states favoured linkage, but labour movements in the developing world were more divided: some focused on the threat to employment, while others saw linkage as a stimulus both to increased productivity and increased labour shares. Furthermore, a broader resistance to linkage is grounded in the argument that both states and capitals should be free to construct local labour regimes uninhibited by such constraints.

Against this background Haworth and Hughes argue convincingly that both the ILO form of labour regulation and that based on the linkage of labour standards to a free trade regime will represent quite complex sites of struggle for control. Indeed, they suggest that 'the capacity for protective legislation to mean different things to different sectors – large scale capital versus SMEs, formal versus informal sectors, children versus adults, women and men, unionised and non-unionised, rural versus urban and so on – would result in its enactment becoming the site of complex and often quite contradictory mobilisations' (1996, 1997). In this context they also note that not only trade-union based forms of organization (from international union confederations such as the ICFTU to rank and file networks), but also other social movements concerned with issues of human and social rights represent important foci of mobilization, albeit on a terrain in which the power of both states and capitals remain formidable.

Three of the contributions to this book, those of Whitehouse and Zetlin, Castle and his colleagues, and Davidson and Taylor, address these issues directly. The first shows that ILO standards have continued to play a significant but problematical role in the regulatory regimes of advanced capitalist states, for they constituted important reference points in the controversies about decentralized bargaining and gender inequality in Australia, but it became increasingly difficult for trade unions to lever gains on this basis within the revised legislative framework.

Castle *et al.* examine the evolving roles of ILO conventions, WTO clauses and state policies in the contrasting context of a major developing society, India, and in respect of another focus of core standards, the regulation of child labour. First they note that the ILO standards on child labour have been very unevenly ratified and implemented, but they also argue that an alternative policy of linkage to WTO agreements, entertained by the US government and by consumer lobbies, is at best likely to have only a narrow impact, affecting child labour in high-profile export-oriented manufacturing but not in other sectors. Secondly they use a comparison across different states within India to show that state policies which combine educational, welfare and regulatory elements have succeeded in diminishing child labour on a broader front, while in backward states child labour has increased. Both this and the increased commitment of the Indian government in the 1990s underline the continuing importance of state policies, even in highly constrained circumstances. Finally they argue that, while the debates about WTO linkage have exerted pressure on developing states to address the issue of child labour, the linkage of national initiatives with a revised and more flexible ILO strategy is likely to be a more productive focus of mobilization by workers and consumers, albeit one which will also face resistance from the proponents of liberalization.

Finally Davidson and Taylor explore the competing agendas of social regulation involved in the social relations of sexual exploitation of indigenous people by tourists, as this has become an important feature of the burgeoning business of world tourism but also an increasing focus of feminist and human rights mobilization against such exploitation. As we noted earlier, they underline the international constraints and domestic priorities which lead to a limited and permissive regulation of these relations by local states, and this underpins the argument that challenges to this pattern need to question the existing social organization and interconnections of gender inequality, sexual exploitation, third world debt and global tourism on a broader front than the contemporary focus on child sex abuse and paedophilia. Thus their analysis not only addresses an important substantive topic but also underlines the relevance of a much broader analytical agenda – concerned with the politics of gender and sexuality as well as class and labour – growing out of the more focused concerns of this volume.

Supra-state Regulation by Regional Trading Blocs?

There remains a last strand to these discussions, concerned with efforts to construct regional forms of such regulation (especially in Europe and North America), which brings our earlier treatment of national regimes of labour regulation in the advanced capitalist states into closer connection with the dynamics and contradictions of supra-state regulation. Here Stone's (1996) recent comparison of the contrasting policies developed through the EU and NAFTA, in the context of the growing transnational mobility of manufacturing capital and threats of a race to the bottom, provides a useful bridge between debates on the strengths and weaknesses of each of these regional regulatory apparatuses. She identifies four emerging models of transnational labour regulation, two in each region, and traces the differential efficacy of each of these options in terms of their implications for inequality and the inclusiveness and political leverage of labour.

In Europe she sees two main lines of approach, both of which seek an 'integrative' outcome in terms of uniformity of legislation across the EU. The first European approach is through pre-emptive transnational legislation, directly applicable to all actors and states within the EU, as in those treaty provisions that govern social benefits for migrant workers or equal pay for men and women. However, the application of such provisions, which gain priority over national legislation, has been limited by inter-state controversy, and especially by British opposition. The second European model depends upon the harmonization of domestic legislation, encouraged by shared institutional incentives towards harmonization but reliant upon unilateral moves by member states. This has sometimes taken the form of EU directives which require national legislation within a given time-frame, as in such areas as minimum standards in redundancies and the Works Council provisions of the Social Charter. In such cases harmonization can tend towards pre-emptive legislation if individuals can seek legal redress for national failures to pursue effective harmonization.

Stone sees one of the strengths of the first European approach as its encouragement of active concertation between states in the development of shared norms. It is a powerful constraint upon internal regulatory shopping so long as the floor of rights is set fairly high, and it may encourage the development of transnational unionism. On the other hand she recognizes that the prerequisite of a consensus among the states makes it unlikely that such regulation will gain wide scope and more likely that common rules will involve 'harmonization downwards', while legislation removed from the national sphere is likely to diminish the leverage of labour unions and their role in politics, as the influence of national unions could become diluted and highly mediated in relation to multilateral agencies.

In the second European variant the continuing importance of national legislation makes the domestic leverage of labour more pertinent, while the greater scope for variable application of standards across countries is likely to generate less uniformity and thus leave more scope for regime shopping. Thus this apparently attractive compromise model could easily tip into pre-emptive mode, with the associated costs of inter-state antagonism and greater distancing from civil society, or through slack enforcement it could quite readily move towards regulatory minimalism. This diagnosis appears consistent with that of several other analysts who have emphasized the diversity of European industrial relations traditions and forms of state regulation and have projected a contest between a two- or three-speed Europe on the one hand (Crouch, 1995) and a creeping movement towards weakened forms of protection on the other (Streeck, 1992b). However, Stone hopes that in the longer run a more self-critical development of this approach, underpinned by a more effective transnational mobilization of organized labour, could perhaps form a firmer basis for effective upward harmonization built upon the more effective involvement of both states and agencies in civil society. Some of these issues are considered in detail in our companion volume (Waddington, 1999).

By contrast, neither of the emergent North American models of transnational labour regulation involves a project of integration, but each relies upon a form of 'inter-penetration' between the legal remits of the member states. The first variant involves a form of cross-border monitoring and enforcement which focuses on the conformity of each member state with its *own* rules. This is a feature of the Labour Side Agreement of NAFTA, introduced to allay the fears of organized labour by addressing 'the enforcement of each country's existing labour laws' in the areas of health and safety, child labour and minimum wages. The formal cross-border procedures of investigation, arbitration and enforcement 'are clearly drawn-out and cumbersome. In addition they are laced with qualifiers and exceptions [which] . . . provide a legal excuse for almost all nonenforcement' (Stone, 1996, pp. 462–3; see also Vosko, 1998a, p. 137). US unions have sought to use these procedures against US employers who fired Mexican workers for union-organizing activities, but without success. The second variant of North American transnational regulation has involved the extra-territorial application of domestic law by one state – primarily the USA – to activities within another, either by Congressional or court decisions which give US legislation 'extra-territorial reach', or as often by executive action by linkage with trading privileges for foreign countries.

Stone sees the NAFTA policy as underwriting a neo-liberal free trade perspective, not simply by failing to develop common labour standards but more actively by encouraging deregulation and a lowering of standards so as to avoid forms of enforcement which might fuel capital flight. She notes that this form of cross-regulation may leave some space for organized labour to mobilize leverage within the domestic political arena, but also how this may be compromised by an acute awareness of the scope for capital to run from more costly regimes. The final, extra-territoriality model is also open to potential labour mobilization within the domestic political arena, and has the theoretical potential to enforce high labour standards albeit on a piecemeal basis. However, this approach is likely to create antagonism rather than efforts to build 'shared norms and standards between nations', while its very piecemeal character limits its efficacy in constraining regulatory competition. Thus neither of the North American models transforms the established political terrain of labour movement activity as much as the European models, and at best they continue to afford organized labour in the USA a very limited space as subordinate partners in a free trade project. In these ways, then, Stone nicely illuminates the interplay between construction and reconstruction of capital–labour relations in specific states (discussed earlier in this introduction and in many of the chapters of this book) and some of the crucial contested issues in the shaping of contemporary regional transnational regimes of labour regulation.

Concluding Remarks

We have reviewed a wide range of literatures bearing on globalization, the interplay between supra-national and national systems of regulation, and the relationship between capital, labour and the state. Evidently, a single volume cannot bear on all the issues that we have identified, and we have cited several, notably those related to the trajectories of the so-called 'developmental states' and many developing states, which the following chapters do not address. The logic of the volume is analytical rather than substantive, in that each of the following chapters addresses an aspect of the links between supra-national regulation, national patterns of class compromise, and more local economic restructuring. Some chapters, such as those of Burnham, Kettunen and Hampson, address these themes primarily by analysing the changing character of national state regimes and their regulatory strategies in response to globalization. Others, by Peck, Whitehouse and Zetlin and Parry *et al.* focus on the linkages between such reformulated strategies and specific forms of the restructuring of national and local labour markets. Finally several of the chapters, especially those of Castle *et al.* and Davidson and Taylor consider particular examples of the relationship between state and supra-state policies as they bear upon the regulation of labour within the global economy. Thus each chapter stands in its own right as a treatment of its substantive topic, but each also contributes to a wider understanding of the processes of labour regulation.

We have argued that extreme accounts of globalization treat the process as an inevitable, ahistorical and actorless trend. It is, instead, driven by identifiable actors, including TNCs and nation states. Such institutions as the IMF and the WTO are not independent of nation states, though they may develop a 'relative autonomy' just as these states have been argued to be relatively autonomous from the capital–labour relation within their borders. As Panitch (1994, p. 87) argues, writers like Cox see the role of international agencies in unduly top-down terms, neglecting the ways in which changes in state agencies reflect a wider process of the restoration of conditions for accumulation: 'the state has, as always, been a fundamental constitutive element in the very process of extension of capitalism'.

We have also argued against views of nation states which imply that they reflect stable social settlements or mere dramatizations of models of Fordism or some variant of corporatism. This is not, however, to celebrate complexity and variety. The core idea is that the state intervenes to manage the capital–labour relation in ways constrained but not determined by this fundamental feature of any capitalist society. Forces beyond national borders impinge on this management in new ways but do not offer one path of development, be it lean production or anything else. Relations between capital, labour and the state, played out within an economic system which is intrinsically unstable and therefore dynamic, shape identifiable systems of labour regulation.

Notes

1. We should also register here some of the important ambiguities associated with a periodization in terms of Fordism, which forms the benchmark for any conceptualization of a transformation into post-Fordism. A key problem with regulationist accounts of Fordism is that they draw together characterizations of the labour process (Taylorism and Fordism), the wage form (high day wages and mass consumption) and state policies (Keynesianism and the welfare state) which are both unevenly implemented and problematically integrated in terms of developments over time and space (see Tolliday and Zeitlin, 1986a; Clarke, 1992; Williams et al., 1992; Peck and Miyamachi, 1994). On the one hand this makes it difficult to pin down at which level the defining features of Fordism or its successors are supposed to operate. On the other it leads to a proliferation of sub-types of Fordism and Taylorism which simply tend to echo the temporal and spatial variety of existing configurations.

2. Furthermore, the impact of transnational locational decisions varies sig-

nificantly between sectors, depending in part upon the extent to which activities are tied to specific locations or are readily transferable around the globe, and in part upon the specific carriers of transnational models of corporate best practice. Thus the idea of a lean production paradigm would not apply at all directly to large parts of the service or public sectors, though in the latter case the dissemination of policies of privatization may lever change in similar directions across different nation states.

3. It is important to emphasize here that we should include within the ambit of international regulatory regimes not only public interstate and supra-state institutions, but also the growing web of private arbitration and bargaining on such matters as tax regimes and bank regulation, in which private corporations and international legal practices and consultancies play central roles (Picciotto, 1996). On the one hand such webs of quasi-private regulation remove the process still further from both state-centred forms of democratic accountability and more direct challenges from below, but on the other hand they do not resolve the contradictory demands of different private capitals and competing state regulatory regimes (Picciotto, 1991, 1996).

4. Here we should also note another strand of analysis, that of the 'new international labour studies', which seeks to challenge the top-down emphasis of much of the IPE literature, including that drawing upon Coxian hegemony theory. This approach focuses attention on class relations outside the dominant capitalist economies and highlights the ways in which both organized and unorganized workers in the 'third world' constitute an active presence in the reconstitution of the international political economy and the recasting of national and international regulatory regimes (see Munck, 1988; Waterman, 1998).

2 THE RECOMPOSITION OF NATIONAL STATES IN THE GLOBAL ECONOMY: FROM POLITICIZED TO DEPOLITICIZED FORMS OF LABOUR REGULATION

Peter Burnham

Introduction

The realization that there is such a phenomenon as the 'world economy', of which all 'national' political economies are a part, presents a serious problem for social science disciplines that have been focused since 1945 on analysing national characteristics. This is the source of the current crisis of sociology, politics and industrial relations when confronted with 'globalization'. Paradoxically the notion of 'globalization' also poses problems for the discipline of 'international relations' which has developed in the twentieth century primarily as a study of the relations *between* states rather than as an analysis of the *medium* in which states exist. There is of course no uncontested definition of 'globalization'. However, Higgott (1997, p. 6) offers a good example of the eclectic IPE orthodoxy, arguing that 'globalization' represents (a) the emergence of a set of sequences and processes that are unhindered by territorial or jurisdictional barriers and that indeed enhance the spread of trans-border practices in economic, political and social domains, and (b) a discourse of political knowledge offering one view of how to make the post-modern world manageable.

The principal responses to the 'globalization' thesis have been either to assert the call of Ecclesiastes that 'nothing much has changed' (there are no new things under the sun) or to proclaim that 'all is new' (and presumably 'history is bunk'). While sceptics and realists line up to dismiss globalist claims and reassert the 'power' of the state (Hirst and Thompson, 1996; Waltz, 1979), liberals point to the retreat and even disappearance of the state as the principal form of political authority (Ohmae, 1995). In contrast to the often quite sterile debate produced by this realist/liberal encounter, this chapter suggests that a return to classical Marxist ideas on the relations between class, capital and state and a focus on the changing nature of the *form* of national state integration into the world economy may offer a more productive approach for mapping recent industrial, political and economic change.

In summary I shall argue three points. First, most approaches to 'globalization' fail to adequately theorize the relationship between states and markets insofar as they see states and markets as isolated, fragmented aspects of social reality existing in a purely external and contingent manner. The result is the populist (and misleading) claim that states have lost 'power' to markets. By contrast Marx's methodology views the relationship as internal and necessary and enables us to understand current change in terms of the recomposition of an organic whole. Second, processes of international restructuring are undertaken by national states in an attempt to reimpose tighter labour discipline and recompose the labour/capital relationship. Global capitalism is still structured as an antagonistic state system and many of the changes which characterize the global political economy are introduced by states in an attempt to solve problems that have their roots in labour/capital conflict. Finally, I shall argue that current governing strategies are usefully characterized in terms of *depoliticization*, which involves a shift from discretion to rules in economic policy, a reassertion of the boundaries separating 'legitimate' political, economic and industrial activity and a fragmentation/devolution of decision-making in numerous arenas. In terms of state regulation of labour, there has been a shift from *politicized* to *depoliticized* forms of management in the global political economy from the late 1980s, and changes in the global system (in many cases authored by states) are now used to bolster governing processes and reassert the boundaries of 'responsible' trade unionism.

States and Markets: Bringing Class Back In

There are a number of diverse approaches which seek to explain recent changes in state/market relations. The most popular frameworks are those that argue a version of 'post-Fordism' (Jessop, 1994b); a 'new global order/ withering away of the state' (Ohmae, 1995; Strange, 1996); and the 'internationalization of the state' (Cox, 1996). I have argued elsewhere (Burnham, 1991, 1997) that these approaches are flawed on three counts.

First, they counterpoise the state and the market as two opposed forms of social organization, stressing how globalization gives the market 'power over' the state with a resulting loss of 'sovereignty' and 'national autonomy'. The weakness of this view is that 'states and markets' are conceived in a reified 'thing-like' manner brought into a purely external relationship with each another. In this regard they follow implicitly the liberal/realist position which separates aspects of social reality and looks for external linkages between disaggregated phenomena.[1] I will argue that notions of externality and structure should be replaced by the dialectical categories of social process and contradictory internal relationship. In this way we can understand the social constitution of states and markets as differentiated aspects of the same set of fundamental social relations. Secondly, the approaches noted above over-estimate the extent to which national states could 'control' capital before 1973 – in this sense by invoking historically inaccurate notions such as the 'Keynesian Welfare State' they support the increasingly implausible idea of a watershed in the global political economy occurring at some point in the 1970s (for a general critique see Matthews, 1968; Tomlinson, 1981; and Glyn, 1995). Finally, they tend to see labour/capital relations as external to the process of restructuring (if deserving of a mention at all) and therefore have little to offer an analysis of the state's regulation of labour.

An alternative approach, and one which places class relations at the centre of analysis, starts from the premise that the relationship between states and markets is internal and necessary (although of course the institutional form of this relationship varies given the historical character of the class struggle). States are an aspect of the social relations of production (a historically specific and differentiated form of those relations) and their 'power' derives from their ability to reorganize labour/capital relations within (and often beyond) their boundaries to enhance the accumulation of capital both domestically and globally (for much greater elaboration see Holloway and Picciotto, 1977; Barker, 1978; Clarke, 1988b, 1991; Burnham, 1990, 1995; Bonefeld, Brown and Burnham, 1995). This interpretation of Marx's approach to the state has been developed most consistently under the auspices of the Conference for Socialist Economists (and in the journal *Capital and Class*). Rooted in Marx's account of the 'fetishism of commodities', this approach dissolves the state as a given category and sees it as a 'rigidified' or 'fetishized' form of social relations (see Holloway, 1994). National states exist as political 'nodes' or 'moments' in the global flow of capital and their development is therefore part of the antagonistic and crisis-ridden development of capitalist society. As Bukharin (1917/1972) argued at the turn of the century, the struggle between 'national states' (which is nothing but the struggle between respective groups of bourgeoisie) is not suspended in mid-air, but is 'conditioned by the special medium in which the "national" economic organisms live and grow' (the world economy). 'National' political economies (and the social division of labour within them) exist only as part of the world economy (and thereby of an international division of labour). Individual states may seek to alter the *form* of their integration into the world economy (through the routes of production, trade and finance) but they remain circumscribed by their ability to enhance accumulation and manage class struggle in both international and domestic arenas.

Recent changes in the global political economy are thus predominantly about reorganizing (rather than bypassing) states, and this recomposition is undertaken actively by states as part of a broader attempt to restructure, and respond to, a crisis of labour/capital relations (manifest in national terms as fiscal crisis, declining productivity, lack of competitiveness, etc.). In the last 25 years the strategies adopted by 'advanced' capitalist states to 'manage' labour and money look remarkably different from the received models of postwar regulation. In many cases, overtly 'politicized' forms of labour management and inflation control involving voluntary restraint, incomes policies and the machinery of tripartism have now given way to 'depoliticized' forms of management which marketize aspects of state activity and shift responsibility for management onto international regimes and independent organizations. In this way they 'internationalize' economic policy-making to the advantage of national governments. This, of course, is a long-standing strategy of national states, seen for instance in the return to the Gold Standard in the 1920s with its associated claims of 'automatic regulation'. The distinctive aspect of current developments, however, lies in the way in which states are able to capitalize on changes which have occurred in financial markets in the last few decades to shore up demands for low inflation strategies which are focused primarily on capping wage settlements.

The reregulation of financial markets (increased capital mobility, the creation of a genuinely integrated global market) in the last twenty years has undoubtedly affected the fiscal and monetary choices open to governments (Thompson, 1995).[2] Since foreign exchange dealers prefer to hold currencies backed by anti-inflationary policies, the search for counter-inflationary credibility is of paramount importance both rhetorically and materially. While in the postwar era, currency markets were driven largely by current account imbalances, now interest rate differentials are the prime determinant of exchange rate movements. The 1980s and 1990s have seen a general convergence in interest rates and any state which adopts a significantly looser monetary policy than the prevailing level risks a depreciation in its currency. Since the sheer scale of flows in the foreign exchange markets rules out reserve intervention as anything more than a short-term policy, monetary policy is, for the moment, inextricably tied to exchange rate management. The net result of this fiscal and monetary environment is that governments have a clear incentive to enhance their counter-inflationary credibility (for further elaboration see Thompson, 1995, 1996; also the debate between Hirst and Thompson, 1996 and Radice, 1997).

However, it is overly simplistic to view these developments as giving 'power' to markets over states. Rather, the reregulation of financial markets provides one of the strongest possible public justifications governments can muster for maintaining downward pressure on wages to combat inflation and thereby achieve price stability (states of course were responsible for the creation of the Eurocurrency markets that developed largely out of interstate rivalry focused on finance, see Van Dormael, 1997). In many key ways therefore, the reregulation of financial markets enhances the 'power' of the state *vis-à-vis* the working class (and employers) since it can be argued forcefully that price stability really is the crucial determinant in the global political economy and lack of 'competitiveness' translates directly into a loss of jobs and profits.

In this environment, where the maintenance of price stability is publicly acknowledged as the first objective of monetary policy (and high wage settlements are seen as a major cause of inflation), governments across the world in advanced capitalist states have attempted to control inflation by adopting 'rules-based' rather than 'discretion-based' economic strategies (Kydland and Prescott, 1977; Keech, 1992). 'Rules-based' approaches attempt to build counter-inflationary mechanisms into the economy by offloading part of the government's responsibility for economic policy onto a non-governmental body. This can be achieved in two ways. First, by offloading onto an international regime, usually an international monetary mechanism, which sets definite rules (Gold Standard, ERM). This attempts to build 'automaticity' into the system, formally limiting government room for manoeuvre. Secondly, by offloading onto a national body which is given a definite role in statute and thereby greater independence from the government (for example moves towards central bank independence). Whereas 'rules-based' strategies are attempts to 'depoliticize' the government's economic policy making (thereby shielding the government from the political consequences of pursuing deflationary policies), 'discretion-based' approaches are highly politicized since national governments play the central role in controlling inflation, usually through formal incomes policies. While 'discretion-based' strategies offer maximum room for manoeuvre (and enable governments to gain immediate credit for successful outcomes) they also carry a higher risk that economic crisis will become a political crisis of the state itself.

In Britain following the governing crises of the Heath/ Wilson/Callaghan years 'discretion-based' strategies have gradually, and falteringly, been replaced by the search for policies grounded in more publicly credible 'rules'. While in the context of the last twenty years this shift is clear (and was emphasized dramatically by Gordon Brown's decision to grant 'operational independence' to the Bank of England, within five days of becoming Chancellor), it is not depicted accurately in terms of unilinear historical development. State management of labour and money proceeds via a series of oscillations (fixed, floating, fixed rate; tighter and looser monetary policy; rules, discretion, rules, etc.) to secure the maximum effectiveness of specific policies. Although much of this may seem somewhat removed from a discussion of the restructuring of class relations, the real significance of the shift from 'discretion' to 'rules' (or from politicized to depoliticized management) lies in how governments use the language of 'external commitments' to legitimate the recomposition of labour/capital relations in the guise of global competitiveness (also see Gill, 1995). These remarks are best illustrated by analysing the change from *politicized* to *depoliticized* state management of labour, focusing in particular on wage policy, in Britain since 1945.[3]

The 'Failure' of Politicized Management in Postwar Britain

Throughout the period 1945 to the mid-1980s the British state adopted a politicized strategy to manage labour which required increasingly elaborate government intervention to persuade trade unions and others to moderate wage demands. In the context of relatively full employment (the product largely of fortuitous structural conditions as the Treasury was later to admit[4]), successive governments sought to regulate labour through moral exhortation (in the national interest), increasing the exercise of centralized authority over wage determination and through the creation of new surveillance and guidance machinery. As I shall indicate, in many key respects the story of state policy in the postwar period confirms the views of Kalecki (1943/1971, p. 141) that lasting full employment is unsound from the government's point of view, causing particular social and political problems, and that large-scale unemployment is 'an integral part of the normal capitalist system'.

As early as 1939, Keynes and others in the Treasury[5] expressed anxiety over the dangers of wage inflation (Cairncross, 1985, p. 399). With wage rates increasing by approximately 11 per cent per annum in the early years of the war, the 1944 White Paper on Full Employment further highlighted the problem of wage control, emphasizing that 'if we are to operate with success a policy for maintaining the high and stable level of employment, it will be essential that employers and workers should exercise moderation in wage matters ... increases in the general level of wage rates must be related to increased productivity' (PRO, T267/8). The response of the Attlee government (calls for moderation in the national interest, tripartite structures and increased intervention in the process of wage bargaining) set the pattern for the next 30 years. In addition to maintaining direct controls on labour (which were gradually phased out under Attlee's first term of office),[6] the government commissioned a series of reports on wages policy, the most important of which in 1946 called for the creation of a 'National Industrial Conference'.[7] Designated as a tripartite body (staffed by government, employers' organizations and trade unions), it was envisaged that the Conference would promote the 'general understanding by workers and employers of the basic economic considerations operative in conditions of full employment' and consider 'relative wage levels in different industries' (PRO, T267/8). Although the Conference was approved by Cabinet in May 1946 (although opposed by Bevin), it soon became clear, in the face of rising wage claims, that the Conference (in the form of the reconstituted National Joint Advisory Council) was an insufficient response to the problem of the wage/price spiral.

In a situation where the government faced the dual problem of attracting labour to 'undermanned' industries and preventing wage increases in others, the majority of state officials by 1947 accepted the view of Archibald Rowlands (Permanent Secretary of the Ministry of Supply) that 'if Ministers were serious about economic planning it was difficult to see how they could leave wage settlements entirely to employees and employers' (PRO, T267/8). The view that the government was required to intervene more positively in the fixing of wages than had been customary in the past, led Cripps to produce, in February 1948, the *Statement on Personal Incomes, Costs and Prices*. While the Working Party responsible for the Statement ruled out setting up a 'Central Appeal Tribunal' to oversee all major wage negotiations, its final report included strict adherence to collective agreements and emphasized that there could be 'no justification for any general increases in wages' (Cairncross, 1985, p. 404). Backed by the TUC, the voluntary wage freeze lasted eighteen months and saw annual wage rises drop from 9 per cent per annum between 1945 and 1947 to 2.8 per cent in 1948 to 1949. However, following devaluation and then dramatic import price rises associated with the outbreak of the Korean war, wage rates began to rise sharply in summer 1950.

The government responded by drawing up plans for a Wages Advisory Council whose function was to 'offer more specific guidance on wage and salary negotiations than the very general pronouncements it had made during the last few years' (PRO, T267/8). The Council would provide advice on all collective negotiations on rates of pay and on how settlements would affect the 'national interest'. It would not be formally independent (as for instance an Industrial Court) and it would be up to government to periodically define the national interest for the Council. Although these plans never materialized as Labour left Office in October 1951, the incoming Conservative government soon arrived at a similar conclusion, proposing in 1952 the creation of a Committee on Wage and Price Stability. In the early 1952 drafts of Butler's White Paper, *The Economic Implications of Full Employment* (finally published in 1956), Treasury advisers distinguished between demand-inflation (exacerbated by the defence programme and raw material shortages) and cost-inflation (produced by the strong bargaining power of trade unions and management slack). It was, they concluded, cost-inflation which produced the wage-price spiral, and unless workers and management 'modify their attitudes and methods in order that there really should be restraint, without losing the flexibility of wage structures', the whole economy was threatened (PRO, T267/9). However, in a pattern which characterized the 1950s and 1960s, the TUC refused to participate in government-sponsored committees oriented specifically towards wage restraint, arguing it was better that the TUC should 'seek to shape Trade Union policy on wages in its own way' (PRO, T267/9).

Between 1952 and 1956 the government faced a series of major industrial disputes involving engineers, shipyard workers, dockers and railwaymen. After a number of abortive attempts to gain the confidence and agreement of workers and employers, the government in July 1956 inaugurated a new Whitehall arrangement for dealing with wages and prices, which provided for more regular meetings of the Permanent Secretaries involved (Labour, Trade, Transport, Fuel and Power and Works) under the overall control of the Treasury (PRO, T267/10). This arrangement produced the proposal for a wage and price 'plateau'. The Treasury suggested there be a series of formal quadripartite meetings between the government, employers' organizations, the TUC and the directors of the nationalized industries. The aim was to 'spread stability backwards', starting with the nationalized industries, going on to private industry and ending up with the unions. However, in the face of opposition from both employers and unions, Eden modified the proposal and on 1 August 1956 saw each set of authorities separately, thereby formally inaugurating the 'plateau'. Nevertheless as wages continued to outstrip prices the Treasury concluded pessimistically by the end of the year that 'all that can be done is to make some speeches and statements to the effect that Suez and its consequences made it all the more necessary that all concerned should exercise restraint in regard to those elements of costs and prices which were in their own hands' (PRO, T267/10).

With the arrival of Peter Thorneycroft at the Exchequer in January 1957 the wage-price problem began to be considered from two angles. First, how to control prices in the nationalized industries (the 'plateau' had pushed many into the red). Secondly, the search for a substitute to the 'plateau' was intensified. By Spring, Thorneycroft had concluded that vague appeals for restraint had failed and without a prompt solution the government would be forced to devalue sterling. Between 1948 and 1956 incomes had risen by 75 per cent and output by only 28 per cent. In a forthright paper delivered to the Cabinet in April 1957 he argued that the main deterrent to wage claims and the main incentive to refuse them in the past was the risk of losing business because prices would be too high. In the peculiar economic circumstances of relatively full employment these factors had to a remarkable degree been removed. He concluded, 'almost everything that has been tried has been worth trying. Often we have had a partial or temporary success or near-success. Nevertheless we must frankly admit that we have failed. On the path we are at present following we are moving down towards an economic and political disaster' (PRO, CAB 129/087). Thorneycroft's solution was to indicate to the country that unrestricted collective bargaining was inconsistent with full employment and price stability. More positive government intervention was a necessity. He proposed that the government take a lead in the process of collective bargaining by announcing a figure for average wage increases based on the national average increase in productivity (the 'guiding light'). More-over, the government would have to be prepared to 'take sides' and be ready for large strikes since he argued it is the public and the currency which suffer from higher costs and prices, not the employers or the trade unions (PRO, CAB 129/087). Under Selwyn Lloyd in 1960 and later Reginald Maudling, the 'guiding light' was adopted first in the guise of a 'wages pause' and then in 1962 in the form of the first official incomes policy with a 'norm' equal to the average increase in national productivity.[8]

By the early 1960s the government was convinced that the problem of inflation was fundamentally a problem of 'autonomous wage pressure' (in other words, demand control could not stop inflation). A report submitted to the Cabinet by the Economic Section in 1961 (PRO, CAB 129/105) echoed Thorneycroft's earlier concerns by concluding:

> The disparity between the rate of increase of average earnings and of GDP per worker is the biggest single danger to healthy growth in the future. The rise in prices in the UK has been greater than in most other countries and has gradually eroded the benefits of the 1949 devaluation. If British costs go on rising at the present rate, not only will this country be unable to sell

enough exports to pay for the rising volume of imports required by the potential rate of growth, but even in the home market British goods will become less competitive, so that imports will rise still further. The deterioration of the balance of payments shows the need to prevent this continuing. Looking ahead there can be no doubt that a continuation of past experience will carry with it a very real possibility of devaluation being forced upon this country. *The essential need is to find a means whereby the national interest is brought to bear on wage negotiations* (emphasis added).

For Macmillan, and for successive governments up until the mid-1980s, the means by which the national interest would be brought to bear on wages would remain politicized through the form of indicative planning and official incomes policies. While the keystone of the first official incomes policy in 1962 was a uniform 'guiding light' (since income rises were restricted to increases in productivity, prices were therefore prevented from reflecting market conditions), after 1964 a fixed universal norm was prescribed, which included prices in order to gain union support.

In February 1965, Wilson replaced the National Incomes Commission with the National Board for Prices and Incomes (NBPI). A pay norm of 3–3.5 per cent was set in April 1965, which could only be exceeded if productivity gains were made (Cronin, 1991, p. 234). This effort to control wages on a voluntary basis collapsed in July 1966. Following the seamen's strike in May, the government introduced a six-month statutory pay freeze along with a set of deflationary financial measures. This was followed by the establishment of wage norms of between 3 and 4 per cent from July 1967 to the fall of the government in 1970. Although Wilson had argued that incomes policies would be pursued alongside controls over profits, dividends and rents, by 1969 it was clear that incomes policies were being used to hold back inflation and maintain profit margins by reducing labour costs. The 1969 White Paper on *Productivity, Prices and Incomes Policy* stated clearly that the government did not believe that any general reduction in the level of return on private capital would be helpful to the modernization of the economy.

Most studies of the Wilson period conclude that the government's attempt to hold down wages and reduce the significance of the shop stewards movement was a failure (Tiratsoo and Tomlinson, 1993; Coates, 1975). A number of factors contributed to this failure. The institutionalized forms of bargaining and consultation which successive postwar governments had set up to contain and co-opt the working class, in addition to twenty years of relatively full employment plus the degree of job control that local unions had achieved, considerably strengthened the power of workgroups and their shop stewards in relation to capital and the state. The strength of labour was evident in wage drift (the difference between national rates and actual local earnings) which characterized motors, docks, shipbuilding and engineering; in the growing pattern of short, local, unofficial strike action which spiralled in the Wilson years; and in the control exercised by the workforce itself over workplace and job security. By the mid-1960s, with inflation continuing to erode the value of real wages (the Retail Price Index increased by 35 points between 1963 and 1970 (Butler and Butler, 1986, p. 382)), over 90,000 autonomous shop stewards in engineering, docks and building produced an explosion of unofficial industrial action which testified to the inability of Labour governments or the TUC to control working-class resistance. This set the backdrop for the infamous report of the Donovan Commission on Trade Unions and Employers' Associations which influenced the strategies adopted by both Wilson and Heath in relation to the 'problem' of industrial relations.

Researchers for the Donovan Commission reported in 1966 that shop stewards 'were active in most industries and firms where unions are recognised' and that most stewards had 'established their right to bargain with management about most of the main aspects of their members' working lives – wages, conditions, hours of work, disciplinary matters and employment issues' (McCarthy and Parker, 1968, quoted in Coates, 1994, p. 106). This situation was characterized by the Commission as one of 'parallel unionism'. In effect, a two-tier bargaining system had been created. The upper tier was the formal structure recognized by law, where negotiation took place between paid union officials and management at an industry level, which the government sought to regulate. The lower tier was informal, not subject to regulation by law, highly decentralized and in the hands of workplace leaders (Jones, 1987, p. 78). The situation was portrayed perfectly by a report of the NBPI (1968) which commented:

> the essence of the problem of applying the incomes policy to Payment by Result (PBR) Systems is that a large part of the increase in earnings under them does not arise from 'claims' or 'settlements' in the accepted sense of the word, and they are often negotiated by individuals or small groups of workers with foremen, rate-fixers or first-line management . . . Thousands of such bargains are struck every day . . . we came across only one instance where a firm was attempting to apply the (incomes) policy to PBR earnings in any way (quoted in Jones, 1987, p. 77).

In short, union officials found themselves with no means of implementing the national agreements they signed. Donovan's conclusions echoed the findings of Board of Trade studies into the first shop stewards movement which grew out of the 'great unrest' prior to world war one (Aris, 1998). Official trade unions could no longer contain and channel the demands of the working class. Disorder in factory and workshop relations threatened to undermine management prerogative and *in extremis* undermine the ability of the state to regulate labour.

Building on the work of Tolliday and Zeitlin (1986b), Coates (1994, p. 109) has recently added some important qualifications to the picture painted by the Donovan Commission. Not only were there wide variations in the influence and activities of stewards in different plants but there were significant variations in degrees of management control even within the motor industry, normally cited as being the most prone to workgroup power. Nevertheless, in the upper echelons of the state the power of labour was viewed with increasing dismay. Government perception was of an impending political crisis produced by the working class whose decentralized form of action seemed increasingly beyond government or official trade union control.

The Donovan Commission's solution was for management to take the lead. In the Commission's view the shift in power to the lower tier should be recognized and effective procedures developed voluntarily to regulate actual pay, constitute a factory negotiating committee and cover the rights and obligations of shop stewards (Jones, 1987, p. 78). Through the centralization and formalization of steward organization, the shift to plant and company bargaining could be recognized and a link could then be re-established between wages and productivity. However, in the event Wilson disregarded Donovan's preference for voluntarism and opted for legislation to contain the strength of the shop stewards in the form of the 1969 White Paper, *In Place of Strife*. Wilson's solution rested on the formalization of the informal sector and called for legislation to provide the government with the legal authority to call a twenty-eight-day 'cooling off' period for each unofficial strike and compulsory balloting for 'official' disputes. These initiatives foundered on the rock of rank and file militancy, central trade union opposition and employer indifference (Hyman, 1975). However, as earnings increased by over 14 per cent in 1970 and as the number of days lost in industrial dispute over the period 1968–70 topped eight million (Jones, 1987, p. 79; Hawkins, 1976, p. 136), the Heath government attempted to push through what has been described as 'the greatest revolution in legal thinking about trade union laws since the Trade Union Act of 1871' (Kidner, 1979).

Heath's Industrial Relations Act 1971, had two, now familiar, objectives. First, it sought to consolidate union organizations as disciplining agencies, by conceding specific bargaining rights in return for 'responsibility'. Secondly, it proposed a range of legislation which aimed at strengthening individual rights against unions, enabling penalty clauses and criminal sanctions to be applied against irresponsible unions (thereby restoring the principle of Taff Vale[9]) and against 'unconstitutional strikers', all to be regulated under the jurisdiction of a distinct Industrial Relations Court. In this way it sought to undermine the organizational strength of workers and, by establishing the right not to belong to a union, it aimed to undermine the closed shop (Lewis, 1983; Bain and Price, 1983).

Whereas the Donovan Commission believed that reforms could be accomplished without destroying the 'British tradition of keeping industrial relations out of the courts' (Heath, 1971), the 1971 Act made the law the main instrument of solving the 'problem' of labour. The legislation, however, proved to be of very limited value, as the TUC instructed its members not to register under the new Act and most employers, anxious not to fan the flames of unrest, neglected to use its provisions (Jones, 1987, p. 86). Heath's policies to tackle wage inflation also came to grief. The Conservative's 'quiet revolution' in government which looked for market-based solutions to the 'inefficiency' of the British economy, formally ended in November 1972 when, after failing to tame the mineworkers, Heath dropped 'de-escalation' as a substitute for a formal incomes policy.[10] In conditions of rising unemployment and inflation, Heath's strategy from November 1972 to his fall in February 1974 was to pursue expansionary policies (culminating in the Barber boom) while imposing a firm incomes policy.

Drawing on initiatives adopted in the USA by Nixon, Heath introduced a three-stage statutory incomes strategy which began with a three-month wages and prices freeze and thereafter sought to moderate wage claims within set limits through an increasingly bureaucratic mode of regulation policed by the Prices Commission and Pay Board. Although Heath's first phase was relatively successful, Russell Jones correctly argues that the government's strategy of combining 'rapid expansion, depreciation of the exchange rate, and statutory incomes policy was fundamentally flawed' (Jones, 1987, p. 96). In the context of a worldwide commodity price boom, a fourfold increase in oil prices at the end of 1973 and the downward float of sterling since the introduction of the floating rate system, any attempt to peg wages within a narrow band – without the support even of the TUC – was bound to end in disaster. When the end arrived in early 1974 (after Heath's second ill-fated confrontation with the mineworkers) the Wilson government found it relatively easy to repeal Heath's Industrial Relations Act[11] but experienced more difficulty, as the 1970s wore on, in controlling wages and inflation.

Labour entered office emphasizing once again its special relationship with the official trade union movement. To blunt the rank and file militancy which had created problems for Labour in the 1960s and brought down the Heath government, the Wilson/Callaghan administration made the fullest possible use of policies of co-option and co-operation (backed by the use of force). Through the rhetoric of the 'Social Contract' (with its National Enterprise Board, planning agreements and Industry Act), Labour invoked the ideology of worker participation, uprated arbitration and conciliation procedures, enacted legislation to uphold employment rights, used productivity deals to promote sectionalism, encouraged the TUC to police 'irresponsible elements' and finally used troops to break strikes (Coates, 1980). Above all, Labour skilfully deployed the threat of imminent economic crisis to gain TUC backing for policies designed to drive down the cost of labour power.

By the first quarter of 1975, 500,000 civil servants had negotiated wage increases of 32 per cent, 100,000 power workers 31 per cent (matching the miners' 31 per cent rise in March) and gas manual workers 34 per cent (Coates, 1989, p. 72). In the face of rampant inflation and a deepening balance of payments problem which had not been corrected by Healey's $3.7 billion loans from private banks and the Shah of Iran in 1974, TUC leaders agreed in the summer of 1975 to impose voluntary pay restraint. Complementing Healey's infamous deflationary budget of April 1975, the government urged rank and file compliance with the pay norm. By the third quarter of 1976 the inflation of basic wage rates had dropped from 33 per cent in 1975 to just 18.7 per cent. Over the same period price inflation fell from 26.6 per cent to 13.7 per cent (Jones, 1987, p. 107). However, as the social and industrial 'benefits' of the Social Contract failed to materialize, and prices continued to rise, Labour's ability to control working-class resistance ebbed away. As Coates (1989, p. 74) explains, the processes which ate away at the loyalty of trade union officialdom, and undermined its credibility and role as advocate and enforcer of pay restraint, were the rising tide of the working-class unemployed and the persistent fall in living standards that accompanied Labour's policies towards the end of the 1970s.

By 1975 it was clear to the state that the politicized management of labour since 1945 had been far from successful. A Special Treasury Study of government wages policy (PRO, T267/28) concluded:

> it can hardly be argued that Incomes Policy has kept our degree of inflation lower than that of our neighbours, and until very recently it could not be plausibly asserted that import price problems had unfairly prejudiced our success. Moreover it cannot be said that the policy has found a formula for a fair or efficient distribution of incomes. Nor is there, in spite of the NBPI's

efforts, any evidence that 'restraint' assisted either economic growth or economic efficiency. Incomes Policy must therefore, to date, be judged a failure.

Depoliticization and Governing Strategies in the 1990s

By the late 1970s the economic conditions that had given rise to relatively full employment in Western Europe had changed. The return of large-scale unemployment, fiscal crisis and the volatility introduced by the switch to floating exchange rates and the reregulation of financial markets enabled the British state to reassess its approach to the regulation of labour. As Kalecki (1943/1971, p. 138) had argued in the early 1940s, 'the assumption that a government will maintain full employment in a capitalist economy if only it knows how to do it is fallacious'. Under a regime of permanent full employment, 'the sack' ceases to play its role as a disciplinary measure and the stronger bargaining power of the workers is likely to increase political instability and lead to problems associated with 'political overload' and 'ungovernability'. As we have seen, the ability of the state to successfully pursue anti-inflationary policies in conditions of relatively full employment is circumscribed fundamentally by the relationship that can be established between government, unions and employers' associations (and the relationship between the latter groups and their members). In such circumstances the implementation of anti-inflationary policies will always threaten to heighten class conflict and ultimately risk the danger that an 'economic/industrial' crisis will become a crisis of political authority itself (Goldthorpe, 1978).

One of the most important lessons of the 1920s (from the viewpoint of the state) was that the onset of recession paradoxically gave governments greater room for manoeuvre in devising strategies to regulate the economy. Switching from a politicized (discretion-based) system to a depoliticized (rules-based) approach enabled the government to 'externalize' the imposition of financial discipline on labour and capital. The stronger (and more distant) the set of 'rules', the greater manoeuvrability the state would achieve, increasing the likelihood of attaining objectives (in this instance, low inflation). This was the logic behind Britain's return to the Gold Standard in Spring 1925 at the prewar parity of £1 = $4.86. The move was subjected to a devastating critique by John Maynard Keynes, who argued that the prewar parity was too high and would impose painful and useless deflation on the British economy (Block, 1977, p. 17). Leading supporters of the return to gold, in particular John Bradbury and Otto Niemeyer in the Treasury, were adamant that the Gold Standard would make the British economy 'knave-proof', free of manipulation for 'political or even more unworthy reasons' (Rukstad, 1989, p. 440). In effect it was judged that the Gold Standard with its 'automatic corrective mechanisms' was the best guarantee against inflation. Similar arguments were employed by critics of the Conservatives' regime of politicized management in the 1950s. Supporters of the Operation Robot plan[12] argued that the rule of the market should prevail over interventionist management and 'if the workers, finding their food dearer, are inclined to demand higher wages, this will have to be stopped by increasing unemployment until their bargaining power is destroyed'.[13] The experience of the 1920s and the criticism voiced in the 1950s were finally heeded in the 1990s in a context where the reregulation of financial markets strengthened arguments favouring the implementation of depoliticized rules-based policies.

The parallel between Britain's return to gold in the 1920s and Major's determination to depoliticize economic policy-making by joining the ERM in 1990 is striking. Both 'regimes' seemed to offer an automatic corrective to inflation and both in the short term were successful in delivering their promise. Although unemployment increased in the 1920s, those countries which had returned to gold at prewar rates of exchange saw a reduction of wages and prices sufficient to reverse much of the wartime inflation. By contrast countries such as France, Belgium and Italy which ultimately returned to gold at parities below those prevailing before the war, 'were unable to prevent inflation from continuing into the mid-1920s' (Eichengreen, 1990, pp. 25–6).[14] In this light the now familiar view that joining the ERM was 'one huge and recognisable mistake' (Jay, 1994, p. 202), is to miss the point that it enabled the government to secure short-term victory in the April 1992 General Election while cutting inflation by almost a third between October 1990 and September 1992. In other words, the decision to join the ERM should be seen as a governing strategy whose success in the short term outweighed the political embarrassment it caused Major once he had attained his election victory. Moreover, as with the return to the Gold Standard many commentators also maintain that the rate on entry to the ERM was much too high. This, however, is to overlook that participation in the mechanism was not motivated by the desire to compensate inflation, wage increases and sluggish productivity by a lower exchange rate. The argument that the rate was too high seems to imply that a devaluation of sterling would have been desirable. However the purpose of joining the ERM was to exert a disciplinary impact on labour and capital, ostensibly imposed from the outside, forcing them to achieve downward pressure on wages and increased productivity, in short, lower unit labour costs.

Since 1990 the British state has sought to externalize the imposition of monetary discipline, first through membership of the ERM and then by moving at least rhetorically to restructure the institutional relations between the Treasury and the Bank of England. Major and Lawson agreed with the Bank of England in early 1990 that Britain would reap substantial benefits from joining the ERM. In particular because periodic exchange rate realignments would now be ruled out, both sides of industry, in Major's view, would be forced to face the long-standing problem of inflationary wage settlements. Thatcher's remedy for the 1980s, that policy should focus on the control of monetary aggregates (the Medium Term Financial Strategy), was weakened as the government found it increasingly difficult to control the money supply, and as different measures of money were seen to contradict each other (see Bonefeld, 1993; Grant, 1993). The prerequisite for sustained ERM membership was a reduction in unit labour costs through lower wages and the intensification of work. The Bank of England made this quite clear:

> The Governor has emphasised that henceforth companies can have no grounds for expecting a lower exchange rate to validate any failure to control costs. The greater stability which ERM membership offers sterling against other European currencies should in itself be welcome to business as it will enable firms to plan and invest with greater certainty. If companies recognise that they are now operating under a changed regime the benefits of lower inflation will accrue sooner, and at a lower cost in terms of lost output, than could otherwise be expected. But if they fail to recognise the constraints under which they now operate the outcome will prove painful to them (quoted in Smith, 1993).

With inflation rising, the ERM offered the government the opportunity to have monetary discipline 'implemented from without' (Sandholtz, 1993). Clearly, the Major administration hoped it could be insulated from the unpalatable consequences of 'economic adjustment' by shifting responsibility onto an international regime. ERM membership, the government hoped, would force employers to compensate for the high interest rate pressure on profits by confronting their labour force to secure lower wage rates and to increase output per worker. A falling exchange rate would no longer compensate sluggish productivity or enable wage negotiators to agree 'unacceptably' high claims. In essence, the ERM replayed the episode of Britain's return to the Gold Standard in 1925. The 'politics of austerity' could now be legitimated in the language of globalization with 'external commitments' uppermost. In many respects, and from the viewpoint of the governors,

ERM membership 'worked'. Inflation fell from 10.9 per cent in October 1990 to 3.7 per cent by September 1992. Lamont heralded the 'sea-change' in attitudes to inflation that occurred in Britain, particularly amongst trade union leaders, since joining the wide band in October 1990. But above all else, this act of depoliticization enabled Major to preside over the second worst recession since the Second World War and survive for a further term of office. In addition to undermining resistance to government policies (significant anti-poll tax riots occurred in April 1990), it secured wage restraint and forced British workers into deteriorating conditions for longer hours (Bonefeld and Burnham, 1996).

Following Britain's exit from the ERM the government began a search for a 'new framework', a 'new anchor', in short, for another strategy to depoliticize economic policy. On 8 October 1992, in a memo to the House of Commons Treasury and Civil Service Committee, Norman Lamont set out the policy framework which would replace the ERM. Counter-inflationary credibility would now be sought by restructuring the institutional relationship between the Treasury and the Bank of England in order 'to make the formation of policy more transparent and our decisions more accountable' (Jay, 1994). In November 1992 Lamont set an inflation target of 1–4 per cent and asked the Bank to assess inflation prospects in quarterly independent reports. With Kenneth Clarke as Chancellor in May 1993, the Bank was given the right of deciding the timing of interest rates. Finally in February 1994, Clarke outlined a new framework for monetary policy decision-making: decisions concerning interest rates would be taken at meetings between the Chancellor and the Governor and minutes would be published with some time delay. Well-publicized disputes between the Chancellor and the Governor led to a questioning of the ability of these halting moves towards central bank independence to constitute an effective counter-inflationary anchor. It is for this reason that the government in 1995 reviewed recommendations to enshrine price stability in statute as the primary objective of monetary policy and follow the Bank of France by creating an independent Monetary Policy Committee within the Bank to oversee the making of policy. In the wake of Blair's victory in May 1997, 'New Labour' completed the reforms begun by Lamont and Clarke. The move to introduce 'operational independence', broadly along the lines of the New Zealand model, has now left the Bank 'free' to pursue an inflation target laid down by a Monetary Policy Committee (for more detail see Bonefeld and Burnham, 1998). Moreover, the government seeks to pursue depoliticizing strategies associated with 'globalization' within the European regional context, through skilful use of the 'convergence criteria' associated with the planned introduction of a single currency. Wage restraint is required in order to keep inflation low and enable the government to bring the benefits of the single currency to Britain. Finally by allowing the National Audit Office to approve the assumptions used in projecting the public finances and by encouraging the IMF to draw up a code of conduct for 'open economic policy' (thereby gaining external validation for policies), Labour has travelled full circle from the IMF intervention at the height of politicized management in 1976.

Conclusion

Globalization we are told, *ad nauseam*, is a multifaceted phenomenon which has transformed both 'structure and agency'. At the heart of the globalization thesis is the claim that the relationship between state, capital and class has changed fundamentally. States are either 'withering away' or becoming 'internationalized'. Capital is now global and 'markets' hold and dispense 'power' in both economic and political arenas. The working class must adjust to a new flexible insecurity and can no longer rely on 'democratic government' (increasingly powerless) to fight its corner. Although this characterization of contemporary society appears persuasive, it is at the same time unsatisfactory. It fails to convince on grounds of theoretical adequacy or historical accuracy and does little to further our understanding of the state's regulation of labour.

Building on Marx's general analysis of state, labour and capital, the approach developed here identifies the internal and necessary unity of state and market in capitalism. Space is thereby opened up to view new developments in the global political economy in terms of the reorganization (rather than bypassing) of states. Moreover, this recomposition is undertaken actively by states as part of a broader attempt to restructure, and respond to crisis in capitalist society. From the viewpoint of state managers, 'politicized' forms of labour management and inflation control involving voluntary restraint, incomes policies and the machinery of tripartism have for the moment given way to 'depoliticized' forms of management which marketize aspects of state activity and publicly shift responsibility for management onto 'external' regimes and independent organizations. In this way depoliticization strategies aim to capitalize on recent changes in the global political economy to the advantage of national governments. Both forms of management have, of course, their limits and contradictions.[15] Acts of depoliticization are highly political and, until well established, risk provoking strong opposition. This was recognized for instance by Keynes in the 1920s when he opposed the return to gold, arguing that the working class would resist a direct reduction in its real wages and so even colossal unemployment would fail to bring down wages and prices to an internationally competitive level. Keenly aware of the political dimensions of economic policy, Keynes concluded that the main result of the new parity would be intensified class conflict and a crisis of the state. Moreover, recent upheavals in global financial markets have led sections of capital and social democratic governments to call for the adoption of 'constrained discretion' – a variant of rules-based management which appears more palatable to a New Labour audience.

By prioritizing strategies of depoliticization and externalization, states have found a novel (but not historically unique) way in which the mythical 'national interest' can be brought to bear on wage settlements. The technicalities of new currency bands, central bank independence, the reregulation of financial markets and single currencies should not obscure our perception that these are means of depoliticization designed to enhance the subordination of labour to capitalist command. 'Globalization' is therefore as much a state strategy as it is a market one (Panitch, 1994). Although individual governments may be bucked by markets, market-based solutions offer governments opportunities to recast labour/capital relations (often in the guise of controlling inflation) without resorting publicly to the 'politicized management' of the period 1945–86. In short, it is much too simplistic to see 'globalization' as transferring 'power' from states to markets. The task for future research is to retain a focus on the centrality of labour/capital/state relations and conceptualize global processes in terms of the recomposition of relations of domination and struggle.

Notes

1. In brief, as Gilpin (1987) argues, most orthodox international relations theorists are 'liberal' in their approach to the 'economy' and 'realist' in their analysis of the state. For an excellent critique of this orthodoxy in international relations see Rosenberg (1993).
2. The term 'reregulation' is preferred to 'deregulation' since in the last twenty years we have seen a complex process of the drafting of new regulations (often new market-oriented rules) rather than a simple lifting of regulations (see Cerny (1993)).
3. Although the following discussion focuses exclusively on Britain, the shift from politicized to depoliticized forms of labour regulation is evident across the globe as former bastions of social democracy (such as Sweden)

show increasing interest in central bank independence, and neo-corporatist models (Germany) seek greater forms of worker flexibility allied to hardline central bank independence. For a discussion of how the language of 'external commitments' is used to depoliticize see Bieler (1998).

4. PRO, T267/12 'Policy to Control the Level of Demand 1953–58' (Treasury Historical Memoranda No. 8, July 1965).

5. Most notably the authors of the Stamp Survey of Economic and Financial Plans 1939.

6. In particular the Essential Works Orders and the Control of Engagement Orders which limited labour mobility.

7. PRO, T267/8 'The Government and Wages 1945–51'. The so-called Nicholson Report was published on 26 March 1946 under the Chairman-ship of E. M. Nicholson, Secretary of the Lord President's Office.

8. In the interim Macmillan formed the Council on Prices, Productivity and Incomes (COPPI) envisaged as an 'independent' tripartite body but which became, with the withdrawal of the TUC, an ineffective academic group which increasingly refrained from criticizing government policy.

9. On Taff Vale, see Clegg, Fox and Thompson, 1964.

10. De-escalation or the N-1 strategy was a policy designed to give a lead to the private sector in wage settlements. Each successive major settlement in the public sector was to be 1 per cent less than the last. In 1972 the NUM submitted a claim for a 30 per cent wage increase to which the National Coal Board responded with 8 per cent in line with N-1. In the wake of the ensuing strike a court of inquiry recommended a 20 per cent settlement which was later agreed by both the NUM and the government. For details see Hawkins, 1976; Jones, 1987, p. 85.

11. The first stage in the repeal was the Trade Union and Labour Relations Act 1974 which restored the presumption that collective agreements were not intended to be legally enforceable. The second stage was delayed until Labour was re-elected with a majority when the Trade Union and Labour Relations (Amendment) Act was passed in 1976.

12. This was a plan to make sterling convertible on a floating rate in 1952. For details see Cairncross, 1985 and Proctor, 1993.

13. PRO, T236/3242 'Setting the Pound Free', memo by Cherwell to Church-ill, 18 March 1952. Cherwell, an opponent of the plan, used this argument to persuade the Cabinet that Robot was a risky strategy for the Conservative government, given their slender overall majority. He nevertheless accu-rately represented the argument of Robot's advocates.

14. Also see Feinstein, 1972, table 65, for an analysis of the movement of average wage earnings and retail prices.

15. The forms of management are not necessarily mutually exclusive. However, governments tend to prioritize one form over another as the guiding principle of their strategy. For example, Major saw the ERM as the cornerstone of economic policy, but this did not preclude the government setting a norm for pay rises in the public sector. See Bonefeld, Brown and Burnham, 1995.

3 LOCAL DISCIPLINE: MAKING SPACE FOR THE 'WORKFARE STATE'

Jamie Peck

A new political-economic orthodoxy seems to be gripping many of the advanced industrial nations. Couched in terms of economic globalization, the supposedly ineluctable imperatives of 'flexibility' and 'adaptability' on the part of labour, and the necessity of confronting 'hard choices' in the field of social policy, this new orthodoxy has it that the only realistic strategy for nation states in these competitive times is a combination of macro-economic austerity, deregulated labour markets and radically reformed welfare provisions. In this context, welfare reform has assumed unprecedented significance, as the once-celebrated principles of welfarism have become subject to unyielding political onslaught. Welfare systems, along with their 'dependents', are now castigated as symbols of outmoded values, as inhibitors of labour market flexibility, and as unproductive drags on the wealth-generating economy. Echoing a familiar refrain of Thatcherite conviction politics, the increasingly insistent plea from politicians of virtually all stripes is that *there is no alternative* to fundamental welfare reform. Cutting costs and appealing to the self-interest of middle-class taxpayers are factors here, but they are not the only factors. The challenge is a greater one: to reform welfarist principles as well as practices, to transform incentive structures as well as institutional structures, to replace passive welfare with active 'workfare'.

> We understand that economic stability is the prerequisite for radicalism in social policy rather than an alternative to it. We must be the parties of fiscal and economic prudence. Combined with it must be reform of the welfare state. The public simply won't pay more taxes and spend more to fund an unreconstructed welfare system ... We are spending. We are taxing. But we

have more poverty and inequality ... Welfare has become passive; a way of leaving people doing nothing, rather than helping them become active (Tony Blair, speech to the Party of European Socialists' Congress, Malmo, 6 June 1997).

Like the US Democrats before it, the British Labour Party has placed welfare reform at the heart of its political programme. According to Tony Blair, 'the greatest challenge for any democratic government is to refashion our institutions to bring [the] new workless class back into society and into useful work, and to bring back the will to win'.[1] As Chancellor Gordon Brown puts it, the new Government's objective is to 'rebuild the welfare state around the work ethic' (quoted in the *Guardian*, 26 June 1997, p. 25).

A striking feature of what is apparently becoming a transnational welfare reform effort is that while the scale and shape of welfare systems differ markedly between, and sometimes within, nation states (see Esping-Andersen, 1996), the current repertoire of reforms share a number of common characteristics. First, the critique of welfarism is increasingly formulated in the language of 'welfare dependency'. Dependency discourses seek to establish the causes of poverty and un(der)employment in terms of individual and even moral failings (see Schram, 1995). One of the principal effects of this discourse, once welfare and welfare recipients have been constructed as the root of the problem, is to legitimate distinctively *anti*-welfare restructuring strategies. It follows that any alternative system must tackle the perceived problem of passivity through 'active' measures designed to reconnect the 'workless' with wage-labour, along with its associated ethics and disciplines. Policy proposals focus increasingly on work and work ethics, the once broad remit of welfare reform collapsing into a narrow preoccupation with welfare *to work*. The emerging orthodoxy has it that systems of welfare, based on the axioms of needs-based eligibility, social entitlement and labour market exclusion, should be replaced by *workfare regimes*, based on selective, active programmes geared to maximizing participation in wage-labour (see Shragge, 1997; Peck, 1999).

This uneven shift from welfarism to workfarism seems also to be associated with changes in the dominant scales and sites of regulation: the ideological 'decentring' of welfarism typically has an institutional analogue in various forms of decentralization, defederalization and localization in welfare processing and programming. While experiences are inevitably uneven, path-dependent and contested, the broad pattern might be characterized as one in which nationally-constituted welfare regimes are giving way to locally-constituted workfare regimes. In the process, new 'models' of reform are being developed at the local level, models which are *themselves* globalizing as they begin to define the terms of transnational policy discourse. One of the ways in which the case for welfare reform is being pressed in Britain, for example, is through a highly selective reading of American experience, as boiled-down versions of the 'Californian model' and the 'Wisconsin model' are deployed to shift the terms of the debate, not least in order to foster the impression that workfare can work (see Mead, 1997; House of Commons, 1998; Matthews and Becker, 1998; cf. Theodore, 1998a).

The rise of local workfare systems does not mean that nation states have somehow absented themselves from the task of welfare reform. On the contrary, nation states remain in many ways the principal actors in the reform process, though increasingly their role is cast as that of an orchestrator or animateur of a tendentially decentralizing system, in contrast to their more managerial, 'hands-on' function under welfarism. More often than not, it is nation states that are leading the attack against welfarism; it is nation states that have opened up the space for local experimentation with work programmes; it is nation states that are galvanizing and lubricating the reform process (see Peck, 1998b). This has certainly been the case in Britain and the United States, where the Clinton and Blair administrations have appealed in different yet related ways to notions of decentralized workfarism in their attempts to institute radical welfare reform (see Theodore, 1998a). Clinton's far-reaching reform of 1996, the Personal Responsibility and Work Opportunity Reconciliation Act, did this by eliminating federal entitlements and 'block-granting' residual welfare/workfare provisions to the states; Blair is beginning to do this through the empowerment of local partnerships and private contractors under the somewhat ironically named 'New Deal' welfare-to-work programme. Though British politicians remain somewhat squeamish about the term 'workfare', this is clearly the thrust of policy. Ruth Lister has characterized the New Deal as 'a further step along the workfare road' (1997, p. 19; see also Philpott, 1997).

It is clear also that much of the inspiration for the current round of British reforms can be traced to the home of workfare, the United States. The USA has accumulated more than 25 years' experience of welfare-to-work programming, though the results have been as mixed as they have been modest (Handler, 1995). The hunger for solutions to what is impatiently referred to as the 'welfare mess' has become such, however, that any indications of 'successful' local programming are immediately seized upon, hyped and remorselessly emulated. This has been the experience of the Greater Avenues to Independence (GAIN) programme in Riverside, California, which following positive research evaluations in the early 1990s emerged as 'most touted welfare-to-work program in the nation' (*US News and World Report*, 16 January 1995, p. 30;

Department of Labor, 1995). California Governor Pete Wilson was moved to describe Riverside as the 'dream county' for welfare reform.[2] Delegations of visitors from around the United States, and from overseas, have since poured into the Riverside GAIN offices, anxious to learn the secrets of this 'work-first' approach to welfare reform in which participants are cycled through an intensive, short-term programme designed to effect rapid re-entry into the labour market. The programme is strictly mandatory, while every effort is focused on getting jobs for participants *quickly*. According to one of the architects of the Riverside method, the fundamental principle is 'the greater good for the greater number':

> I've got to keep my investment in service restricted to the most minimal level it could *possibly* take in order to get a person a job. So how *few* services can I render and still get somebody employment, so that we can reach out and touch many more welfare recipients' lives? . . . We had to become a kind of Wal-Mart organization. We had to keep our costs down, our overhead down, and deal in volume. And we had to have satisfied customers, which is the business sector, if we're going to get repeat business.[3]

One of the reasons why the Riverside approach has attracted such attention is the way that it marries a distinctive, no-nonsense philosophy with positive evaluation results (see Gueron, 1996). The California GAIN programme was celebrated in Labour's *Road to the Manifesto* as an example of 'world's best practice' in work-based welfare reform (Labour Party, 1996, p. 9).

As a practical manifestation of the philosophy of workfare, the Riverside programme presents an opportunity to consider some of the wider *labour-regulatory* impacts of such work-first approaches to welfare reform. Local workfare experiments of this kind are more than fads of social policy; they are at the leading edge of contemporary attempts to transform regulatory norms in the lower reaches of the labour market. Workfare is not simply about making the poor work; more fundamentally, it is also about making flexible labour markets work. The Riverside strategy is concerned to enforce both work and work values in the context of a deepening moral panic over the work ethics of the poor, coupled with the continued deterioration of low-income labour markets. Work-first workfare is about realigning welfare provisions, incentive structures and work expectations in the light of the realities of flexible employment. It aims to (re)socialize welfare recipients for contingent work. As one of Riverside's managers explained,

> Employment, that's education itself . . . It's also socialization. You learn self-discipline and those sort of traits. You learn how to temper your personality

... I think we sort of got off the track, probably in the sixties, about the value of work ... We forgot that employers do education and training on the job, training people in their way of doing things ... and how really important that is. Instead we had government doing it, or sending them off to school.[4]

This chapter presents a critical analysis of Riverside's work-first approach to workfare, outlining its methodology and considering its role in the process of labour control. It will be suggested that local workfare systems of this kind presage the installation of a new regime of labour control, locally-applied (see Peck, 1996; Jonas, 1996), imposing what in some ways are nineteenth-century regulatory norms in the context of contemporary 'flexiblizing' labour markets. The remainder of the chapter is divided into four parts. It turns next to an outline of the broader context of the workfare offensive, defining workfare *vis-à-vis* welfare as a political-economic strategy. Following this, the Riverside method is examined, prior to a consideration of the ways in which work-first approaches are contributing to a reworking of regulatory norms in the labour market. The chapter is concluded with a comment on the role of work-first approaches and the difficulties of policy transfer in what is fast becoming a transnational workfare offensive.

The Workfare Offensive: Terms and Terminology

It would be quite wrong to portray the workfare offensive as some unmediated, homogenous, 'Americanization' of social and labour market policy. In reality, workfare philosophies, practices and programmes have different inflections in different countries, reflecting political traditions and institutional structures. The term 'workfare' itself is highly elastic, its meaning often varying with the context in which it is used (see Standing, 1990; Peck, 1998c). It is necessary to be sensitive to these variations in meaning and signification, but it is equally important to be clear about what, in generic or abstract terms, workfare stands for. While the origins of workfare lie in a series of quite narrowly defined welfare-to-work experiments in the USA, the term is 'now used in a much broader sense to include, as a condition of income support, the requirement that recipients participate in a wide variety of activities designed to increase their employment prospects' (Evans, 1995, p. 75; see also Noël, 1995; Mead, 1997). More broadly still, workfare is taken by some as a paradigmatic indicator of 'post-welfarism', as a transition of sorts is identified from welfare states to workfare states (see Jessop, 1993; Shragge, 1997). For present purposes, workfarism is generically defined in terms of the following three criteria:

- individually, workfarism is associated with *mandatory* programme participation with a view to behavioural modification, in contrast to the welfarist pattern of entitlement-based systems and voluntary or optional work programme participation;
- organizationally, workfarism involves a *systemic* orientation towards work and labour-force attachment, displacing welfare's bureaucratic logic of eligibility processing and benefit delivery;
- functionally, workfarism implies an ascendancy of *active* labour market inclusion over passive labour market exclusion.

These workfarist principles are becoming embedded in rather different ways in the post-welfare settlements which are currently being engineered across parts of north America and western Europe (see Noël, 1995; Martin and Sunley, 1997), but as a set of principles it is clear that they diverge significantly from those of welfarism. Table 3.1 summarizes some of the more telling contrasts between established welfare structures and emerging workfare strategies. Where welfare stands for the principles of needs-based entitlement and universality, workfare stands for market-based compulsion and selectivity. Where welfare stands for passive income support, workfare stands for active labour market inclusion. Where welfare constructs its subjects as claimants, workfare reconstitutes them as jobseekers: the status of being *on* welfare is replaced by the transitory experience of being processed back into work *through* workfare (see Dean, 1995).

Welfare and workfare also imply alternative modes of labour regulation. While welfarism was fundamental to the stabilization of Fordist wage relations, to the regulation of incomes and demand, and to the reproduction of industrial labour during the postwar 'Golden Age' (Gough, 1979; Lipietz, 1987), workfare strategies are being pursued in a very different kind of labour market. There is a brutal but undeniable logic in the way that workfare aggressively mobilizes workers for low-waged work. Under conditions of wage and employment polarization, workfarism maximizes (and effectively mandates) participation in contingent, low-paid work by churning workers back into the bottom of the labour market, or by holding them deliberately 'close' to the labour market in a persistently 'job-ready' state (see Swift, 1995). It constitutes its subjects as active agents, denying a stable mode of existence outside the wage-labour market to all but the irredeemably 'unemployable'. In Offe's (1985) terms, it represents a shift from principles of labour market exclusion to those of labour market inclusion. The OECD (1990, p. 88) characterizes this transition as one in which systems of labour market regulation based on passive income support are being displaced 'by a combination of

Table 3.1 *Welfare structures and workfare strategies*

	Welfare structures	Workfare strategies
Ideological principles	Entitlement	Reciprocity
	Aid distributed on basis of need	Enforcement of work and work values
Objectives/rationale	Reducing poverty through income transfers	Tackling welfare dependency through promotion of work
	Responding to manifest social need	Maximizing labour market participation
Dominant discourse	Need and entitlement	Work, personal responsibility and self-/family-sufficiency
	Social work/bureaucratic codes and norms	Business/employment service codes and norms
Means	Passive income support	Active labour market integration
Labour-regulatory function	Exclusion from wage-labour	Inclusion into wage-labour
	Socially-sanctioned recipient groups defined on basis of ascribed/categorical characteristics	Market-determined treatment groups defined on basis of job readiness
Subject/state	Welfare recipient	Job seeker
	On welfare	*Moving through* workfare
Social relations	Determining entitlements of passive subjects	Interventionist case management of active subjects
Hierarchy	Centralized control	Centrally-orchestrated devolution
	Limited local autonomy in programme design, entitlement and eligibility	Increasing local discretion over programme design, entitlement and eligibility
	Management by input controls and sanctions	Management by output targets and incentives
Delivery	Bureaucratic; line management ethos	Flexible; local market ethos
	Process and input orientated	Output and outcome orientation
	Standardized programmes	Variegated programmes
Work/work programme participation	Limited	Extensive
	Voluntary	Mandatory; ethos of compulsion

Source: Peck, 1999.

active reintegration policies, positive incentives to search for work and a safety net in the form of minimum income security'. Workfare systems are more 'active' in the sense that they are systemically organized around the goal of maximizing employment for designated social groups (such as the young unemployed or lone parents). They also seek actively to adjust the self-images and labour market expectations of welfare recipients, transforming 'those attitudes, affects, conducts and dispositions that present a barrier to the unemployed returning to the labour market, and alienate them from social networks and obligations' (Dean, 1995, p. 572; see also Offe, 1985).

As the centrepiece of an 'active' regime of labour regulation, workfare can be seen as a strategy for the social reproduction of the contingent labour supply. Workfare seeks to compensate for the weakened 'demand pull' of contingent labour markets, the capillary action of which has been ruptured by job instability and low pay. Willfully misinterpreting this as an individual/ motivational problem, and conveniently sidestepping the structural economic explanation of deficient labour *demand*, workfare seeks to counteract the weak pull of contingent work by inducing a concerted push from welfare. According to workfare advocate Lawrence Mead (1997), welfare recipients will only be reconnected with the world of work with the right combination of 'help and hassle'. For Mead, compulsion is the defining feature of effective workfare programmes because it is this which triggers the push from welfare. But this assumes that jobs are available for 'activated' welfare recipients to enter. When an adequate supply of decent-paying jobs is absent workfarism is likely to have deep and adverse effects both on the 'self-formation' of welfare recipients, who are forcibly engaged in the governance of their own subordination to contingent work (Dean, 1995), and on the structure of labour markets, where it reinforces the downward drag on pay and conditions (Peck, 1996). Workfarism therefore represents a far-reaching regulatory strategy.

> Workfare should not be a short-term program to existing welfare clients, but a long-term program to destroy the culture of poverty ... what's most important is not whether sweeping streets or cleaning buildings helps Betsy Smith, single teenage parent and high school dropout, learn skills that will help her find a private sector job. It is whether the prospect of sweeping streets and cleaning buildings for a welfare grant will deter Betsy Smith from having the illegitimate child that drops out of her school and onto welfare in the first place – or, failing that, whether the *sight* of Betsy Smith sweeping streets after having her illegitimate child will discourage her younger sisters and neighbors from doing as she did (Kaus, 1986, p. 27).

Under workfarism, the economics of the workhouse are being reworked, as local responses are fashioned to cope with the continued casualization of labour markets. In America's central cities in particular – the primary sites of the 'welfare mess' – deteriorating pay and conditions at the bottom of the labour market have produced serious shortages of entry-level jobs paying decent wages (Danziger and Gottschalk, 1995; Capelli et al., 1997; Theodore, 1998b). Pay and conditions at the bottom of the US labour market have actually fallen below the regulatory floor established by the welfare system. A demand-side resolution to this imbalance between low-waged work and welfare might involve the raising of wages and employment standards in the contingent labour market. The Riverside approach, on the other hand, represents a radical supply-side strategy: cut welfare and reregulate contingent workers. It creates contingent welfare as a means of enforcing contingent work. Welfare ceases to exist as a temporary shelter from the vagaries of low-wage labour markets. In addition to exerting a downward pull on wider regulatory standards, such models recall the workhouse principle in standing as a persistent reminder of the price to be paid for unemployment. Under workfare regimes such as the Riverside model, welfare recipients are aggressively 'jobclubbed' into private-sector jobs. This has the effect, within local labour markets, of driving down both the reservation wage of the unemployed and the prevailing market wage for low-paid workers, while also further destabilizing the contingent labour market. In transferring yet more of the costs and risks associated with contingent employment to workers themselves, workfare may also be performing a basic regulatory function, in mobilizing a 'job-ready' supply of workers for the very bottom of the labour market.

Work-first, California-style: The Riverside Method

California's counties have been developing a range of approaches within the state's GAIN programme since the mid-1980s, ranging from education and training-orientated models (or the 'human capital development' method) to work-first, job-search-based approaches (known as the 'labour force attachment' method). A detailed three-year evaluation of GAIN in six counties conducted by the Manpower Demonstration Research Corporation (MDRC), concluded that the work-first approach was the most cost-effective way of moving welfare recipients (most of whom are single mothers) back into work, while the results for the human capital approaches were much more mixed (Riccio, Friedlander and Freedman, 1994; Gueron, 1996). The MDRC study tracked the experiences of an 'experimental' (on-programme) group and 'control' (off-programme) group over a period of three years. Across the six research sites, the outcomes could best be described as modest, but very strong results were achieved in the one site which had most single-mindedly pursued a work-first strategy, Riverside County, an expanding suburban area east of Los Angeles. Over three years, Riverside generated average earnings gains of $3,113 (49 per cent) for experimentals relative to the control group, while reducing welfare payments by an average of $1,983 (15 per cent). Most strikingly for policy-makers, every public dollar invested in the Riverside programme resulted in $2.84 being returned in the form of reduced welfare costs and increased tax receipts.

MDRC concluded that the Riverside results were 'the most impressive . . . yet observed for a large-scale welfare-to-work program' (Riccio, Friedlander and Freedman, 1994, p. 3). Although MDRC was quick to emphasize the dangers of 'overpromising' on the basis of these results,[5] politicians at the state and federal level seized on the Riverside model as concrete evidence that workfare could work. Following the passage of federal welfare reform in 1996, the work-first package has become an even more attractive one, because the new block-grant system requires states to meet exacting caseload reduction/work placement targets while actually eroding the resources available for training and employment programmes. States are consequently confronted with strong financial incentives to reduce the welfare rolls by way of minimum-cost interventions and to place recipients in 'real' jobs, rather than induct them into (costly) education and training programmes (see Edelman, 1997). The federal reform process has placed a premium on low-cost, short-term meas-ures, thereby raising the real prospect of a 'race to the bottom' in welfare standards and confirming the predictions of those critics who have been concerned for some time that, 'Riverside is the future' (Handler, 1995, p. 84).

In the context of an increasingly frenzied process of welfare reform in the USA, attention has focused on those features of the Riverside policy package which might be 'transferable' to other areas. The programme evaluation and policy transfer literature emphasizes five key features of Riverside's work-first approach: first, there is a pervasive emphasis on job search throughout all elements of the programme; second, this is reinforced by the continuous incantation of a strong 'employment message'; third, participation is strictly mandatory; fourth, a system of 'intensive case management' effectively 'perso-nalizes' the case worker–client relationship, permitting the close tracking of individual job search activities; and fifth, the programme is operated under very tight financial parameters, including the use of performance-based incen-tive systems for individual case workers and for local GAIN offices, thereby ensuring that high throughputs of participants can be achieved at low cost. All this is undergirded by a forcefully-articulated programme philosophy: 'Each day in employment is a good day.' The Riverside approach is based on the notion that even the most menial job can be a 'learning experience' for the programme's 'welfare-dependent' clients, whose shortcomings are represented in behavioural and attitudinal terms. In short, work is promoted as the antidote to welfare dependency.

> In America's past there was a belief that if you worked hard, did good work, and were reliable, you would eventually prosper. This belief is still valid. Proof of this is evident in the success of our GAIN clients ... Employment, however modest, teaches and reinforces very basic, yet essential, skills necessary for acquiring and retaining employment, that many people take for granted but not all of us have, such as: setting the alarm clock; getting to work on time; accepting supervision; learning to complete tasks reliably; getting along with co-workers; and, dressing appropriately for work.[6]

The Riverside programme deploys a fairly conventional range of services – including job clubs, individual client counselling, assisted job search and basic education provision – but is distinctive in the aggressive way it seeks to convey its 'employment message' to clients and the exhaustive emphasis which is placed on moving participants into work as quickly as possible. According to MDRC President Judith Gueron,

> More than any other place I know of, this program communicates a message of high expectations. When you walk into a GAIN office in Riverside, you are there for one purpose: to get a job. At orientation, job developers announce job openings; throughout, program staff convey an upbeat message about the value of work and people's potential to succeed. If you are in an education program ... you are not marking time, as you can in some locations ... [S]taff who are closely monitoring your progress will insist that you look for a job. Finally, if offered a job by a job developer, you have to take it or have your grant reduced ... Under this regime, welfare *feels* temporary.[7]

The cornerstone of the Riverside method is the job club/job search function, into which most participants are directly channelled. This intensive component of the programme contains many familiar elements, such as help with the completion of job applications and search techniques, but also seeks to strike at the heart of the 'pathologies' ascribed to the welfare population by drawing attention to the 'differences between a working lifestyle and a welfare lifestyle ... The participant is encouraged to look at what he/she can do *now* as a start toward a working lifestyle' (Riverside County DPSS, 1994, p. 7). Crucially, clients must learn to follow the rules: a strict set of rules, mirroring those pertaining in the labour market itself, are enforced on the programme. This is epitomized by the list of 'Job Club Rules' which are bluntly outlined for the benefit of every participant:

1. Be on time – 8.30 to 12.30
2. Dress for success
3. Full class participation
4. No criticisms
5. No food
6. No drink
7. No gum
8. Daily job search

While occasionally terse, the tone of the programme is generally up-beat and positive. Programme workers adopt a business-like approach, which is more akin to that of a private employment agency than a traditional welfare office. Yet the climate of coercion clearly impacts on the relationship between case workers and their clients. The majority of participants are mandated to attend the programme and the threat of benefit sanctions is a real one. Of the eight largest counties in California, Riverside has the highest rate of sanctions for non-compliance. As the programme's director has put it, 'It is not optional. You don't have the luxury, if you're a welfare recipient, to stay home. In fact, we *insist* that you come here ... but if they don't even come and show up, we will cheerfully reduce their welfare grant.'[8]

The Riverside model resonates with conceptions of 'welfare dependency' in striving actively to inculcate a 'basic work ethic', employment itself being viewed as a 'gradual socialization process'. Encouraged to regard 'any job as a good job', participants usually find themselves rapidly reintegrated into the labour market, albeit typically in a low-wage, entry-level job. Riverside's 'stepping stone' philosophy holds that participants are more likely to be able to move into a better-paying job if they are already in work. In the words of a Riverside job developer, 'My philosophy is any job that will get you back out into the job market, it's going to have some potential. You might be really nice to a customer that you're giving a Big Mac to, and they might be the president of some company that wants to hire you. You just never know.'[9] GAIN staff are themselves assessed and rewarded on the basis of their record in achieving job placements: each must place a minimum number of clients in work every month in order to qualify for salary bonuses. Over the years, these job targets have been gradually ratcheted up, subjecting programme staff themselves to intensification and speed-up, while driving down unit job-placement costs.

Active job development is another distinctive characteristic of the Riverside programme. GAIN staff are all hired with a view to developing jobs for clients, including scanning newspapers and looking out for 'help wanted' signs. Marketing techniques are aggressively used to promote both the general concept of GAIN and the specific merchandise of the 'job-ready' applicant, who can if necessary be with an employer that very afternoon. Programme staff make no secret of the fact that employers' needs and preferences are paramount, 'thoroughly screening participants prior to referral for a hiring interview' and being 'sensitive to the needs of the employer' (Riverside County DPSS, 1994, p. 8). Achieving 'job readiness' (at the minimum of service intervention and the lowest cost) is the overriding goal. The essence of the programme is to drive down costs while maximizing the flow-through into employment, to maintain strict discipline while relentlessly promoting the virtues of work.

Workfare as Labour Control: The Regulatory Logic of the Work-first Method

What California's Republican Governor, Pete Wilson, likes about the Riverside approach is that it cuts costs while aggressively enforcing a vision of the work ethic commensurate with the realities of the (low-wage) labour market:

> If you simply say we are going to educate you and train you but never require that you go to work, a lot of people are never going to go to work. [The Riverside model] is, I think, creatively impatient ... It's sort of like having a mother or father in the household who's saying, get out and get a job, go ahead and better your lot by getting some additional education but in the meantime start paying some rent.[10]

The Riverside approach seeks to overcome one of the paradoxes of workfare, that for all its rhetorical attractiveness, implementation tends to be considerably more costly than passive income support (see Butler and Kondratas, 1987; Rector and Butterfield, 1987; Tanner, 1996). It differs from traditional approaches to workfare (based on the compulsory participation of welfare recipients in 'community service' jobs) by effectively mandating rapid entry into the wage-labour market, at whatever wage and under whatever conditions: go to work, or face sanctions. This method appears to dovetail neatly with the current imperatives of welfare restructuring in the USA, for it offers the promise of enforcing work while cutting costs. There is consequently a significant degree of 'fit' between the economics of state-level welfare reform and the apparent potential of this 'local solution'.

Measured in narrow terms, the Riverside programme has certainly been effective in moving people from welfare to work, but it is important not to exaggerate what has been achieved. In part, the Riverside results look so striking due to the historic pattern of failure in welfare-to-work efforts in the United States: this is a field of at best very modest results (see Gueron and Pauly, 1991; Friedlander and Burtless, 1995; Handler, 1995; Blank, 1997). The Riverside results may be the 'most impressive yet achieved', but they are far from conclusive. The MDRC data revealed that the Riverside experimentals were only $52 per month better off than their counterparts in the control group, that about two-thirds of the experimentals were not working at the time of the year-three interview, and that almost half never worked during the entire three-year period (Handler, 1995). While the Riverside programme was propelling people into work it was not lifting them out of poverty. Most who found work did so only at low wages, often requiring top-ups from welfare benefits in order to raise them to subsistence levels. As MDRC's Judith Gueron has conceded, if ending poverty rather than tackling 'welfare dependency' is the policy objective, then Riverside does not provide the answer: 'the downside to Riverside is that families weren't moved out of poverty. People didn't get better jobs. If that's your goal, you have to make a larger investment to get there.'[11]

Although the Riverside model may look like effective welfare policy, it represents a rather perverse form of labour market policy. According to Lawrence Mead, the strength of '[e]fficient programs like Riverside' is that they 'stress placement in *available* jobs with the minimum of extras'.[12] Practically speaking, the main achievement of the Riverside programme is to *accelerate* entry into low-wage employment (Gueron, 1996). The work-first strategy is predicated on the twin assumptions that the local labour market has the capacity to absorb a continuous flow of welfare recipients and that such transitions can be achieved with fairly minimal support. More specifically, it depends on the existence of a very turbulent, high turnover labour market, one which produces a plentiful flow of (entry-level) vacancies. Given that the Riverside programme effectively provides a forced labour supply for such jobs, while also covering much of the cost of recruitment and induction, it can be seen as an indirect subsidy to low-wage employers. So while the Riverside strategy speaks to the preoccupation in the USA with 'welfare dependency', it is actually likely to exacerbate the problem of *working* poverty by forcibly crowding welfare recipients into the bottom end of the labour market.

Consequently, one of the longer-run effects of work-first strategies may be *further* to destabilize the contingent labour market. Competition for low-wage jobs will intensify as labour market participation rates are gradually raised by workfare programmes, but this need not necessarily mean that the number of jobs in low-wage labour markets will also rise. On the contrary, the same amount of work may have to be 'shared' by a larger number of labour market participants, leading to job fragmentation and falling wages. Work-first workfare may be partially successful in its goal of replacing welfare dependency with wage dependency, but it may do so at considerable cost. Paradoxically, one of the enduring concerns of US welfare reformers has been the problem of 'repeat usage' of welfare, a problem which has been typically misdiagnosed (in supply-side terms) as a measure of chronic welfare dependency, when the reality is that (in demand-side terms) it reflects the chronic instability of low-wage *jobs* (see Pavetti, 1993; Blank, 1997; Capelli, *et al.*, 1997). Work-first workfare may serve to intensify this problem of instability. As such it clearly will not resolve the contradictions of contingent labour markets (see Peck, 1996), though there may be a sense in which it serves a regulatory function in *containing* some of these contradictions. Experiences in Riverside and elsewhere suggest that work-first approaches perform this containment function by deepening control over the mobilization, deployment and reproduction of contingent labour. Work-first workfare performs this local labour control function in at least four ways: by acting as a deterrent to current and potential welfare users; by instilling strict programme discipline and 'appropriate' forms of work socialization; by destabilizing the experience of welfare receipt; and by increasing the potential and actual substitutability of labour. Each of these mechanisms of local labour control are now briefly examined in the context of the Riverside experience.

First, the deterrent effect. An important feature of workfare programmes is their capacity to disrupt, and therefore deter, welfare claims. Levels of individual intervention and personal surveillance under Riverside's 'intensive case management' system are considerably higher than is the case under conventional welfare arrangements. Some claimants will go to work to avoid the intentional 'hassle' of the GAIN process, others may already be working. So the very *threat* of mandatory participation induces some welfare recipients to deregister. In fact, there tends to be a significant dropout rate at all stages in the administration of workfare programmes, an effect which Mead (1992, p.

172) terms the 'workfare funnel'. Riverside staff drew attention to this deterrent effect in different ways:

> There is some subset that we don't really understand yet. They're working already and it's not reported. What the [GAIN process] does is flush that to the surface. They say, oh yeah, I'm going to work tomorrow, and they've been working for three months. But they haven't told us, and they aren't going to tell us because they'll go to jail! . . . So people go to work literally before they have any real contact [with the GAIN programme itself] but much more of that happens after they have been involved with [GAIN].[13]

> Sometimes they go to work when they get a letter from GAIN saying that they're coming in [to begin the programme]. *They know*. And like all communities, there's a lot of communication. I'm sure in the [welfare] community, they know. So here's a letter from GAIN. They're going to put me through this process. And they begin to look for work . . . Some people go to work so that GAIN will not bother them anymore.[14]

Workfare programmes therefore exert an influence over the population of claimants, indeed across the 'welfare community', through their ability to impose work, job search and other activities. Workfare advocates insist that the programme is effectively exposing fraud, but while this may be part of the picture, the deterrent effect operates in a more complex fashion. Work requirements alter the trade-off between welfare and work, because in requiring attendance at a GAIN office (and subsequently at work) they render untenable 'passive' claims, those not involving wage-labour. While anti-welfare rhetoric tends to have it that all such claimants were either working illegally or watching daytime TV, the evidence is that most will have been raising children while working (legally) in part-time jobs (see Blank, 1997). In enforcing waged work, workfare also 'deters' these activities.

Second, programme discipline and work socialization. The highly interventionist methodology of the Riverside programme serves a related regulatory function: it mimics the rules and conventions of low-wage labour markets through the operation of a high-discipline programme environment. As the programme's director has explained, 'It's really simple; you've got to be all over every client like flypaper! Every day. "Okay, you said yesterday you were going to do this and this, what have you done today?"' (quoted in Bardach, 1993, p. 19). The Riverside programme gets 'all over its clients' by checking up on job search activities and imposing exacting participation rules. Tardiness and inappropriate dress are penalized, as strict codes of time discipline and 'business-like' dress are enforced (see Figure 3.1).

MANDATORY DRESS CODE

PROPER DRESS for men and women (respectively) for interviews or participation in a Job Club/Job Search activity is as follows.

MEN	WOMEN
Shirt and Slacks	Skirt and Blouse
Appropriate Shoes	Dress
Socks	Nylons (Hose)
Neat and Clean	Neat and Clean
Clean Fingernails	Appropriate Shoes

IMPROPER DRESS

ABSOLUTELY:	NO	Spandex pants (short or long)
	NO	Short skirts (must be at least knee length)
	NO	Shorts
	NO	Tank tops
	NO	Theme tee shirts
	NO	See-through tops
	NO	Hats
	NO	Sun dresses
	NO	Mid-rift tops
	NO	Extreme hairstyles
	NO	Tennis shoes
	NO	Jeans/Levis

Appropriate dress is necessary to participate and be successful in your job search. If you choose not to comply with these guidelines you will be referred to your counsellor.

Source: Riverside County DPSS.

Figure 3.1 *Riverside's workfare dress code*

The purpose of micro-regulatory strategies such as dress codes is to prepare GAIN participants for the world of work, to ensure, in other words, that they are 'job ready'. As a Riverside manager explained,

> 'Job ready' doesn't mean that they are trained to do something, it means they are ready to work ... A large portion of our clients are not in general terms job ready, and that's why they get a job, they lose a job, because they're not going to take any stuff off anybody, and if they want to go home, they go home, and if they don't want to come in, they just don't show up. This is the basic problem that we're talking about with low-income, welfare-

type people ... it's the attitude that has to be overcome. And the way we've gone about doing that is by constant pressure, relentlessly applied. Until they get a job, and they hold a job. Or they leave the area![15]

The supply-side logic upon which work-first programming is predicated locates the causes of labour market instability and under-employment firmly with the (assumed) attitudes and predispositions of those in the welfare population: the argument goes that jobs are lost not because contingent work is inherently unstable, low-paid and exploitative, but due to the attitudes of 'low-income, welfare-type people'. Workfare programmes internalize this analysis, functioning to socialize, acclimatize and acculturate welfare recipients for contingent work (see Vosko, 1998b). This is where the methodology of work-first differs from human-capital-based models of workfare, given that the latter involve investments in education and training with a view to *raising* the employability level of participants, while the former aim simply to 'attach' workers to *available* jobs, typically at the bottom of the labour market.

Third, destabilizing welfare. Workfare programmes like Riverside seek explicitly to destabilize the welfare experience by invoking scenarios based on threats and opportunities which point only in one direction – off welfare and into work. As a programme manager put it, 'I don't believe in stable welfare ... It causes people to drop out of school, enter crime, become involved in drugs, the whole thing. It's a terrible punishment to inflict on somebody.'[16] This reworks one of the oldest axioms of poor relief, that welfare provisions should not be permitted to undermine the imperative to work: the objective is to 'spur people to contrive ways of supporting themselves by their own industry, *to offer themselves to any employer on any terms*' (Piven and Cloward, 1993, p. 34). So, a feature of the work-first method is that participants must be exposed to a determined 'push' from welfare. According to Judith Gueron, one of the main impacts of the 'tough and conservative' Riverside model is that the welfare experience is made to '*feel* temporary'.[17] A case worker explained how this approach is applied in the practice of a client interview:

I draw a line on a chart, for 'welfare' going down: The governor proposes a cut in the grant; your child turns 18; another child goes to live with her father ... then I draw another line starting just under the welfare line but going up: You get a raise; you quit and get a better paying job; you get a promotion ... Well, maybe the best the line will do is stay flat, but unlike welfare it won't go down (quoted in Bardach, 1993, p. 7).

'Motivation' in the Riverside programme is consequently secured not simply through esteem-building but also through the deliberate exploitation of uncertainty and fear, coupled with the systematic erosion/withdrawal of alternative means of subsistence. Following the federal reforms of 1996, there is a sense in which this workfarist logic has become a systemic one in the USA, as all recipients are now confronted with federally-sanctioned time limits, allowing maximum lifetime claims of no more than five years. States are allowed to impose shorter time limits if they wish to, as many have (see Children's Defense Fund, 1996).

Fourth, labour substitution. Work-first workfare programmes constitute what amounts to a forced labour supply for entry-level jobs, weakening the bargaining positions of all low-wage workers by raising the constant spectre of substitution. The Riverside programme prides itself on providing for what employers want: a constant supply of 'job ready' recruitment candidates. As an employment specialist explained, 'I listen to what employers need in terms of an employee, and then I try to meet their needs ... I can't guarantee that a person is going to work out at the job. No one can guarantee that, but I can guarantee if someone doesn't work out I can replace them with another worker' (quoted in Riverside County DPSS, 1994, p. 47). An effect of the Riverside method is to engineer a persistent over-supply of 'job ready' labour for the lower reaches of the labour market, tipping the balance of power further in favour of employers and constituting a drag on pay and conditions. The Economic Policy Institute has calculated that the recent US welfare reforms will result in pay levels in the low-wage labour market falling by an average of 11.9 per cent, and by more in states (like California) where there is a large welfare population (Mishel and Schmitt, 1995). Other studies have demonstrated that there is already a real shortage of entry-level jobs, particularly in America's central cities. Once welfare recipients enter these crowded urban labour markets, this situation will deteriorate still further (Theodore, 1998b).

In the longer term, there is also a real possibility that employers will begin to restructure their recruitment and labour process strategies in order to exploit the forced labour supplies of workfare workers. Under this scenario, workfare programmes would be not only eroding but actually pulling down the floor of pay and employment conditions at the bottom of the labour market, fuelling job polarization and casualization tendencies and resegmenting the low-wage labour supply in the process. There may be a sense, then, in which workfare programming contributes to a perverse 'regulatory fix' across the lower tiers of highly competitive, deregulated labour markets, transforming the nature of work as well as welfare in the process. Work-first programmes like Riverside are distinctive in that they seek actively to *remake* the contingent labour supply, deliberately overturning the established incentive structures and modes of calculation among the welfare/low-wage population decisively in favour of waged work.

Conclusion: Transnational Workfare?

Local workfare experiments are playing an important and potentially transformative role in reshaping regulatory conventions and power relations in contingent labour markets. A case in point, the Riverside programme is an institutional manifestation of a no-frills 'hard workfare' philosophy: it sets out deliberately to destabilize the experience of welfare receipt, propelling programme participants into the lower reaches of the labour market with the minimum of delay, the minimum of cost and the minimum of support. Programmes like this are transforming experiences of both welfare and low-waged work: denied the right to subsist *on* welfare, the poor are now being processed *through* workfare, as they are forcibly rotated through contingent jobs. Riverside's active enforcement of daily job search, its remorseless inculcation of pro-work messages and its relatively high 'success rate' in moving individuals from welfare to (low-wage) work have afforded the Riverside 'message' great potency in the struggle to 'end welfare as we know it'. And just as the project of welfare reform is fast becoming an international one, so also are examples of 'successful' work-based programming taking on a much wider significance.

Work-first strategies will continue to prove attractive under conditions in which public finances are strained, anti-welfare sentiments are running high and where there is frustration with traditional welfare programmes and services. But while the work-first method may give the impression of a quick fix, it is in fact anything but. The effectiveness of such programmes, as even their advocates concede, is highly contingent on the state of local labour markets. This means that policy transfer is inevitably difficult, perhaps especially to countries like the UK, where the structures and dynamics of the labour market are markedly different (see Mead, 1996, 1997). Welfare-to-work programmes which yield high job-placement rates in the rapid-turnover labour markets of edge-city California, or in the buoyant economies of suburban and rural Wisconsin, are not likely to be anything like as effective in the inner cities or coalfield areas of Northern Britain. This serves to underline the fact that while workfare strategies may have powerful political support, and while they may yield striking results in some localities, they are not unproblematic. As their perverse consequences for contingent labour markets illustrate, workfare strategies are contradictory. Likewise, the politics of welfare reform in which they are enveloped are also complex and unpredictable.

As the Blair Government contemplates radical reform of the British welfare state, this might give cause for reflection. While academics and consultants peddle the principles of workfare for British policy audiences and while so much international attention is focused on America's bold experiment with decentralized welfare reform, even Lawrence Mead cautions us 'not [to] assume that what works in America would necessarily transfer to the UK' (1997, p. ix). In the UK, there is a very real danger that welfare-to-work policies will prove least effective in precisely those areas where they are most needed: areas of high unemployment and weak labour demand. Britain's 'welfare mess' has a very particular geography, a geography which may render many off-the-shelf workfarist 'solutions' effectively untenable. The uneven geography of labour demand, and the differential capacities of welfare-to-work strategies which follow from this, constitute perhaps the fundamental challenges for Labour's welfare-to-work programme (Holtham *et al.*, 1998; Peck, 1998a).

Thus far, however, there is little evidence that the course of policy is set to change significantly, certainly not to embrace strategies like job creation which at the present time seem irredeemably associated with the rejected lexicon of 'Old Labour'. Instead, redoubled emphasis is being placed upon 'welfare dependency' analyses and the (workfarist) forms of supply-side strategy which tend to follow in their wake. Perhaps most controversially, given the hitherto sacrosanct principles of uniformity and universality in the Beveridgean model of welfare, there is growing evidence that Britain's path towards workfarism will also be associated with decentralization and the emergence of a 'mixed economy' of local welfare provision. A recent assessment of lessons for the UK from American welfare-to-work experiments, for example, produced cross-party support for the principles both of mandatory programming and local experimentation:

> The federal nature of the United States allows for experimentation with different welfare schemes in different states ... The United Kingdom would benefit from greater flexibility and experimentation. More pilot schemes and geographical experiments, particularly when focused on areas with low unemployment, might also allow for quicker, more focused evaluation and monitoring ... We recognise that the British economy does not have the demand for labour that the American economy provides. The British labour market has, however, undergone profound changes: there is overall employment growth and an increase in part-time, temporary and more flexible work patterns. These labour market changes provide the right

opportunities to reform the social security system. We believe that the British social security system should be more closely tailored to work requirements for claimants (House of Commons, 1998, pp. viii, x).

As welfare-to-work experimentation spreads and as dependency discourses are progressively entrenched, there is a real possibility that workfarist practices will become more and more generalized, for all their weaknesses and inequities. In this sense, workfarism is taking on the features of a transnational regulatory project. Different versions of workfare are fast becoming policies of choice among political leaders, particularly those seeking to make a virtue of the 'hard choices' which lie ahead in the field of social policy. In Britain at least, work-based welfare reform has already been established as one of the defining policy agendas of the Blair administration. Labour has embraced the once-controversial principles of compulsion, privatization and localization in welfare-to-work programming. They represent significant steps along the road to workfarism. There can be little doubt as to the inspiration for this strategy. As the Prime Minister stressed in his first major speech after taking office, delivered in a poverty-stricken housing estate in south London, 'The initiative on jobs and welfare that I launched [in May 1997] with President Clinton was born out of a recognition that this is a shared problem and not one unique to Britain. We can learn from each other's experience, and we can also co-operate to find common solutions.'[18]

Acknowledgements

The research reported here was supported by the Harkness Fellowships programme of the Commonwealth Fund (New York) and by the Leverhulme Trust (Research Fellowship 10896). Thanks also to Paul Edwards, Tony Elger, Andy Jonas, Martin Jones and Nik Theodore for helpful comments on an earlier draft of the chapter. Responsibility for its final contents, of course, remains mine.

Notes

1. Speech at the Aylesbury Estate, Southwark, 2 June 1997.
2. *San Francisco Chronicle*, 20 April 1995, p. A25.
3. Senior executive #1, Riverside DPSS, interview with author, October 1995.

4. *Ibid.*
5. *San Francisco Chronicle,* 24 January 1995, p. A2.
6. Federal Document Clearing House Congressional Testimony, 28 February 1995, Lawrence E. Townsend Jr, US Senate Labor and Human Resources Committee.
7. Federal Document Clearing House Congressional Testimony, 15 March 1994, Judith M. Gueron, House Ways and Means/Human Resources Welfare Revision (emphasis added).
8. Quoted from *MacNeil/Lehrer NewsHour,* 1 August 1995, transcript #5283.
9. *Ibid.*
10. *Ibid.*
11. *San Francisco Chronicle,* 24 January 1995, p. A2; *MacNeil/Lehrer NewsHour,* 1 August 1995, transcript #5283.
12. Federal Document Clearing House Congressional Testimony, 9 March 1995, Lawrence M. Mead, Senate Finance Welfare Revision (emphasis added).
13. Senior executive #2, Riverside DPSS, interview with author, October 1995.
14. Manager #2, Riverside GAIN programme, interview with author, October 1995.
15. Manager #1, Riverside GAIN programme, interview with author, October 1995.
16. *Ibid.*
17. Federal Document Clearing House Congressional Testimony, 15 March 1994, Judith M. Gueron, House Ways and Means/Human Resources Welfare Revision (emphasis added).
18. Tony Blair, speech at the Aylesbury Estate, Southwark, 2 June 1997.

4 REGULATION, RESTRUCTURING AND REGENERATION IN COALFIELDS: THREE EUROPEAN CASES

Chas Critcher, Dave Parry and Dave Waddington

The decline of the European coal industry and its impact upon mining regions provide rich material for the analysis of the simultaneous processes of managing industrial restructuring and regenerating local economies.

> Experience suggests that a coal restructuring programme should have two clear objectives in order to minimise negative social impacts: (a) to get working age miners into alternative jobs quickly; (b) to diversify the regional economy's structure and markets over the medium term (International Economic and Energy Consultants, 1995, p. 4).

These processes require regulation by the nation state, and also by the EC above and the local state below it.

This chapter examines three contrasting case studies. In the UK, the mass of the industry was closed down, save for a privatized rump, itself with an uncertain future. Apart from a very few indigenous initiatives, regeneration policy was restricted to demand-side features, especially labour reskilling and the encouragement of small business, a policy executed through local branches of quangos. The consequence has been local economic collapse and social disintegration in the affected areas. By contrast in Germany the long-term decline of the industry has been managed through a gradual and negotiated series of national agreements, buttressed by indirect subsidies and guaranteed markets. There have been concerted efforts to induce local economic regeneration involving co-operation between federal, regional and municipal government and between the public and private sectors, all co-ordinated at a local level. Although this has not wholly prevented burgeoning unemployment, mining localities have been spared the drastic economic and social consequences of mass closures and local economies given time to restructure. The third case, of Spain, differs again. Until the late 1990s a highly unprofitable industry has been wound down very slowly, mainly because of the political influence of regional government and the organized labour movement. This political success has prevented significant measures to regenerate local economies which remain highly dependent on coal. A protectionist policy, with high levels of direct subsidy and guaranteed markets, has not prevented pit closures and loss of employment, merely postponing the demise of the industry and ensuring that its consequences for local economies will be devastating.

These three patterns – of drastic closure regardless of local consequences; limited protection and managed decline with organized efforts to regenerate the local economy; and large-scale protectionism without significant regenerative effort – offer case studies of deindustrialization and economic regeneration in coalfield areas. We present material on three comparable areas in each nation: South Yorkshire in the UK, Asturias in Spain and North Rhine Westphalia in Germany. In addition to established studies we draw on our own programme of work (Critcher, Schubert and Waddington, 1995; Parry, 1996) including a specially commissioned study on Spain (Vazquez and Del Rosal, 1995).[1] We focus on four aspects of the regulation of change and regeneration. First, there is the extent to which apparently economic decisions are directed by political structures, cultures and ideologies. Second, we examine the 'policy mix' of strategies, their adequacy and the models of change they endorse. Third, we consider the role of institutions charged with responsibility for economic regeneration, especially their 'institutional thickness': how densely they are networked into other economic, political and social agencies at the local level. Finally, there is the question of the effectiveness of local strategies in a global economy.

Initially we establish the decline of European coal, the differential position of national economies within it and their distinctive economic and political characteristics. The middle part of the chapter considers the specifically local impacts of decline management and economic regeneration in the three areas in order to give an empirical grounding to these theoretical considerations, which are reconsidered in the conclusion.

The Three National Coal Industries

Coal in a Global Market

Coal's share of the expanding global energy market had declined from 60 per cent in 1950 to 35 per cent by 1970 (Chadwick *et al.*, 1987). The potential for

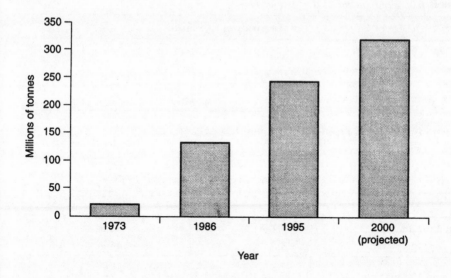

Sources: Sadler (1992) and McCloskey Coal information.

Figure 4.1 *World steam coal trade*

a global market in coal remained limited only so long as most production and consumption remained within national boundaries. From 1973 to 1986, the international shipping of steam coal increased six times and doubled again by 1995 (see Figure 4.1).

Effects on the European coal industry were postponed by the oil crises of the 1970s which motivated national governments to aim for national self-sufficiency in energy. But as the crisis receded, a declining demand for energy coincided with new sources, especially gas. Cheap coal imports became available from South America, Asia and the former Communist bloc. As a consequence, coal production began to outstrip demand. The world price of steam coal fell by over 50 per cent in five years, from $60 per tonne in 1982 to $26 per tonne in 1987 (Sadler, 1992).

In Europe, as late as 1990, electricity generation was still 40 per cent dependent on coal. Sixty per cent of the EU market was served by member states (McAven, 1993). In this globalizing market for energy and coal, the European industry generally was becoming marginalized. The future viability of the industry in a globalized context was put into question. However, in each of the three countries – the UK, Germany and Spain – the position of the coal industry was rather different.

Table 4.1 *Hard coal production (million tonnes)*

	UK	Germany	Spain	total
1980	128.2	94.5	16.6	239.3
1985	90.8	88.8	16.3	195.9
1990	89.3	76.5	19.6	185.4
1994	47.8	57.6	18.1	123.5

Source: International Economic and Energy Consultants (1995, p. 1).

Table 4.2 *Variations in coal production and employment (per cent) 1980–9*

	UK	Germany	Spain
coal production	-21.3	-18.4	+1.5
coal employment	-65.6	-22.0	+1.0

Source: Vazquez and Del Rosal (1995, p. 10).

Table 4.3 *Deep-mined coal 1992*

	UK	Germany	Spain
output (million tonnes)	61.4	71.8	13.8
output per man year (tonnes)	1840.0	916.0	483.0
average costs (ecu per gigajoule)	2.58	4.88	6.99
direct subsidy (ecu per tonne)	nil	62.3	24.8

Source: Parker (1994, pp. 28–9).

The Three Industries

Nationalized as a mass industry in 1947, the UK coal industry was privatized as a tiny rump in 1995. In the 1980s, it became almost totally dependent on the newly privatized electricity utilities. Conservative governments adopted a strategy of massive rationalization, prior to privatization. Nonetheless, the UK coal industry was the most efficient in the EU. As Tables 4.1 to 4.3 show, in the early 1990s the UK coal industry had a higher rate of productivity and lower costs than either Germany or Spain, making its price the most internationally competitive, though still well below that of coal imported from outside the EU. In principle the UK industry was the most able to retain a place in the global economy, given some direct or indirect subsidies or guaranteed markets. On economic grounds alone, the UK had the most viable coal industry in the EU.

The German coal industry played a major role in the postwar reconstruction. Ruhrkohle, a private corporation founded in 1968, owns most of the deep coal mines. A high degree of mechanization cannot resolve the geological problems of coal extraction. Government subsidies have maintained but rationalized the industry despite fierce competition. During the 1980s the industry lost 19 per cent of its production and 22 per cent of its workforce. As Tables 4.1 to 4.3 show, Germany produced more coal than the UK in the early 1990s but at a higher cost and price, the latter three times the international market price. Economically, German coal is not a very viable industry. Arguments in favour of its retention have to use other criteria.

In Spain, coal's contribution to economic development peaked in the 1950s and 1960s, as a consequence of Spain's isolationism and commitment to energy self-sufficiency. But by the 1980s the effects of liberalization, economic competition and especially entry into the EC meant that such an uncompetitive industry became ever more vulnerable, heavily dependent on the energy supply industry and the contracts with it brokered by government. These guaranteed markets enabled expansion when the rest of the European industry was in steep decline. In the 1980s, it actually increased production and employment by between 1 and 2 per cent. The state-owned HUNOSA dominates the industry, accounting nationally for 35 per cent of coal employment and 42 per cent of production. Its hard coal is of poor quality, high in ash and sulphur content. It lies in geologically problematic strata. The mines are small and production methods are crude. As Tables 4.1 to 4.3 show, the industry has a lower rate of productivity and higher costs than the other two countries. The price of its coal is nearly three times that of the UK, four and half times that of the international market price, prompting the comment that 'HUNOSA is probably the most uneconomic coal mining operation in the world' (Parker, 1994, p. 54). The economic case for the Spanish coal industry is non-existent.

Thus at the beginning of the 1990s, the most economically viable industry, that of the UK, was contracting fastest and the least economically viable in Spain contracting the slowest, with Germany intermediate on both counts. Politics rather than economics was driving the course of each national industry, especially whether, why and to what extent national governments were prepared to subsidize it: 'the size of the gap between the cost of EU-12 deep-mined coal and international prices . . . remains the basis of the politics of coal in these countries' (Parker, 1994, p. 29). In Spain and Germany the rate of subsidy actually increased in the late 1980s when it was decreasing in the UK.

Table 4.4 *GDP and energy dependence*

	UK	Germany	Spain
GDP per capita 1990 (US dollars)	12,270	14,730	8,990
Energy balance (equivalent oil tonnes)	- 6.9	-147	-55.1
Per cent of energy imported	-15.2 (surplus)	54	61

Source: Cole and Cole (1993).

National Economies in a Global Energy Market

The national economy's general position in the world market and its degree of energy self-sufficiency are presented for the UK, Germany and Spain in Table 4.4. The UK's economy operates at a level below that of Germany but well above that of Spain with a per capita GDP of $12,270 per inhabitant. However, its energy position is by far the most favourable, being only 6.9 million tonnes short of a production/consumption balance. Its energy production comes in the main from offshore oil and gas and it has the largest coal reserves in the EU.

Germany has until recently continued to maintain economic growth with a 1990 per capita GDP of $14,730. It has a very highly developed industrial base and is heavily dependent on imported energy resources, despite its significant domestic coal industry. The balance of energy production to consumption was considerably worse with a 147 million tonnes of oil equivalent shortfall.

Spain's economic development has been retarded by isolationism and an agrarian economic base. In 1990 its per capita GDP was $8,990. Economic growth is centred mainly in the north east from Valencia through Cataluna. In terms of oil equivalent, Spain consumed 55.1 million tonnes in 1990 more than it produced.

Political Context

In the UK, government policies from 1979 to 1997 reinforced the highly centralized nature of political power. Centrally determined budgets with strictly enforced spending 'caps' limited the powers of regional government (in England the county councils) and local government. To enforce their policies, government made extensive use of quangos (quasi-autonomous non-governmental organizations), unelected bodies funded by central government, designed to circumvent the expression of local political interests. This reflects the state's power to enforce central decisions. There is no interface between the centre and the regions in which regional views can find coherent expression and require account to be taken of their interests. Governing parties can also afford to ignore regions where other parties dominate, since their influence is confined to the municipalities.

Neo-liberal ideologies of the market were brought to bear on all aspects of government policy. Opposition was neutralized at every turn. Regional disparities were perceived as the natural outcome of market forces in which government had no right to intervene. Until recently, the UK has been characterized by the centralization of power in a politically polarized, economically uneven and socially divided society.

The reconstruction of postwar West Germany helped develop consensual goals of 'social peace' within the 'social market'. Towards that end, long-term planning for economic and social policy has been the guiding principle, even for the ruling Christian Democrat Party. Consensual planning as a practice has been endorsed by the constitutional framework. The federal structure of the country means that key elements of political and economic policy lie with the regional government. The *Länder* habitually negotiate with municipalities and other interest groups. Such institutionalization of consensus has important consequences for the processes of both industrial restructuring and regional economic regeneration.

In Spain, the democratic constitution which evolved after democratization took account of nationalistic claims by defining regions as 'Autonomous Communities' with considerable legal and financial powers. Regional and municipal authorities are responsible for more than a third of all public expenditure. Though nominally having a federal structure, Spain has considerable tensions between central and regional governments, especially in regions with nationalistic aspirations. Negotiation between central government and regions is inherently conflictual. The early dominance of Spain's socialist party, the PSOE, generally helped in relations with regions where the same party dominated. But the party's programme to modernize Spain has encountered difficulties wherever it affects the interests of regions where its political support is strongest.

Political structures and ideologies were an important determinant of policy in relation to the coal industry and coalfield communities. Whatever solutions emerged, they were likely to be directed from the centre in the UK, consensually negotiated in Germany and compromised in Spain. Such factors did not necessarily predetermine the policy outcomes but affected the mix and institutional forms of policies.

Table 4.5 *Mining in the local economy: comparison of key economic indicators (1990)*

Indices	Measure	Norm	UK South Yorkshire		SPAIN Asturias		GERMANY North Rhine Westphalia	
			Current	Trend	Current	Trend	Current	Trend
A Industrial structure								
1 Importance of mining	% all extractive and manufacturing jobs	20%	-	↗	+	↗	0	↗
2 Importance of large industries	% plants > 500 workers	30%	-	↗	+	↗	-	=
3 Importance of SMEs	firms employing < 800 workers	35%	++	↗	++	↗	++	=
B Geography and environment								
4 Communications infrastructure	subjective	—	0	=	-	=	+	↗
5 Environmental quality	subjective	—	0	=	+	n/a	+	↗
C Population								
6 Mobility	population increase/decrease	national average	-	↗	n/a	↗	n/a	↗
7 Migrant population	place of birth	national average	0	n/a	-	=	+	↗
8 Proportion of youth	under 20	national average	-	↗	—	n/a	0	n/a
9 Proportion of older population	over 55	national average	n/a	n/a	=	n/a	+	n/a

Table 4.5 *Continued*

			Area 1		Area 2		Area 3	
			State	Trend	State	Trend	State	Trend
D Standard of living								
10 Affluence	disposable income	national average	−	↗	−	↗	+	↗
11 Housing	subjective	—	−	↗	−	↗	0	↗
E Employment								
12 Level of unemployment	% unemployed	national average	++	↗	+	↗	++	↗
13 Youth unemployment	% under-24s unemployed	national average	+	↗	+	↗	0	↗
14 Female employment	% females economically active	national average	−	n/a	−	↗	−	↗
F Education								
15 Average attainment	post-16 education places	national average	−	↗	n/a	n/a	−	n/a
16 Vocational qualifications	any certification	national average	−	↗	n/a	n/a	0	n/a
17 Educational provision	subjective	—	—	=	0	=	+	↗

Key

Current state
++ much greater than national norm
+ greater than national norm
0 near national norm
− below national norm
— well below national norm

Trend
↗ trend upwards
= no change
↘ trend downwards
n/a information not available

Source: Adapted from Thomas and Faist (1992).

Introduction to Case Studies

Table 4.5 summarizes a range of salient factors for the three regions studied here. The data demonstrate that Asturias and South Yorkshire share character-istics often thought typical of coalfield areas: poor communications; population loss; low levels of income, housing, female employment and educational standards; and high levels of adult and youth unemployment. It has also been argued that mining communities generally have tended to be culturally insular and supported by organizations and institutions which were resistant to change and interference from outside, while at the same time being reliant on state assistance through subsidies and maintenance through the 'social wage' (Hudson, 1994). However, North Rhine Westphalia as a region shares few of these characteristics.

The UK: South Yorkshire

South Yorkshire, a sub-region and former county council, is located in the region of Yorkshire and Humberside. From 1966 to 1986, this region lost 9.7 per cent of its total workforce, and 35.7 per cent of those in manufacturing. Comparable national figures were 4.4 per cent and 27.6 per cent respectively. From 1981 to 1985, 70,000 mining jobs were lost. Regional unemployment at 8 per cent is near the national rate but in some ex-mining localities in South Yorkshire it is three times higher.

Decline Management

The UK coal industry had been in steady decline since the start of the 1960s but the industry retained its centrality to the energy market and the National Union of Mineworkers (NUM) retained substantial influence. The year-long strike of 1984–5 called over British Coal's plans for wholesale closure was eventually defeated by the Thatcher government and the hold of the union effectively broken. The government could then implement its strategy of closing most of the industry and privatizing the remainder.

Between 1985 and 1992, 119 pits closed and employment fell from 177,000 to 44,000. In 1992, proposals to close most of the remaining collieries promp-ted widespread and spontaneous protest. The government responded by postponing immediate closures, commissioning parliamentary reports and offering aid packages to the areas affected, but these were merely stalling tactics. Eleven pits were closed with a loss of 30,000 jobs. In coal-dominated areas of South Yorkshire such as the Dearne Valley, all the mines were closed with minimum consultation. Local resistance was bought off by attractive lump-sum redundancy terms, cushioned by central government and European funds, at an estimated cost of £6.6 billion (International Economic and Energy Consultants, 1995).

Despite the massive reduction in employment, the switch to gas turbines and the preferential treatment of nuclear power, the privatized industry remained a substantial supplier of domestic energy but its long-term future remains uncertain. Part of the privatization package was an agreement with the power-generating industry ensuring a short-term market for coal, which was due for renegotiation in early 1998. The new Labour Government extended this agreement for three months while it considered the future of the industry. In July 1998 it announced a programme aimed at revitalizing the economies of former coal regions through the promotion of new industries.

Regeneration

National regeneration policies have been explicitly designed to bypass local government. Quangos such as Urban Development Corporations and Training and Enterprise Councils (TECs) have been the main instruments of central government strategies. Local organizations of these bodies have frequently been required to submit competitive bids for government aid programmes.

In 1990 the government set up 82 TECs in England and Wales (with equivalent bodies in Scotland), which are limited companies with a brief to plan and deliver training to promote and support the development of small businesses and self-employment within their area. TECs exist in the three main South Yorkshire towns (Barnsley, Doncaster and Rotherham). In practice, three-quarters of their budget is spent on training schemes for the unemployed. TECs lack local connections and inspire little confidence in local authorities or businesses. Their powers are limited: they can neither enforce nor co-ordinate training within industry. Targets and priorities are set by central government rather than local interests (Peck, 1994). Despite all these deficiencies, the TECs were entrusted with the government's aid programme announced in 1992.

Also important is British Coal Enterprise (BCE), a wing of the nationalized industry established in 1984 with a brief to provide training opportunities for redundant miners and support for small businesses in mining localities. In effect, BCE has concentrated largely on processing redundant miners through short-term training schemes or alternative employment, usually unskilled and poorly paid (Witt, 1990; Turner 1993). BCE's claim to have created over 100,000 employment opportunities nationally between 1984 and 1994 has been countered by other estimates of 16,000. For Yorkshire, revised estimates suggest 3,100 jobs assisted rather than BCE's claim of 21,875. By contrast, the total of coal jobs lost locally was 47,000 (Fothergill and Guy, 1994).

Following the political turmoil of 1992, a package of regeneration measures was implemented by such agencies. Assisted Area Status and Enterprise Zones were also introduced to streamline the renewal process but very few regeneration initiatives were rooted in local communities. An exception to the generally fragmented, piecemeal and nationally imposed attempts at regeneration is the Dearne Valley Partnership (DVP). An area of 20 square miles with a population of 80,000 in the heartlands of the coalfield, it had lost all but one of its pits by 1995. It has been described as 'probably the most polluted and despoiled area within the UK' (Salt, 1995, p. 70). In 1994, three local authorities impinging on the area formed the DVP, with representatives from the local authorities, businesses and community organizations. Successful in a bid under City Challenge, it adopted a supply-side strategy of land reclamation and development, and improved infrastructure, especially roads and reskilling, with the flagship project of a university college. The first year's land reclamation target was met. How far this agency can actually generate local employment remains unclear.

Implications

The overall effects of local economic regeneration have been minimal, as measured by inward investment, small business activity, job creation, re-employment and outcomes of training (Turner, 1993; Critcher, Parry and Waddington, 1995). Unemployment in the coalfield areas of Yorkshire is 22.8 per cent and 27.8 per cent in pit villages (Beatty and Fothergill, 1994). Forty per cent of ex-miners become long-term unemployed and 20 per cent withdraw from the labour market. The rest are employed in service industries in predominantly unskilled, poorly paid and often casual jobs.

The case of the UK coal industry and the mining regions is a test-bed for the effectiveness of neo-liberal policies towards the decline of traditional industries and the regeneration of older industrial areas. No attempt was made, in a nation rich in gas and oil reserves, to moderate the emergence of a global energy market. Political structures, notably the absence of a regional tier of government, allowed central government to dictate its terms, which were also based on the breaking of the last bastion of organized labour. Such ideological considerations also drove regenerative strategies, which assumed that rendering the labour force more skilled and flexible, together with some aid to small business, would be adequate.

These assumptions could never have been a sufficient basis for regeneration in principle and were not in practice. The institutional means for realizing these objectives were primarily quangos which 'brought' central government policy to the locality without consultation or control. The consequences were the closure of the industrial base of local economies together with regenerative measures of a mostly cosmetic kind. In the UK, ex-mining communities have become zones of apparently permanent social and economic exclusion.

Germany: North Rhine Westphalia

North Rhine Westphalia is the main coal area of Germany, producing 86 per cent of its hard coal from mines on the edges of smaller towns in this region. Though an older industrial area than South Yorkshire, it has many modern characteristics, such as developed transport, financial and small business infrastructures. Regional unemployment is nevertheless higher than the national norm.

Decline Management

Occupying a strategic role in the postwar economic recovery, German coal production rose between 1946 and 1957. However, the increasing availability of oil and gas caused a crisis in the industry in 1958. The private industry dispensed with two-thirds (400,000) of mining jobs in fifteen years, with no planning or special social security provision. In 1968, the remaining 26 mines involving 85 per cent of coal production were consolidated into one company, Ruhrkohle AG. Privately owned by the steel industry and power generators, its economic targets were to be set by the federal government.

After the brief respite of the oil crises, capacity was further reduced in the 1980s as a result of declining steel demand, despite guaranteed sales to power generators. By the 1990s, continuing competition from other energy sources and EU pressure to reduce subsidies rendered the industry economically vulnerable. Coal production halved between 1957 and 1990, from 150 to 70 million tonnes, and was due to halve again by 2005. The national strategic plan for coal, 'Coal Concept 2005', made a commitment to preserve the industry, based in part on the guaranteed but shrinking markets to power stations and the steel industry. Nevertheless, 5,000 jobs a year were scheduled to go.

Ruhrkohle's annual subsidy, of DM8.2 billion in the early 1990s, is to be reduced to 7 billion by the year 2000. It operates through the *Kohlepfennig*, an 8.5 per cent levy on energy bills, and the *Jahrhundert Vertrag*, which obliges the electricity companies to burn 40 million tonnes of coal per year. The government is pledged to continue direct subsidy at least until the end of the century.

A key element in restructuring has been the diversification and adaptation of the mining industry itself. In 1993 Ruhrkohle employed 75,000 workers directly in mining and another 25,000 in other activities such as land reclamation, waste and product recycling. These latter activities generated 50 per cent of turnover in 1995 (Hessling, 1995).

The management of restructuring has taken place with the agreement of the main trade union federation, the IG Bergbau (which subsequently merged with the chemical workers' union to form IG Bergbau-Chemie-Energie), who even agreed to a reduction in hours and wages to accommodate downsizing. Restructuring programmes made extensive use of transfer between pits and early retirement, reducing the miners' average age to 32. As these possibilities were exhausted, formal redundancy was rejected in favour of training schemes (Davies, 1993; Beenken, 1995). Volunteers to leave the industry were offered training while in employment, receiving two-thirds of their average wage. It is unclear how many miners have taken advantage of a new extended scheme since it was introduced in 1995.

Especially important in this continuously negotiated decline is the Campaign for the Future of Coal-Mining Areas (ZAK), a federation of union, employer and local government representatives. ZAK is committed both to retaining a restructured industry and to local economic regeneration and expects consultation over proposals for either (Steingraber, 1995). However, the combined pressures of the costs of German reunification, a downturn in the national economy, pressure from the EC to remove subsidies and environmental protests have cast doubt on protectionist policies for coal. Government proposals in 1996 to hasten the rate of closure provoked mass demonstrations in mining areas and the plans were hastily revised. The new agreement, negotiated in 1997, involves reductions by 2005 in subsidy from DM9.3 billion to 5.5 billion, in production from 47 to 30 million tonnes, in employment from 84,000 to 36,000 and in mines from 18 to 8. Even this may not satisfy the EU; the balance of forces sustaining the management of decline is very fragile.

Regeneration

Regeneration plans in North Rhine Westphalia were first drafted during the 1958 crisis. By the late 1960s the *Land* announced the first of a series of regional regeneration plans to improve the infrastructure of housing, traffic, education and recreation, with subsidiary emphases on land reclamation and increases in training, private investment and regional promotion. Technology transfer was added in the late 1970s. By the early 1980s, the crisis in the steel industry and attendant political protest prompted three new plans, one for the region as a whole, one for coal and steel areas and one for land reclamation. However, their implementation was not to be the direct responsibility of the *Land*; instead the region was divided into fifteen sub-regions, each of which was to have regional boards or conferences. Comprising local authorities, chambers of commerce, trade unions and local community organizations, they would instigate regenerative projects.

Typical of the German approach was the founding of the East Ruhr Development Agency. In 1992 the *Land* government proposed that land reclamation should be handed over to an independent agency and offered DM10 million of start-up finance. Within eight months a limited company had been set up involving four major city or district councils, their chambers of commerce and trade associations, as well as five of the biggest non-mining firms in the region. Its brief was to initiate, co-ordinate and monitor projects, each involving a separate company. The target was to reclaim and develop 200 hectares of land (Esterman and Roxlau-Hennemann, 1995).

Evidence of the effects of such initiatives is widespread. In the first six months of 1991 almost 12,000 new companies were registered in North Rhine Westphalia, a quarter of the national total. In 1965 there was no university; now there are six in addition to six polytechnics and eleven technology centres. Major private sector companies, formed into the *Inititativeskreis Ruhrgebeit*, invested DM5 billion and committed DM4.5 billion of investment in the region in the first two years (Hudson 1992). New employment opportunities have been encouraged by the setting up of industrial parks and the fostering of entrepreneurship (Esterman and Roxlau-Hennemann, 1995; Noll, 1995; Buhr, 1995). Land renewal and reclamation have been the most obvious policy successes and Ruhrkohle is one of the companies at the forefront of the new environmental services industry (Wagner, 1995).

Implications

The German coal industry has been maintained by a series of subsidies under increasing economic and political pressure (Schubert and Brautigam, 1995). North Rhine Westphalia remains significant within the coal industry but Ruhrkohle is less and less centred on coal. Unemployment has risen, especially among the young. In 1994 the national rate was 8.1 per cent; in the Ruhr 13.3 per cent. The precise effects of retraining are hard to quantify. Some observers admit that miners have been reluctant to leave the industry, preferring the established industrial structure and mining culture. There have been considerable strides in land reclamation and development, in the transport infrastructure and in educational provision. Small business start-ups are impressive.

The cumulative impact seems to have been to insulate North Rhine Westphalia from the worst excesses of deindustrialization. Partly explicable by the region's relatively favourable positioning in the national economy, it is also the outcome of specifically political attitudes, structures and decisions. Regional elections make all political parties sensitive to mining votes. The federal structure has enabled North Rhine Westphalia to influence national policy decisions.

Both restructuring and regeneration have involved a co-ordination of all affected parties. Local institutions are as much the products as the instigators of such dialogue which has necessitated 'a new understanding of the role of the state and its players in economic policy ... based on non-hierarchical relationships i.e. on co-operation with those affected in the economy and society' (Schubert and Brautigam, 1995, p. 45). The search continues for 'new forms of dialogue and cooperation between the state, institutions and companies' (Noll, 1995, p. 118).

The German case as evident in North Rhine Westphalia contrasts sharply with the UK. The effects of the emergence of a global market in energy have been moderated in view of the potential social costs of the economic collapse of the coal industry, which has itself been diversified. Policy objectives have been on both the supply and demand side. Partnership and decentralization is institutionalized at the local level. The political culture is committed to dialogue as an inherent process across the board. However, the recent groundswell of opinion among the finance community against the managed economy and some envy of the 'British solution' to economic restructuring pose a considerable threat to the model of change management in North Rhine Westphalia. The social and economic exclusion evident in the UK could yet be the fate of mining communities in Germany.

Spain: Asturias

The once powerful Asturias region has slipped from fifth to twelfth place in the league table of prosperity in Spain. Production and income per capita are significantly below the national average. From 1955 to 1985 Asturias lost 15.7 per cent of all its jobs, but 51 per cent of manufacturing jobs. Comparable national figures showed a gain of 1.8 per cent in jobs, and a manufacturing loss of 18 per cent. With redundancy disguised as retirement, the unemployment rate, at 20 per cent, mainly of young people, is just below the national average.

Central Asturias has 40 per cent of Spanish hard coal production, and 40 per cent of the workforce. HUNOSA accounts for 82 per cent of employment and 66 per cent of production. Production costs are over twice the national average. Despite increases in national production, Asturias' share of coal production fell from 67 to 53 per cent between 1970 and 1992. Mining jobs decreased by a third from 32,000 to 21,000. The number of pits halved in the 1980s with just fourteen left (Vazquez and Del Rosal, 1995, p. 19). The Asturian coalfield is the least efficient and most vulnerable in the national coal industry.

Decline Management

The response to the long-term crisis in the Spanish coal industry was the nationalization of eighteen mining companies in 1967 into HUNOSA. Its operations were protected by import tariffs, guaranteed prices, contracts with thermal power stations and direct subsidies to production costs. Spain's entry into the EC jeopardized these protectionist policies. Existing subsidies and agreements were initially modified to make them apparently compatible with EC regulations but by the late 1980s the government was under increasing pressure to produce a programme for the rationalization of the industry. Commitments were made for a progressive reduction of direct subsidy and a programme of contraction for the industry as a whole, yet in the 1980s six restructuring programmes failed either to reduce the massive state subsidy or to improve productivity.

The negotiation of such plans has always been complex and highly con-flictual, with many different interests represented by the company, unions, regional and local government, political parties and even the Church. Such plans were designed to protect rather than reform the industry and its jobs. None of these plans had the desired impact: production and employment decreased, productivity remained static and costs increased. The net result was an increased level of subsidy from central government. By the 1990s this burden had become intolerable and in the EC's view anti-competitive.

Two further restructuring plans were produced for 1991–3 and 1994–7. The 1991–3 plan, produced after much argument, reduced the 18,000 jobs by a third by progressively reducing the retirement age to 55. HUNOSA bore the cost of high levels of pension and social security entitlements. The 1994–7 plan aimed to maintain existing levels of production while cutting the workforce by another 2,000, reducing the retirement age to 47, and improving technology. HUNOSA would diversify into waste recycling and environmental regeneration.

The attempted phasing of contraction, and the use of early retirement and social security to soften its impact, only postponed the time when wholesale closure would be proposed as the only viable solution. The Minister for Industry did just that in late 1996, with a leaked document indicating that existing deals with the electricity industry would not be renewed. Following widespread political protest, a new agreement was reached in May 1997. HUNOSA would by 2000 reduce its production from 2.5 million tonnes to 2.1 million tonnes and its workforce from 10,000 to 7,000. The EU, wanting a reduction of production to 1.5 million tonnes, refused to sanction the agreement, provoking a national strike in January 1998. The future of the industry seemed more uncertain than ever.

Regeneration

The two restructuring plans of the early 1990s included very little by way of local economic regeneration. The government produced but failed to resource a Plan for Asturias; nor did it fund the regional government's own plan. Regeneration thus became the responsibility of several agencies set up mainly by regional government with different briefs and organizational structures. The two most important have been the Institute for Regional Development (IFR) and the Business Assessment and Promotional Service (SAYE).

Founded in the mid-1980s, initially to attract inward investment, the IFR subsequently diversified its activities into land reclamation and development; applications for EC aid; support for exports; and financing of R&D and small businesses. The SAYE targets small businesses. Both have offices in the main municipalities. Other agencies include the Foundation for the Promotion of Applied Scientific Research and Technology, a joint initiative between the regional government and the University of Oviedo, concerned with technology transfer; and EXPORTATSUR, a grouping of private company exporters. Additionally, there are development agencies in nine municipalities, business centres, chambers of commerce and local branches of the state-owned national Innovation Company (ENISA) offering small-scale grants for business innovation.

Vazquez and Del Rosal argue that this apparently 'wide institutional base for economic promotion ... presents significant deficiencies in terms of organisational structures and demonstrable results' (1995, p. 69). One index of the success rate is the four-year (1989–93) achievement of the SAYE. It claims to have supported two thousand projects producing six thousand jobs. On average, each project cost 26 million pesetas (£100, 000 at 1997 prices) and produced three jobs, a cost per job of 9.2 million pesetas (£35,000). Vazquez and Del Rosal conclude that 'the performance of these organisations has involved considerable effort and huge financial resources, often disproportionate to the results obtained' (1995, p. 70).

More local is the Society for the Development of Comarcas Mineras. A joint venture of HUNOSA and a wing of the IFR, this is designed to generate venture capital for new and existing businesses. From 1989 to 1993 it invested 5,800 million pesetas (£23 million at 1997 prices) in twenty companies, producing 677 new jobs (£35,000 per job). This operates alongside HUNOSA's diversification programme and various forms of EC aid. Assessing the overall results in the Comarcas Mineras, Vazquez and Del Rosal note considerable improvements in land reclamation, environmental improvement and transport but only marginal gains in job creation or small businesses. This they attribute to four types of deficiency in regenerative agencies. First, they are fragmented, lacking in co-ordination, often overlapping in jurisdiction and unable to establish a 'critical mass' of activity. Secondly, they are wholly public sector activities with insufficient involvement of local business, so are not integrated into the local economy. Thirdly, they are excessively bureaucratic organizations, lacking in flexibility or clear targets. Fourthly, they lack long-term objectives, and short-term goals are frequently subject to political interference. Consequently, economic regenerative strategies and agencies are inadequate to the task of halting the apparently irreversible decline of the local economy.

Implications

In Spain the objective of protecting jobs has until recently overridden those of making the industry viable or regenerating the local economy. The pressures towards distributive measures proved stronger than those towards economic efficiency. The consequence for Asturias is a steep decline in the overall level of economic activity. Young men and women have been hardest hit, with little prospect of any but the lowest grade of jobs. Mining locality unemployment stands at 25 per cent, and 40 per cent of the unemployed are under 25 years old.

We find in Spain a set of responses quite different from those in either the UK or Germany: outright protectionism, with extremely high levels of direct and indirect subsidy. Although the need to restructure the industry has been recognized, the actual process has been tortuous and modernization has proved impossible. Central governments, fearful of political ramifications, have been unwilling to enforce a closure programme. All restructuring programmes have been fiercely contested by an alliance of regional political interests, holding tacitly the expectation that the state should provide them with jobs, however uneconomic, and with a dominant strategic objective to wring concessions out of the state. Restructuring programmes were fatally compromised by this balance of political forces. Regenerative agencies rely heavily on regional government, lack co-ordination or clear goals and exclude the private sector. Dialogue here has been largely an adversarial process of bargaining. In Asturias there persists a basically unviable industry, on which the region remains highly dependent. The decline of the industry and attempts at economic regeneration have been haltingly managed. Its demise, and the further decline of the region, seem imminent.

Conclusions

Assessing the precise regional effects of the regulation of industrial decline and economic regeneration is complex, since other potential outcomes remain unknown. Comparative study of the kind undertaken here must acknowledge variations in national politics, energy economics and the 'positioning' of the region which comprise 'the proliferation of special factors that inhibit direct comparison between cases' (Ferner et al., 1997, p. 59). Nevertheless, one simple criterion is how far the gross outcome avoids the standard fate of older industrial regions: structural unemployment, skill imbalances, physical neglect, depopulation and social disintegration (Albrechts et al., 1989, p. 2). This is essentially the position in South Yorkshire's ex-mining communities and the burgeoning reality in the Asturias. Only North Rhine Westphalia has avoided this scenario. In considering the exact reasons for the German 'success' and the relative failure of the other two we shall reconsider the themes outlined in the introduction: the policy mix, the role of institutions and the importance of social dialogue, before considering the relative importance of the global, the national and the local in structuring responses to economic decline.

The Policy Mix

Decisions about the deindustrialization and economic regeneration of regional and local economies are ultimately determined by political factors at the level of the nation state: 'it is difficult to provide a full evaluation of policy response as long as an inadequate understanding persists of the social and political relations within which policy mechanisms and behaviour are embedded' (Albrechts *et al.*, 1989, p. 5). Parker's (1994) argument, that the differences between restructuring policies in the three nations are explicable in terms of politics, is incontrovertible. UK policy is driven by the centralized nature of the state, the clarity of its energy policies and its resolve to isolate and break the radical miners' union; that of Germany by a decentralized state, a more equivocal energy policy and its willingness to negotiate with a more moderate mining union. We might add that in Spain the rigidities of regional autonomy, the absence of an energy policy and the militancy of the union and the region all helped to delay effective action of any kind. It is therefore crucial 'how the balance of opposing internal political forces determines the rate of change', so that the prime consideration 'is not about fundamental strategic direction but about politically acceptable phasing of decline' (Parker, 1994, p. 76).

This determination of the economic by the political also applies to local regeneration policy. Martin (1989) has reviewed the six options available: reindustrialization; industrial de-maturation; tertiarization; reskilling and flexibilization of the workforce; infrastructure renewal; and financial reorganization. The decision about which mix of policies to adopt reflects national political views of both the ends and means of economic renewal. Germany's approach is to maximize involvement in a comprehensive plan, and is the only one to incorporate all of Martin's options, including the regulation of dematuration through the diversification of Ruhrkohle. In the UK there has been an unwarranted assumption by national government that retraining and SME support will restimulate the local economy. Spain vacillates ineffectually between these two models. With the UK it resorts to what Hudson (1992) calls welfare regulation, with heavy spending on pensions and unemployment benefit, as opposed to economic regeneration. Such short-term measures may mitigate the worst effects of deindustrialization but have no effect on the local economy. They are produced by political influences, in the UK a zealous belief in market forces, in Spain the extreme political sensitivity of the industry and its regions. Essentially the same contrast between comprehensive planning and piecemeal short-term measures is found at the level of institutions.

'Thick' Institutions

The important factor for economic institutions is recognized to be their degree of 'thickness', not their size or number but how they are interlocked with other significant political and economic institutions locally and with the state nationally. Hudson (1992) notes that the local institutions may either resist or welcome change: this is a persistent difference between such institutions in Spain and Germany. Resistance in older areas is more likely because existing institutions favour political and cultural continuity rather than economic change. Hence the problem for such areas is to develop new kinds of institution 'which would allow more of a smooth and incremental adaptation of local economic and social life to the broader exigencies of national state policies and global political-economic change' (Hudson, 1992, p. 212). Hudson remains sceptical about the viability of the necessary institutional reform.

Our case studies suggest that institutions at both regional and local level do matter, though their effects may be uneven. In the UK, the failure of central government localism to induce thick institutions enabled fast closure but prevented economic regeneration. In Spain the coalition of interests rooted in local institutions resisted industrial change and ignored regenerative change. In Germany, the creation of new institutions through a 'conference' structure ensured their dense networking. If institutional thickness of local institutions and regulation via regional government are prerequisites for successful regeneration of the local economy, they are clearly identifiable in North Rhine Westphalia, conspicuous by their absence in South Yorkshire and present only in politically oppositional form in Asturias.

Social Dialogue

Resolution to policy dilemmas is thought to lie in social dialogue: constructive discussion of policy options among producers, workers and consumers. Discussing the example of social dialogue set by the European Coal and Steel

Community (ECSC), Ferner *et al.* (1997) distinguish between effects on three different types of countries. They suggest dialogue would have happened anyway in those countries 'with strong legal measures in support of social dialogue', of which Germany is the prime example. Nor was there any effect on countries where 'liberal market philosophies' co-exist with 'weak processes of social dialogue', the UK being the most extreme case. Where the model has had most effect is 'in countries . . . where a legal framework for dialogue exists but is to varying degrees fairly weak or uncertain', an example being Spain. This typology is very accurate for economic regulation in coal mining areas in the UK and Germany. The case of Spain is more complex, since the typology begs the question of why, if the legal framework exists, the processes are so weak. The explanation is political. Whatever the constitution may say, the key factors are the balance of power between central and regional government and, crucially, prevalent working assumptions about the balance between dependence and autonomy for the regions. That is why the EU cannot induce dialogue where the conditions for it do not exist: 'The vitality of dialogue in each member state . . . is to a large extent determined by the national institutional, cultural and legislative frameworks within which social dialogue is being conducted.' (Ferner *et al.*, 1997, p. 69).

Global, National, Regional, Local

The fundamental importance of the regional level of regulation is universal but any particular region is a unique economic, political and cultural formation (Amin and Thrift, 1995). A generally applicable formula for regional development is a chimera. 'Regulatory systems are not portable structures, achieving similar results wherever they are deployed, but are in fact deeply rooted in local social structures' (Peck, 1994, p. 169). A basic principle may still be prescribed, that effective regional policy 'implies the decentralisation of powers of planning and implementation to the local level' (Martin, 1989, p. 48). This does not, however, specify how the local, the regional and the national need to operate in concert and the conditions needed to bring this about. The basic necessity is that the respective powers of the national, regional and local levels should achieve a kind of balance. Trigilia may be right to stress that regeneration poses 'a regulative problem of a regional nature' (cited in Peck, 1994, p. 165) but this is not simply a question of an institutional tier, though that may be a prerequisite. It has to be effectively interlocked with the central state, as it is in Germany but not in Spain. Similarly, the local should mean not penetration by the region but a genuine autonomy. In all this, a feedback loop of political communication is vital. If that is absent, the structure will not operate with the required degree of flexibility.

As the German case shows, even that may be insufficient if the national is unevenly related to supranational institutions. EU commitment to free competition acts against subsidies necessary to the management of decline. In both Germany and Spain it is the EU which objects to planned contraction. To then proclaim commitment to regional development of older industrial areas seems somewhat hollow (Ferner *et al.*, 1997, p. 61). In short, regulation at the local, regional and national level, however well designed and executed, may be insufficient if at the supranational level there is no regulative system. As Peck and Tickell (1994, p. 292) emphasize, the search for appropriate instruments of economic generation – 'a new institutional fix' – is spurious while there is no attempt to meet the need for the 'construction of a new global regulatory order'. The 'hollowing out of the state' gives regions regulatory responsibility without power while supranational systems have power without responsibility (1994, p. 311).

Our most optimistic case, North Rhine Westphalia, may in the long term reposition itself as a region in the German and European economy but has exerted no influence over the global energy markets which have caused the demise of its coal industry. Limited protection for the rump of the industry is under constant challenge from European regulations designed to ensure free competition. Nor can the *Land* necessarily exert control over the national energy policy and attempts to revise it in the light of economic problems following reunification.

On the basis of recent events, we cannot agree with the view that 'with appropriate action and public and private initiative, the social impact of coal sector restructuring can be minimised and a more secure future for the coalfields can be foreseen' (International Economic and Energy Consultants, 1995, p. 9). The balance of political forces which has given some support to the coal industry and its areas seems likely to tilt against them. Although the basic problems of the European coal industry are economic, their resolution is a matter of political will. We cannot be sanguine about the likely outcome.

Note

1. This international comparison was funded by an extension of an original grant from the Economic and Social Research Council to study the UK mining industry (Grant L206252004). The authors gratefully acknowledge the ESRC's support.

5 THE NORDIC MODEL AND THE MAKING OF THE COMPETITIVE 'US'

Pauli Kettunen

At the same time as the nation state is said to be eroding in the globalizing world, reflections on different 'models' which refer to nationally organized forms of social life remain vivid and popular. Expressions such as the 'Japanese model', 'German model' or 'model of New Zealand' are frequently used in public discussion. The 'Anglo-Saxon model', 'Rhine model', or 'Nordic model' claim similarities among some countries, but even here one talks about institutions within nation states. While there are different forecasts concerning a convergence or divergence of models, such 'model consciousness' questions any simplistic story of globalization. However, it would be an understatement to take the discussion of models as just an indicator of the fact that globalization has not yet proceeded as far as the most enthusiastic proponents of the globalization thesis suggest (see Hirst and Thompson, 1996; Beck, 1997). Rather, this model consciousness is to be seen as a way in which national perspectives are reproduced, not despite but through globalization.

In this chapter the relationship of the Nordic model of labour relations to globalization is discussed. The 'Nordic model' refers to national institutions in the five Nordic countries, Denmark, Finland, Iceland, Norway and Sweden. I will not, however, just adopt this concept instrumentally, but take seriously the historicity of the model discussion. What follows is not primarily an account or a forecast concerning the impacts of the processes called globalization on the national institutions called the Nordic model. My primary interest concerns a particular type of power: the power of defining the agenda, in this case the agenda of working-life issues.

The notion of a Nordic model – as well as 'models' in general – has been articulated in the 1980s and 1990s within a discourse in which national institutional arrangements are compared more intensely than before from the point of view of competitiveness. The concern with international competitiveness is, of course, far from novel. However, there are new types and new imperatives of competitiveness which mediate the structural power of transnationalized financial markets and transnationalized enterprises into national contexts. 'We', within a given national framework, are supposed to make ourselves attractive and competitive to those who make decisions about the flows of money, investments and the location of production and jobs, and who compare national conditions from a transnational perspective. The talk about models expresses the crucial role of comparisons in economic and political practices. These comparisons are an aspect of continuous self-monitoring *reflexivity* and, thus, a mechanism for reproducing and articulating various 'imagined communities' (Anderson, 1983), notably national communities, within the processes of globalization.

As they concentrate on arguments concerning the best way of making and keeping 'us' competitive, not only critics but also proponents of the 'Nordic model' contribute to the taken-for-granted status of the imperatives of competitiveness. No doubt the social implications of various competition models and strategies differ. In any case, the way in which 'our' competitiveness preconditions the agenda of working-life issues tends to mean that 'we' is defined through collective and individual competitiveness. Here an ideological reproduction of (above all, national) communities and mechanisms of social exclusion are two sides of the same coin. I argue that this is true even of those competition strategies that point out competitive advantages of social regulations and are advocated by many defenders of the Nordic model. For my argument, a historical approach is necessary.

The Nordic Model

There is an ideological charge in the 'Nordic model'. In political debates, it is mostly a concept of those who wish to defend the welfare state and collective institutions of industrial relations (see Schiller, 1994). The concept is criticized by those who are critical of the institutions referred to in this fashion. In particular, some employer representatives have denied the existence of a single Nordic model (e.g. Myrdal, 1995). There is also scholarly critique, emphasizing various differences between the industrial relations systems (or welfare states, or regimes of accumulation) in the five Nordic countries, or pointing out that despite remarkable similarities the institutions themselves are national (Strøby Jensen, Due and Madsen, 1994; Neal, 1994).

True, not only 'model' but also 'Nordic' is a problematic term. However, important historical facts are ignored if one rejects the attribute 'Nordic' because the institutions of the regulation of labour are not seen as Nordic in a supranational sense but nationally Danish, Finnish, Icelandic, Norwegian and Swedish. Even the argument stressing past and present differences between the national institutions misses a crucial point. Admittedly, the institutions *are* national and there *are* remarkable differences between them as well as remarkable similarities with traditions and states of affairs outside the Nordic countries (especially in those other small European countries to which Katzenstein, 1985, applies the concept of 'democratic corporatism'). Nevertheless, there has been both an experienced Nordic context in which national identities and institutions have been shaped and an inherent Nordic element in the different national identities and institutions in Denmark, Finland, Iceland, Norway and Sweden.

The Nordic context contains much more than a juridically single labour market and the freedom of crossing borders without a passport since 1954. It has been institutionalized through communication and co-operation not only between state authorities but also – since the late nineteenth century – between all sorts of voluntary organizations, such as trade unions and employers' organizations (Østergård, 1997, pp. 42–5). Inspired by the wide cultural and communicative connections beneath the level of governmental and intergovernmental politics, some commentators have constructed visions of *Norden* as a 'mega-region' in the Europe of regions (Joenniemi, 1994), although they have been somewhat discouraged by the different stands which the five Nordic countries have taken regarding the EU. Denmark (since 1973), Finland and Sweden (both since 1995) are EU members. Only Finland, however, was among the first members of the EMU in 1998, whereas Norway and Iceland have only joined the European Economic Area (EEA).

The different positions taken with regard to European integration do not, however, indicate some drastic break in the history of Nordic co-operation. This history displays how 'the Nordic element has never lastingly gone beyond national frameworks' (Sørensen and Stråth, 1997b, p. 19). The Nordic identity was developed in the nineteenth century as an element within national identities. As such it has never attained an independent existence beyond them. From another perspective the same idea may be expressed by saying that *Norden* has served as a frame of reference in which national differences have been identified and national institutions formed.

Through the strengthening of Social Democracy in the 1930s, 'Nordic' became associated with democracy. At that time the notion of Nordic democracy primarily confronted the threat of fascism, including, for example, the mythological '*Nordische Gedanke*' of the German Nazis. 'Nordic democracy', however, did not just refer to similarities of existing circumstances. The concept could also work as a criterion of a critique of society, as it did in the Social Democratic wing of the Finnish labour movement from the 1930s. Finland was a Nordic country, yet it did not properly meet the democratic demands inherent in 'Nordic'. This was one argument of the Finnish trade union leaders in the 1930s, as they attempted to break the political legitimacy of the policies of Finnish employers who, unlike their colleagues in Denmark, Sweden and Norway, refused to accept the principle of collective agreements (Kettunen, 1995, pp. 268–70).

In part, intra-Nordic comparisons and connections have been conditioned by tough competition in the world market. For example, during the twentieth century the competition between the Swedish and Finnish wood processing industries has frequently contributed to the willingness of the Swedish trade unions to help improve the bargaining power of the Finnish trade unions. The latter were much weaker until the Second World War and indeed until the 1970s, and failed to show the Social Democratic internal unity that was evident in the Swedish trade union movement.

In any case, it is also possible to defend the concept of the 'Nordic model' by referring to actual institutional similarities in the regulation of labour which, since the beginning of the 1970s, have been common not only to the 'core' Scandinavian countries – Sweden, Denmark and Norway – but also to the 'peripheral' countries of *Norden*, Finland and Iceland (Lilja, 1992; Gudmundsson, 1995). Those common characteristics can be roughly listed as follows (see e.g. Bruun, 1994; Kauppinen, 1994; Kjellberg, 1983, 1998):

– a high degree of employee organization, including the public as well as the private sector, white-collar as well as blue-collar workers, female as well as male employees;
– a high degree of employer organization;
– the absence or insignificance of organizational divisions within the workers' union movement based on ideological rivalry;
– the existence of separate, strong organizations of white-collar employees;
– relatively centralized national organizational structures;
– however, at the same time, a strong presence of trade union organization at workplace level;
– a nationally institutionalized hierarchical system of collective bargaining;
– the priority of collective agreements rather than direct statutory interventions in the regulation of employment relationships;

– tripartite co-operation between trade unions, employers' organizations and government, promoted by the strong position of Social Democracy in the political system as well as the trade unions.

While neo-corporatist institutions have formed a strong link between industrial relations and the development of the welfare state, the welfare state has had a major impact on industrial relations by creating a large public sector and making possible the high participation of women in working life outside home, often in public-sector jobs. At the same time there is a clear gender segmentation in the labour market (Hirdman, 1990; Julkunen and Rantalaiho, 1993; Therborn, 1995, pp. 61–2).

To be sure, not only are the national routes to the 'Nordic model' different and the 'model' itself in transition in different ways in different countries, but every point on the list above could also be used as a variable in a comparison which would aim at clarifying differences of traditions, present practices and future prospects between the Nordic countries. Thus, for example, in Norway union density, although far above the average of EU or OECD countries, is somewhat lower (under 60 per cent in the middle 1990s) than in Denmark, Finland, Iceland and Sweden (80–90 per cent) (ILO, 1997, p. 236). The difference is at least partially due to the fact that in Norway unemployment benefits are not organized on the basis of union unemployment funds. On the other hand, Norway, with her particular oil-based capacities for managing the international recession of the early 1990s, has in the 1980s and 1990s shown a more stable and less challenged continuity of 'traditional' neo-corporatist modes of compromise and regulation than the other Nordic countries have (Bruun, 1994; Dølvik, 1994).

Denmark has been the Nordic forerunner in the history of collective agreements since the Danish 'September Compromise' of 1899, the first agreement in the world between national peak organizations of workers and employers, including a model-shaping combination of the principles of collective bargaining and management's prerogative to hire and fire workers and to direct them at work (Scheuer, 1992, pp. 171–3). In the long run, Denmark has also been the most consistent among the Nordic countries in preferring collective agreements to legislation in the regulation of employment relations (Bruun, 1990, p. 37), despite her tradition of legislative solutions to wider industrial conflicts when the parties fail to achieve a compromise (as happened, for example, in May 1998). But in regard to organizational structures the 'Danish model' has been exceptional in the Nordic context. The strength of craft-based unionism (combined with the existence of so-called general unions) makes the history of the Danish trade union movement different from the Swedish, Norwegian and Finnish union movements, in which the principle of industry-based unionism early achieved a dominant position.

Finland was, in turn, a Nordic exception until the end of the 1960s due to a relatively low degree of unionization, political splits in the trade union movement and notoriously 'low-trust' elements in labour relations (partly stemming from the Civil War of 1918 and in many ways still being experienced in the 1970s). However, since the beginning of the so-called incomes policy era in 1968, neo-corporatist practices have occupied a very strong position in Finland even by Nordic comparison, with a tighter intertwining of labour market negotiations and governmental policy measures than in Sweden or Denmark. In any case, many features of the 'Nordic model', especially high union density, became a reality in Finland in the 1970s (Lilja, 1992).

At the same time, however, the 'model' was severely challenged at its heart, Sweden. The celebrated 'spirit of Saltsjöbaden', signifying the legacy of the basic agreement of 1938 between the Swedish central organizations of trade unions (LO) and employers (SAF), was not working as it had during the postwar decades. A crucial economic policy element based on the highly institutionalized party relations in the labour market had been the active labour market policy, which included solidaristic wage policy not least as a means for structural rationalization within the national economy. This so-called Rehn-Meidner model faced difficulties in the 1970s and thereby failed to contribute to economic growth and the competitiveness of export industries (Pontusson, 1992a, 1992b). The political confrontations concerning economic democracy and workers' co-determination in the 1970s (Schiller, 1988) preceded a new constellation of power in the 1980s. Backed by the new structural power of their 'exit' option (see Hirschman, 1970) in the world of free capital mobility, the big Swedish-based multinationals wished to get rid of nationally-centralized collective bargaining (once initiated by employer organizations) and tripartite institutions. 'After a long-lasting sickness the "Swedish model" is dead', the chairman of the peak organization of Swedish employers announced in 1990 (Pestoff, 1991, p. 98; Rehn, 1996, p. 188).

The 'death of the Swedish model' – or, for that matter, of the Nordic model – has proved to be an exaggeration (see Kjellberg, 1998). But regardless of the actual fate of the model, the discussion about the death or survival of the Swedish, Scandinavian or Nordic model has been very important for the history of the 'model'. Indeed, the model concept first attained wider use as it began to refer to something that was seen as being challenged; as something to be rejected or defended.

From the growth of Fascism during the 1930s until the end of the cold war, Scandinavia and especially Sweden were often said to represent the 'Middle

Way' or 'Third Way'. The frame of reference consisted of confrontations between rival universalist visions of social transformation. There was also a strong universalist charge in the very notions of the 'Middle Way' and the 'Third Way'. Not only insiders but also many outsiders (in the first place, Social Democrats) saw the Swedish and Scandinavian postwar developments as exceptionally consequential steps in a universally valid direction of progress. These countries seemed to follow the direction declared to be universal, for example, through the organizational principles of the ILO (tripartism) and through the postwar programme of the same organization, the Philadelphia Declaration of 1944, which included the principles of collective bargaining, the representation of workers and employers in economic and social policy-making, the aim of full employment, and a trust in a welfare-generating linkage between social equality and economic growth.

The political power of this vision diminished remarkably during and after the 1970s through the international neo-liberal offensive which was inter-twined with the decline of the 'Fordist' paradigm of capitalist development and then with the collapse of so-called really existing socialism. Characteristic enough, at the beginning of the 1980s the 'Third Way' was provided with a new meaning in the Swedish political vocabulary. It meant now a Social Democratic attempt to find an alternative both to Keynesian and neo-liberal economic policies (Rehn, 1996, p. 180; Åmark, 1992, p. 88). A more permanent change was, however, that the static and statistical metaphor of 'model' was substituted for the historicist metaphor of 'way'. This carried more than just a shift of words. It involved a change in the meanings of and relationships between time, space and politics.

The previous metaphor of (the Middle or Third) 'way' implied three intertwining ideas: that there was a continuous line from the past to the future, having a certain direction; that there was an ongoing worldwide political struggle concerning the right way along which national societies were sup-posed to proceed in history; and that the code of this future direction was inherent in the present society. The concept of model, in turn, was adopted in a context in which the future was confronted with the past and conceived of in terms of unavoidable 'new challenges'. This kind of confrontation between past and future is certainly no new postmodern mode of thought. Neither is an emphasis on historical continuities excluded from the current model discus-sion, as is shown by the so-called institutional approach and analyses of 'path-dependency'. However, the context in which the functions and mean-ings of working-life institutions were defined had changed, as had those functions and meanings themselves.

As a mode of conceptualizing change and motion, the primarily temporal notion of social progress was first declared to be dead by postmodernism and then displaced by the primarily spatial notion of economic and cultural globalization. It seems to me that crucial implications of this shift of horizon can be traced by looking at the ways in which institutions and discourses of labour regulation have been connected with the *idea of society*. In part this problem concerns modern 'society' in general, yet it also concerns historical specificities of 'society' in the Nordic political cultures.

Society and Immanent Critique

Nordic 'society' has been defined by the nation state, as modern 'society' in general has been (Giddens, 1984, pp. 163–4; Lash and Urry, 1994, p. 320). Further, Nordic 'society' has involved a notion of national economy in which an easy adoption of the idea of the national economic interest has been combined with an awareness of a dependence on external factors. In this respect the Nordic countries probably share a lot with other small open economies.[1] However, there is something particular to the Nordic conception of the way in which 'society' and 'state' are related to each other. They are tightly intertwined and even identified in the Nordic political languages.

In political programmes as well as in the language of ordinary people it is more frequently 'society' than 'state' that is supposed to carry responsibilities for the welfare of people or to guarantee rights to individuals or to put limits on private interests in the name of the general or public interest. The conceptual mix of state and society has a history remarkably longer than the era of a large public sector or welfare state or neo-corporatism. In some historical explanations the traditions of independent peasant and local self-government as well as the absence of conflicts between state and (Lutheran) church are pointed out (Aronsson, 1995; Trägårdh, 1997). Importantly, the intertwining of 'state' and 'society' cannot simply be interpreted as an indicator of an illiberal subordination of society to state. It can also mean that the legitimacy of state or public power is based on its capability to involve associative principles of 'society' (see Trägårdh, 1997, p. 260). The role of collective negotiations and agreements is to be seen in this context. The preference for mutual agreements between organized collective parties rather than direct statutory interventions in the regulation of employment relationships does not indicate a confrontation between 'state' and '(civil) society'. Rather, in Sweden, Denmark and Norway from the 1930s (though only after the Second World War in Finland) regulation through collective agreements became an inherent principle of a 'society' which represented not individual but general, not private but public interests.

There is a further dimension to this concept of 'society'. It has not just referred to an existing state of affairs, for society has been thought to be a historical actor with its own normative standards, containing the code for its future change and reform. This understanding of society includes the idea of immanent critique (see Gronow, 1986, pp. 165–76; Calhoun, 1995, p. 23). The normative standards of society have been assumed to serve as criteria through which it is able to criticize and revise itself. To be sure, this kind of thought is not an exotically Nordic one; the general modern notion of progress is an obvious ingredient here. Nevertheless, without being in a position to develop an adequate comparative investigation, I would suggest that such immanent critique has played a somehow special political role in the Nordic countries. Factors contributing to this mode of thought have been ethnic and cultural homogeneity and a particular type of conformity based on the Lutheran tradition (Stenius, 1997). Homogeneity and conformity have by no means implied an absence of class conflicts and class consciousness. Rather, the nation as 'imagined community' (Anderson, 1983) could offer a moral code against which individual and local experiences of suppression and injustice could be contrasted and thus generalized as political class consciousness (see Kettunen, 1995, pp. 262–3). The idea of a society being able to criticize and revise itself was then, in the 1930s, promoted by the particular historical class compromises between workers, farmers and bourgeoisie and – mostly in the case of Sweden – by the hegemonic political position of reformist Socialism.

Not only the contents of what were conceived of as the normative standards of the 'society' but still more the possibility of applying them as criteria of social criticism were matters of hegemonic struggle. Here the famous concept within Swedish Social Democracy from the inter-war period, the People's Home (*folkhem*), is a good, albeit unique, example. The Social Democrats adopted the metaphor of home, so popular among the right-wing nationalists, and proved that the social circumstances did not fulfil this criterion. They consequently attached new political meanings to this metaphor (Larsson, 1994). Under the conditions of the increased political power of Social Democracy, the gap between normative standards and social reality was then to be filled by the action of the labour movement and by public planning relying on scientific knowledge. In this way, in turn, the Social Democrats reshaped the values and norms which could be conceived of as normative standards of the society and, thus, as criteria of immanent critique and the basis for political action and planning. In the very same process, Social Democracy made itself the central factor of national integration.

As to the patterns of the regulation of labour, one can historically identify two intertwined ideological elements that have served as criteria of an immanent critique of society. The first is the idea of a *party symmetry* in the labour market, and the second is a faith in the possibility of a *virtuous circle* between different interests as well as between politics, economies and ethics within national society. As I see it, the modes of thought and action in which these ideas formed criteria for an immanent critique of society have actually faced the 'new challenges' of globalization more fatefully than the formal institutions of the 'Nordic model' have done. This means that the functions and meanings of the institutions are perhaps changed in rather subtle and unnoticed ways.

The Ideology of Parity

Let us first look at the idea of symmetry between the labour market partners. It is a part of the mode of thought sometimes called the 'ideology of parity' (Bruun, 1979). In this – far from exclusively Nordic – ideology a basic assumption claims that the worker is the weaker party in the individual employment relationship, requiring protection through legislation and collective agreements. At the collective level, however, parity is realized in negotiations and agreements between organized workers and employers. The state (or, often in the Nordic languages, 'society'), as the representative of general interests, is supposed to guarantee preconditions for this parity.

It must not be overlooked that in the Nordic countries, as well as in other Western countries, this ideology of the regulation of labour has historically contributed to a justification of hierarchical work organizations. At least in principle, it has made the practice of collective agreements compatible with the definition of supervisory rights as the managerial prerogative of employers. The ideology of parity has also left scope for the justification of hierarchies as functional necessities, conceived of in terms of technical control and efficiency (see Miller and O'Leary, 1989). One could say that the ideology of parity has reproduced tensions between three distinct rationalities which mediate between workers' life-worlds and the systemic conditions of living. Two rationalities are inherent in living by wage-work: that of the *seller of labour power* and that of the *subject of the labour process* (see Kern and Schumann, 1984). The third important rationality here is that of *citizenship*. Obviously, it has been difficult to project the rationality of an equal citizenship into the context of wage-work relations and hierarchical work organizations (see Winner, 1995). One can also argue that the system of collective bargaining, insofar as it follows the logic of selling and buying labour power, tends to reduce qualitative issues of working life into issues concerning the price of labour power and the quantity of labour exploited. The rationality of the subject of the labour process tends to be subordinated not only to the hierarchy of work organization but also to the market logic of employment relationships.

Inherent in the ideology of parity is the assumption of a common general interest above divergent particular interests. This assumption was actualized in the prehistory of the Swedish Saltsjöbaden Accords of 1938. Through the increased strength of collective organizations the probability had grown of industrial conflicts causing big losses not only to the two parties but also to the 'third party' and, thus, 'society'. This view, primarily raised on the political agenda by bourgeois groups, came to be shared by trade union leaders and employer representatives alike. Furthermore, in the late 1930s both had motives, albeit different ones, to avoid direct interventions by the (Social Democratic) government regarding the problem of 'industrial peace'. The result was an agreement on principles and procedures of collective party relations on various levels. The 'spirit' of the agreement included the idea that the labour-market parties reciprocally recognized the particular and legitimate nature of their interests and were committed to taking into account the universal interest through their mutual compromises.

However, this is not the whole picture. Party symmetry not only worked as an idea for regulating labour-market conflicts, a principle of 'conflict-based corporatism' (see Pekkarinen, Pohjola and Rowthorne, 1992b) or an ideological disguise of the basic asymmetry of capital and labour (see Offe and Wiesenthal, 1985). Wider meanings were attached to this principle. In the 1930s the Nordic Social Democrats, especially the Social Democratic trade union leaders, included the symmetry of labour-market parties in the concept of 'Nordic democracy'. The Social Democratic movement was able, probably most successfully in Sweden and least successfully in Finland, to establish the parity of labour-market parties as a normative standard of the 'society' itself, which could then be turned against the prevailing asymmetries. Trade unions were oriented to extend the field of party relations. This not only meant that trade unions achieved a wider and more legitimate role in industrial relations. At least equally fundamental was that capitalists, and somewhat later even state and municipalities in their role as employers, were defined and organized as a 'party' with (no more than) particular interests. The widening of party relations meant a wider field of issues in which employers had to recognize the particularism of their interests. It is worth noting that industrial democracy in the Nordic countries has mostly been conceived of in terms of practices that are connected with the system of collective agreements, for instance the institution of shop stewards. Separate arrangements for employee participation (cf. *Betriebsräte* in Germany) have been either relatively unimportant or tightly integrated with collective party relations (Knudsen, 1995).

On another level, the principle of party symmetry was extended through tripartite procedures in economic and social policies. While an interest in controlling suspected outcomes of the democratic political process was an obvious motive for employers' acceptance of such procedures, trade union representatives saw them as a democratization of the mode in which 'society' upheld its universal interests against particular capitalist interests. The participation of labour organizations in the functioning of 'society' made it easier to move from the notion of the working class as the bearer of universal emancipatory interests to that in which 'society' was given a corresponding historical role.

The Ideology of the Virtuous Circle

The recognition of and compromises between divergent particular interests were also assumed to serve the universal interest in other ways than by preventing destructive conflicts and widening democracy. Compromises would realize and reinforce a virtuous circle between different interests within a national society. In the 1930s, in Sweden, Denmark and Norway (though much more weakly in Finland) the notion of national economy began to be based on new ideas of cumulative economic success (Mjøset, 1986, pp. 60–3). Reflecting the class structure, a virtuous circle connected the interests of worker-consumers and farmer-producers as well as those of workers and employers. Confidence in such positive-sum-games was institutionalized in the class compromises which initiated the period of Social Democracy in the Scandinavian countries. These class compromises included the political coalitions of 'workers and farmers', or Social Democrats and Agrarian Parties respectively, and the consolidation of national systems of collective labour market negotiations and agreements (only the former part applying to Finland before the Second World War).

The idea of a virtuous circle included something more than just organized economic interests promoting each other. Those interests were situated in a wider ideological context of 'society'. The society was expected to be built more and more on industrial wage-work. Yet, the normalcy of wage-work presupposed not only various forms of disciplinary power and 'social engineering' in relation to workers' everyday lives. To put it in very general terms, wage-work had also to be reconciled with three different ideological elements: the spirit of capitalism; the utopia of socialism; and the idealized tradition of the Nordic independent farmer. The first adjustment was a problem common to all Western societies. The second was common to those Western European societies in which the Social Democratic labour movement was strong. The third problem, the ideological adjustment of industrial wage-work to the tradition of the independent farmer, was especially indigenous to the Nordic countries, the idealizing invention of this tradition being an inseparable part of the rise of Nordic nationalisms in the nineteenth century (Kettunen, 1995).

Through the class compromises of the 1930s the values of *efficiency, solidarity* and *equality* – which in a way reflected the spirit of capitalism, the utopia of socialism and the idealized tradition of the independent farmer – acquired in the political culture the status of being normative standards of the society itself. And still more: the idea of or the faith in a virtuous circle between these values, connecting the spheres of economies, politics and ethics, became a normative standard of the society. Apparently, this was particularly true in Sweden, where Social Democracy gained greater power in defining the political agenda than in the other Nordic countries. Esping-Andersen (1992, p. 44) writes of 'the emergence of a synonymity between the Social Democratic movement, political democracy, economic prosperity, and social welfare' following the depression of the early 1930s.

The labour movement accepted that economic growth and thus the rationalization of production were necessary in order to create resources for social welfare and equality. At the same time, bourgeois groups and employers accepted that the collective organization of labour and the widening of workers' social rights could bring positive economic results, not least in respect of industrial peace (Schiller, 1989, pp. 222–5). Somewhat paradoxically, the needs and interests of capital, or employers, gained a moral and political legitimization as the needs and interests of the working class gained an economic legitimization.

In this ideological context the relations between 'parties' in the labour market were supposed to include not only *compromises* between conflicting labour market *interests* but also *co-operation* between groups fulfilling different *functions* of enterprise and society. Here traditions, which were 'invented' in Hobsbawm's (1983) sense, played a role in the service of industrial modernization. Functionalism could be combined with the paternalism of rural industrial communities, which were typical of industrialization in Sweden as well as Norway and Finland (see Larsson, 1994; Hampden-Turner and Trompenaars, 1994, pp. 239–40). There was a common principle in paternalism and functionalism: everybody had to be a useful part of the whole. And there were pre-industrial, traditional grounds for this principle in agrarian rationality, which had its material roots in Nordic natural conditions and contributed to a linkage of egalitarianism with this principle.

The functionalist notions of enterprise and society were, no doubt, ambiguous as to the role of conflicts and compromises between divergent interests. They could justify the defence of management prerogative and the limits of collective bargaining. However, they also made possible a conception of enterprise as a functional whole that was supposed to represent universal interests in relation to particular interests of both employer and employees (Kettunen and Turunen, 1994, p. 74; Flodgren, 1990, p. 124). A horizon was opened to a continuous widening of the field of issues in which employers would be obliged to admit the particularism of their interests, i.e. the widening of symmetrical party relations.

Society, then, was supposed to represent the universal interest in relation to both enterprises and labour-market parties. True, on the macro level of society there was a permanent tension between the principles of compromise and planning. In recent research, two orientations have been identified in the history of Swedish Social Democracy, one combining the promotion of labour-market compromise couched in terms of the ideology of parity with an acceptance of rationalization at company and workplace level, the other wanting to subordinate labour-market compromises as well as business economies to national economic and social planning (Appelqvist, 1996). In any case, the postwar Swedish and more general Nordic agenda of working-life issues was, until the 1970s, shaped by a discourse according to which labour-market 'parties' produced cohesion, efficiency and democracy in 'society', which at the same time was seen as both the subject and the object of rational political planning.

Where Are the Parties?

In the 1980s and 1990s the survival of 'society' has been questioned in debates on modernity and postmodernity, and on globalization. The modern concept of society is considered to be somehow too strong and holistic to stand the 'crisis of modernity' (Touraine, 1995) or too limited, too tightly connected with the system of nation states, to keep its political and analytical power in the era of globalization (Lash and Urry, 1994). It is appropriate to ask whether the specific Nordic notion of society is especially 'outdated' or, at least, exposed to the pressures of change. There are, indeed, obvious critical points concerning the capability of Nordic 'society' to grasp the contemporary reality. It is not difficult to observe that the 'parity-ideological' symmetry of labour-market parties is one of those critical points. There are at least three aspects inherent in this problem.

First, it is now more difficult than in earlier times to define, identify, organize and centralize the 'parties'. Concerning individual employment relations, it is practically and juridically hard to say who or what an 'employer' is in a multinational enterprise which has the complex structure of a corporate group and a wide network of subcontractors (Bruun, Nielsen and Töllborg 1994). The definition of 'employee' becomes troublesome, too. Not only are employee relationships being redefined as a result of the mass unemployment that has shaken the foundations of wage-work society in the 1990s, especially in Finland but also in Sweden, but the practice of 'atypical' (short- and part-time) employment relationships is being extended in the name of flexibility and is perhaps even becoming typical. Further, enterprises are trying to promote both flexibility and involvement in work organizations by making use of methods which blur the difference between wage-work and entrepreneurship and, by the same token, challenge the idea of the employee as the weaker partner in the wage-work relationship.

In consequence, the organizing of collective parties on three levels, namely at the workplace, within each branch and on the central national level – the crucial mode of thought and action in the Nordic regulation of labour – faces big problems. It is true that the rate of unionization has remained very high in the Nordic countries, and that in Finland and Sweden the insecurity of living during the mass unemployment of the 1990s has made people even more willing to seek security and protection from trade union membership (Bruun, 1994, p. 38; Kjellberg, 1998). However, the high rate of unionization has not stopped the Nordic mode of organizing collective parties becoming problematic. In abstract terms, this mode may be characterized as concentration through centralization. The concentration of labour interests was believed to presuppose organizational centralization, corresponding to the concentration and centralization of capital. Since the beginning of the twentieth century this was, for the Nordic trade union movements, the way of producing working-class solidarity and rational action in accordance with the fundamental processes of capitalism (Kettunen, 1994, pp. 115–25). This tradition does not fit well into the picture of new company structures drawn by Bennett Harrison, for whom the main tendency is 'concentration without centralisation' (Harrison, 1994, pp. 8–12; cf. Venneslan and Ågotnes, 1994).

Secondly, there is a growing asymmetry between the actors as regards their ability to act on the same 'level'. There is the transnationalized perspective of capital and the locally and nationally tied perspective of labour (cf. Pekkarinen, Pohjola and Rowthorn, 1992b). Globalization, as temporal and spatial restructuring of social practices, means an increasing mobility, but also, and in fact more fundamentally, increasing differences in mobility between different factors of production. As a researcher of the ILO puts it, 'the real *problématique* of globalization is, arguably, the growing disparity between the mobility of labour and capital' (Campbell, 1994, pp. 186–7). Foreign direct investments have increased rapidly since the early 1980s so that, for example, half of the jobs of the 30 biggest Finnish companies were located abroad by the middle of the 1990s (Ali-Yrkkö and Ylä-Anttila, 1997).

Reflexivity in the form of comparisons becomes ever more vital to all those involved in industrial relations, but the temporal and spatial perspectives of different actors are shaped in very different ways. Thus, the leaders of multinational corporations and actors in the finance market compare local and national conditions from a transnational perspective. Meanwhile employees and their representatives are also supposed to be able to compare local and national conditions, those of 'us' and those of 'others', but in these comparisons their perspectives take local and national conditions as their points of departure. Through this reflexivity, globalization may mean that national and local identities will be anchored in workers' everyday life more consciously than before. This can be seen as an aspect of 'glocalization' (Robertson, 1995) or 'the global institutionalization of the life-world and the localisation of globality' (Robertson, 1992, p. 53).

The complex and rapidly changing corporate structures create new kinds of interest conflicts (e.g. between the local production units of a group) and interest communities (e.g. between local managers, trade unions and political authorities). Here the spatial ties of people still show their vital role. But it is not easy to deal with these new interest conflicts and communities within the modes of thought and action which have been oriented to the institutionalization of clearly identifiable parties on clearly identifiable levels in a national society.

A logic different from that of Nordic-type hierarchical party relations is represented by those forms of co-operation in multinational groups which are established by the European Works Councils Directive of 1994 (Directive on the establishment of a European Works Council or a procedure in Community-scale undertakings and Community-scale groups of undertakings for the purposes of informing and consulting employees, 94/45/EC). This co-operation can be understood as a modest attempt to compensate for the growing asymmetry of capital and labour by means of representative practices for the promotion of the reflexive capacities of employees.[2]

True, the key concepts of the EU language on the 'social dimension' – 'social partners' and 'social dialogue' – may only imply the attainment of a higher institutional level of 'parity-ideological' party relations. For the Nordic trade unions, the promotion of this kind of discourse and practice on the

European 'level' is a way to defend the Nordic model. While there is the threat of international economic deregulation resulting in national social deregulation, this has to be opposed by transnational (European) regulation. However, the relations of European 'social partners' are above all a form of corporatist social policy-making and much less an institution within industrial relations, let alone a level of collective bargaining and industrial action (Strøby Jensen, Madsen and Due, 1995; cf. Ramsay, 1997). The rhetoric of parity conceals the fact that the preconditions for the idea of symmetric parties on various levels of industrial relations have weakened remarkably. The very metaphor of 'level' has lost a lot of its analytical capacity.

Thirdly, an important premise of 'parity-ideological' party relations has weakened, namely the recognized particularism of employer interests. By making heuristic use of Jürgen Habermas' distinctions of different principles of decision-making procedures, it is possible to state that the principle of *compromises between conflicting interests* has given way to the principle of the *fulfilling of given functional necessities*, which are now explained by globalized competition. Then, for the fulfilment of these necessities there is – as the wonderful lessons of human resource management (HRM) can be interpreted – a need for a *discursive, communicative rationality* (for example, in the form of 'direct participation'), through which the given common interest will be clarified and innovatively promoted. This is, in a sense, contrary to Habermas' thesis of the 'colonisation of the life-world', according to which the instrumental and functionalist rationalities of system (economy and administration) tend to push themselves into the field of the communicative rationality of life-world (Habermas, 1981). In the lessons of HRM, communicative rationality is revitalized to serve the instrumental or functionalistic rationality of system (see Altvater and Mahnkopf, 1993, pp. 129–30).

It is possible to understand 'industrial relations' and 'management' as two different practical and discursive ways of dealing with working-life problems. The relationships between these two perspectives have varied and changed. In the context of this conceptual distinction we can say that, after the 1970s, the perspective of 'management' has gained the dominant position in defining the agenda of working-life problems (see Dulebohn, Ferris and Stodd, 1995, pp. 29–38). In the Nordic countries, as elsewhere, employers have accelerated the integration of pay determination and work organization; wage systems have been individualized and, more systematically than before, pay has been transformed into an instrument of management (Kjellberg, 1992, pp. 134–5). The power of management in defining the issues is indicated, for instance, by the vocabulary of working-life reform. In the new rhetoric of HRM 'direct participation' gives an impression of more democracy than 'indirect participation' through trade unions and the representative institutions of industrial relations (Sisson, 1996).

Instead of trying to draw issues of 'management' into the field of 'industrial relations' (or 'party relations'), efforts are made by trade unions and public authorities to prove that including (parity-based) institutions of 'industrial relations' in the field of 'management' would be profitable. This is a profound shift of the perspective on working-life problems. But it is important to note that this kind of defence of parity-based representative industrial relations is not totally unsuccessful in the Nordic countries. After addressing some pre-requisites for such a defence, I will, however, point out its problematic implications regarding the criteria of 'us' and the contents of 'society'.

New Meanings for Old Institutions?

The demand for 'structural reform' of working life is loud in the Nordic countries, especially in Sweden and Finland. There is a clear confrontation between employers and trade unions concerning the reform of labour law. In Sweden, in particular, the once very strong tripartism no longer functions as it did, and employers' criticisms of the old 'model' have been harsh (Kjellberg, 1992; Köykkä, 1994). However, a drastic deregulation, as has taken place in New Zealand, is not a very plausible scenario for any Nordic country (Bruun, 1995; Lange, Wallerstein and Golden, 1995).

Some traditional arguments for a representative industrial relations system are still very much alive, including the need for economic calculability and social conflict regulation. Trade unions and other protagonists of the Nordic model argue for the continuous significance of these objectives, pointing out that the Nordic traditions of collective bargaining are in this respect a source of competitive advantage. Many employers agree; the Danish employer representatives perhaps have the least reservations (see Jensen, 1995; Fleming and Søborg, 1995). In Sweden, besides the tendency toward a decentralization of collective bargaining there have been tendencies toward recentralization during the 1990s, though with a more active government role than used to be typical of the 'Swedish model' (Kjellberg, 1998; cf. Visser, 1996). In both Sweden and Finland the shifts of the political colour of governments have influenced employer organizations' choices. Among the employers there are signs of pragmatism, as well as different positions according to, for instance, the branch and size of enterprises, resulting in an unwillingness to be bound to any single 'model', as the policy of the Finnish employers in the early 1990s has been characterized (Kauppinen, 1994, p. 316). As the low rate of inflation and the restriction of public spending are primary policy objectives, there are, in many cases, obvious benefits in centralized collective labour market regulation. The presence of the 'exit' option of the so-called open-sector enterprises, insofar as it can be interpreted in terms of the unavoidable imperatives of economic competition, may even contribute to this kind of national consensus.

What I find most notable here, however, is the line of argument according to which central elements of the Nordic model could and should be saved by modifying the old institutions to serve new knowledge-based national, local and workplace strategies for competitiveness. In these strategies the key issue is the promotion of competitiveness, through such features as product and process innovation, training, increased competence, stronger attention to 'human capital' through 'human resource management', and greater involvement of employees in work processes and enterprise through 'direct participation'. The vision of 'Nordic' institutions in the service of such 'good' competitiveness attracts the defenders of the Nordic model.

To be sure, the importance of international competitiveness is no novelty, especially in the Nordic countries which have been small, open economies vitally dependent on export. Competitiveness in the world market was a crucial issue within the virtuous circle I described above. On the other hand, it has often been pointed out that this vulnerability to destabilizing external factors has been a major impetus for social corporatism in small European countries (Katzenstein, 1985; Pekkarinen, Pohjola and Rowthorn, 1992b).

There is, then, a continuity from the previous conception of a virtuous circle to the argument that collective regulation of labour relations generates competitive innovativeness. Still more, it is worth noting that the vulgarized Keynesian description of the virtuous circle between growing consumption and growing production – with the emphasis on the demand side – has never been the whole story in the Nordic countries (see Elam, 1994, pp. 63–4). Beginning in the 1930s there was a remarkable supply-side interest in the socio-political orientation of the Scandinavian Social Democrats. The promotion of social equality was held to be the means for releasing human productive capacities and, thus, the means of promoting economic effectiveness (Kettunen, 1997). Hence, there seem to be historical preconditions in the Nordic traditions which can both promote and soften the change that Jessop calls a 'tendential shift from the Keynesian welfare state ... to a Schumpeterian workfare state' (Jessop, 1994a, p. 251), the latter being oriented:

> to promote product, process, organisational and market innovation in open economies in order to strengthen as far as possible the structural

competitiveness of the national economy by intervening on the supply side; and to subordinate social policy to the needs of labour market flexibility and/ or the constraints of international competition. (*Ibid.*, p. 263).

Insofar as a 'Schumpeterian workfare state' is becoming a reality, there are several possible variants of it, including variants that adopt many elements of the 'Nordic model'. In any case, there is a promise here that the nation state can preserve an active even though profoundly changed role.

As former issues on the national agenda of policy-making (especially those of monetary policy) are transformed into external, irresistible conditions, the national 'us' may be ideologically strengthened. The commonplace mode of discussing globalization includes two sides regarding the relationship of economies and politics. One side represents the notion of transnational economic necessities limiting the range and alternatives of national policies and, thus, justifying political choices as an unpolitical fulfilment of unavoidable requirements. On the other side, the concept of globalization is associated with the assumption that the new economies represent a field for innovative imagination with an infinite scope of alternatives, based on a new freedom of markets and enterprises from political as well as spatial or territorial ties. Though the former side implies a reactive role of the nation state, the latter suggests that there are plenty of opportunities to argue for an active role of the nation state. It can be noted, for example, that Porter's (1990) 'cluster analysis' and 'diamond model' rapidly achieved remarkable popularity among the Nordic industry policy planners. No doubt, his thesis on the vital role of a national 'home base' even to globally operating enterprises contributed to his popularity (see Nordiska Ministerrådet, 1991; Penttinen, 1994). Furthermore, a key concept of the 1990s in the Nordic and more general OECD discussion on competitiveness has been a 'national system of innovation', which addresses the significance of nation state and national institutions for innovation-based competitiveness (Johnson and Lundvall, 1991).

The neo-Schumpeterian emphasis on innovation and its institutional framework may support a revitalization of the idea of a virtuous circle between economic rationality, social integration and a care for human subjectivity. Such tones are to be found particularly in discussions of education and training. In one of their 'joint opinions' the European 'social partners' declared in July 1993 that 'there is wide-reaching consensus ... in regarding the improved quality of education and vocational training as one of the major priorities in terms of increasing employment, the competitiveness of firms and social cohesion' (*Social Europe*, 1995). Much of the ideological power of knowledge, training and innovation in the Nordic countries stems from the promise that competitiveness and its preconditions in the global economy can – or even must – be seen from a wider perspective than that of neo-liberal deregulation.

For the trade unions it is easy to accept, at least in their programmes, a 'value-added' competition strategy, which is based on innovation, training and participation, as an alternative to the 'cost-based' strategies of social dumping and low-wage competition (e.g. Nordiska Metall, 1993; the attributes of each strategy are drawn from Locke, Kochan and Piore, 1995). It is not difficult to find theoretical and empirical arguments for the positive, active role of trade unions in such good strategies on national, local, company and workplace levels (Gustavsen *et al.*, 1995; HF-B/LO/NHO, 1997; Locke, Kochan and Piore, 1995; Naschold, 1994). There seems to exist, after all, the opportunity to go beyond merely reactive arguments against neo-liberal demands for deregulation. Furthermore, active participation in the issues of production and contents of work would seem to involve the promise of a solution to a problem found in the old institutions of working life: the tension between the two horizons of the wage-worker, as seller of labour power and as subject of the labour process.

In the Nordic traditions there are some particularly favourable preconditions for this kind of new orientation. While the system of collective bargaining bears a structural tendency to strengthen the logic of the selling and buying of labour power and to transform issues of production into issues of distribution, the Nordic institutions also include prerequisites for involving the collective representation of labour-market interests in work-process issues. The 'parity-ideological' labour-market compromise has been connected with a consensus concerning the legitimacy of technical and organizational rationalization, and to varying degrees issues of this kind have 'traditionally' been included in the field of collective bargaining.

In an international comparison, one might also say that in the Scandinavian countries there are some specific traditions of intermediation between the horizon of the seller of labour power and the horizon of the subject of the labour process. Reflecting their specific histories of industrialization, in Denmark (and in Iceland) the category of 'craft' has been more important than in the other Nordic countries. For the Danish trade unions it is possible to exploit the tradition of craft-based unionism with respect to the new requirements of knowledge-based competitiveness 'by giving greater emphasis to professional qualifications and training' (Scheuer, 1992, p. 194). In Norway there is a traditional emphasis on the articulation of local interests within the nationally centralized structure of decision-making. There are also historical experiences of combining 'socio-technical' workplace-level innovations with efforts to achieve 'industrial democracy', the best-known of which are the experiments led by Einar Thorsrud and Fred E. Emery in the 1960s (Venneslan, 1990; Naschold, 1994, p. 34). In Sweden, besides similar experiments since the 1970s, there is the older avant-gardist tradition of active labour power policies, in which the principles of full employment, solidaristic wage policies and increased productivity were more or less successfully combined and, furthermore, questions of the quality of labour power were placed on the agenda of collective labour relations (Sihto, 1994). In Finland the issues of technical and organizational rationalization have traditionally remained in the sphere of management power to a greater extent than in Denmark, Norway and Sweden. However, the previous failures to follow Scandinavian models in questions of production and work organization have also been a target of some self-criticism in the Finnish trade unions, and they may see in the 'new challenges' a chance for widening perspectives of action (see Alasoini, Kauppinen and Ylöstalo, 1994, pp. 48–9; Ilmonen, 1996; Ilmonen and Kevätsalo, 1995).

An important factor, common to all Nordic countries, is the strong presence of trade unions at the workplace level as well as at the level of national policy-making (Kjellberg, 1983, 1998). This means that a decentralization of industrial relations could be compatible with an active role for trade unions and shop stewards (Lilja, 1997, 1998).[3] In all Nordic countries a tendency can be identified that is celebrated in an article on 'Norway's social partners' joint action programme for enterprise development' (HF-B/LO/NHO, 1997). Many examples can be seen, both at sector level and in individual enterprises, of the social partners developing projects and strategies together. The development of new co-operative traditions between sector organizations and the social partners at enterprise level, which can be regarded as both a supplement and an alternative to the more traditional types of negotiation, provide a flexibility in Norwegian working life that is relatively unique (p. 89).

The strong unionization of professional employees should also be noted in this connection. Through their organizations a combination of professional and instrumentalist work orientations has been channelled into the field of interest articulation and collective bargaining. The separate organizing of professional employees is, in part, rooted in a Tayloristic concept of work organization and, politically, in the reluctance to be bound to the labour movement. These historical preconditions are losing their significance, for example in the new forms of co-operation in multinational groups (Bruun and Kettunen, 1995, p. 41). However, the separate organizations of professional employees also reflect special problems of many female-dominated public sector jobs and labour relations. In this sense, they are consciously contributing to the transformation of the paradigmatic concept of work. This contribution of the female-dominated trade unions concerns, for example, the ways in which the loyalty of the welfare service employees to their clients or patients should be taken into account in the representation of interests (Julkunen and Rantalaiho, 1993). Raising this question may offer ideological support to the new concept of manufacturing production, in which the production processes and the workers themselves are supposed to be able to reflect the needs of the customer.

True, value-added strategies with strong union participation are far from self-evident to employers. In Sweden employer organizations have shown explicit reluctance to link collective relations between labour-market parties with the new practices of promoting competence and innovative work organizations (SOU, 1992, pp. 90–1). In Denmark and Norway this kind of confrontation is much less significant. One might also note that, since the 1970s, the pragmatic orientation of Finnish employer policies has differed from the reideologized policies of the Swedish employers. In general, nevertheless, the common rhetoric on training, innovation and competence does not manage to conceal the fact that enterprises often calculate these issues from the perspective of short-term costs rather than long-term investment. Meanwhile, it should also be noticed that, through the conflicts concerning the actors and contents of competition strategies, the role of competitiveness itself as the centre of the agenda is strengthened. Trade union critiques of 'narrowly' economic arguments actually contribute to the power and legitimacy of the discourse of competition, as the unions focus on developing 'wider' arguments for economic competitiveness; seeking to prove, for example, that security in employment relationships is a necessary precondition for a competitiveness based on the commitment, competence and innovativeness of employees.

By making use of the distinction between 'industrial relations' and 'management' as two ways of thematizing working-life issues, it can be noted that bringing institutions of 'industrial relations' under the umbrella of 'management' is a significant part of the Nordic trade unions' strategies for rescuing parity-based institutions. The trade unions are, for example through their Nordic co-operation, seeking an active role for themselves in projects for competitive work organizations and production systems in which workers would be able and obliged to 'continuously develop their competence' (Nordiska Metall, 1993).

This aim is based on the readily defended argument that the development of work organization and the development of competence are necessary for each other. Most notably, this argument holds for new requirements for communicative and self-monitoring skills, or reflexivity, which are required of individuals as well as organizations. However, there are big problems in the basic orientation of such reforms. Not all people are successful in the tough competition to improve their competence. In addition, there is the severe problem, which is particularly acute in Finland in the 1990s compared with other Nordic countries or even other European countries, that many people lack the ties to work organization necessary for developing these competences, because they lack a job. Furthermore, this lack cannot be compensated by means of continuous training, despite the significant role of training in employment policies and the various public projects for preventing social exclusion by means of training. The gospel of training might partly be seen as a way of 'legitimating the silent co-existence of those inside and outside the new economies'.[4] Be it silent or not, it is a co-existence of 'reflexivity winners' and 'reflexivity losers' (Lash, 1994, p. 130).

Conclusion

The Nordic trust in a virtuous circle between economic growth, widening democracy and increased equality used to imply that equality and solidarity were means for economic effectiveness and goals for which economic growth, in turn, was supposed to serve as a crucial means. During the postwar decades, until the 1970s, this trust widely coloured the public horizon of expectations. It was not just a matter of forecasts. The notion of a virtuous circle contained a notion of the normative standards of the society, by means of which that society itself could be criticized. In their efforts to control their own life, people, especially workers, could have a dual relationship to 'society'. As individuals and members of social groups and classes, they had the possibility of blaming 'society' for the hard conditions of their life and, at the same time, of seeking support from that 'society' for their troubles and experience of subordination.

The ways in which the national 'we' is sustained and reproduced in the political responses to globalization have continuities with this older ideology of the virtuous circle. First, this is to be seen in the criticism of a 'narrow' understanding of competitiveness. In the Nordic traditions of social thought there exist prerequisites for an argument in which a wide spectrum of socially and ethically valued achievements and objectives are proved to be competitive advantages. This argument has not been that unsuccessful, so far, in defending 'parity-ideological' forms of industrial relations. It would not be correct to claim that the new imperatives of competitiveness have excluded social, ecological or moral points of view from the agenda. Rather, the power of those imperatives is indicated by the fact that so many 'good things' can be included and, in this way, subordinated to the argument of competitiveness. This is what tends to happen when the 'Nordic model' is compared with other 'models'. Political and moral points of view lose their autonomy. Here the new discourse on competitiveness differs from the old ideology of the virtuous circle, as for the latter equality was both a goal and a means.

There seems to be a tension in contemporary Nordic discussions of the role of equality, between what are presented as institutional preconditions for competitiveness and the way in which the contents of competitiveness are conceptualized. Participatory practices in working life, including traditional 'indirect participation' via trade unions and even high social norms, are considered not only as 'rigidities' but, rather widely, at least in rhetoric, as competitive advantages, as factors promoting the commitment of workers and the innovativeness of enterprises and their managements. This implies a trust in the egalitarian preconditions for national competitiveness. At the same time, however, true membership in a competitive community – 'inside the new economies' (see Sabel, 1994, p. 143) – is deemed a matter of individual competitiveness. This, in turn, involves communicative and innovative skills and talents and reflexive capabilities of monitoring oneself from the point of view of competitiveness. To be sure, it makes a difference whether or not an individual's opportunities to make her or himself competitive are shaped by more or less egalitarian systems of education and training. It also makes a difference whether or not the encouragement of knowledge-based competition in working life is connected with collective institutions of social regulation. But in any case, the legitimacy of blaming 'society' as well as seeking for support from 'society' has weakened. You have to blame yourself for your lack of competitiveness. Given this point of departure, equality tends to lose even its instrumental value.

'Europe between competitive innovation and a new social contract' is the headline of an article by Riccardo Petrella, a leading figure in the social research organization of the EU. Petrella does not start by contrasting 'bad' cost-based competition strategies with 'good' value-added strategies, based on innovation, training and competence. Rather, he questions the discourse of competitiveness itself. His alternative to the national and European struggle for 'competitive innovation' is 'a new social contract', which would necessarily be global by nature (Petrella, 1995). True, there are attempts to give new impetus to the old argument from the nineteenth century, according to which international economic competition is not just a constraint on national social policies but the basis of international social regulation. In accordance with the traditional internationalist emphases of the Nordic labour movements, Nordic trade union representatives have often spoken of the need for international or transnational regulations and multinational collective action in order to control multinational companies and cross-national financial transactions. This has not, however, been the dominant ideological and practical way in which the increased disparity between the mobility of capital and labour has been responded to. In the 1990s the more powerful tendency has been toward transforming 'society' into a kind of generalized 'national system of innovation', in which 'we' would be defined through individual and collective competitiveness.

Acknowledgements

This paper has been written as a part of my research on changing international aspects in Finnish industrial relations, funded by the Academy of Finland, and in connection with the Nordic research project on 'The Future of the Nordic Model (NordFram)'.

Notes

1. However, the ways of defining this interest have been different according to historical differences of political hegemony in the respective countries. Some Finnish economists and sociologists have pointed out that in Finland economic as well as social policies have been more subordinated to the so-called economic necessities than in other Nordic countries (e.g. Kosonen, 1993).

2. As Rolf Utgård, union representative at board level in the Kvaerner Group puts it: 'it is necessary to work internationally because capital is working more and more effectively and actively internationally, and capital is in a position to take advantage of international competition to tighten up on the employees. This is why we need information on what things are actually like in other countries. When plant-owners say that legislation and working conditions are such and such in England, we need to be able to check on whether that is true' (Mjelva, 1995, p. 29).

3. Mauri Kavonius, Head of the Research Division of the Finnish Union of Metalworkers, describes current developments: 'The main thrust of efforts from the employers' side has been towards decentralisation of the collective agreement system, and breakdown of the level of protection afforded through collective bargaining. Various concessions have been

made by the workers, including allowing working hours and some other things to be negotiated locally under the new stipulations for collective agreements. Through these concessions, the Metalworkers have been able to keep these issues within the framework of collective agreements and thus under the control of the Metalworkers' Federation' (Bruun and Kettunen, 1995, p. 40).

4. Here I apply Sabel's speculation concerning the role of minimum income to the role of training. According to him, 'In northern European countries with strong democratic traditions some alliance of progressives urging the attractive possibilities of leisure in a post-material society and conservatives anxious to keep the poor off the streets might press for a legal right to a minimum income, thus removing poverty from the national political agenda and legitimating the silent co-existence of those inside and outside the new economies' (Sabel, 1994, p. 143).

6 BETWEEN CONTROL AND CONSENSUS: GLOBALIZATION AND AUSTRALIA'S ENIGMATIC CORPORATISM

Ian Hampson

The concept of 'globalization' captures a number of economic and political processes that pose major challenges for states and union movements. These include: major shifts in world trade facilitated by developments in the technologies of transport and communications (Dicken, 1992); the integration of national manufacturing sectors within a global organization of production increasingly dominated by transnational corporations; the rise of a global organization of finance increasingly independent of national politics – indeed, to which national politics is increasingly beholden; the dominance of economic liberal ideology in restructuring policies; and the decentralization of industrial relations and the decline of unions (Martin and Schumann, 1997). About a decade ago Lash and Urry proclaimed that these factors among others indicate capitalism's 'disorganization', and that 'corporatist' political structures are no longer viable (Lash and Urry, 1987).

In this context the 'Australian model' has attracted considerable interest, since it appeared to show that successful industrial adjustment overseen by 'corporatist' structures which preserve and even enhance unions' position in national politics is possible (e.g. Archer, 1992, p. 376; 1995, pp. 86–7, chapter 9; Kyloh, 1989; Ogden, 1992). Indeed, Kyloh goes so far as to suggest that industrial restructuring in Australia is particularly interesting 'because it has been largely directed by the political and industrial leaders of the labour movement' (Kyloh, 1994, pp. 344–5). Such an interpretation has been attractive to left political movements in a number of countries, including Britain (Frankel, 1997, p. 4). The vantage point of the late 1990s provides a suitable degree of hindsight with which to evaluate the Australian experience with 'corporatism', in particular since 1996 saw the labour movement's conservative political opponents returned to power in a landslide election victory.

Archer, Kyloh and other writers eulogize the period from 1983, the year in which the Australian Labor Party (ALP) came to power after a long period of conservative incumbency. The Australian Council of Trade Unions (ACTU) and the ALP signed a historic 'Accord' agreement that ushered in a classic corporatist pattern of politics in which union leaderships trade the wage restraint of their members for a promised influence over a number of arms of public policy – in particular industry policy and industrial relations policy. But the resulting veneer of consensus masked sometimes intense conflict and some crucial defeats for organized labour over the terms of industrial adjustment, and the forms in which Australia's institutional arrangements were being recast. These defeats are instructive for governments and labour movements contemplating similar political strategies. Perhaps the main lesson to emerge from the Australian experience is the incompatibility between union influence on policy and economic liberal approaches to industrial adjustment. In Australia, this mix made the 'corporatism' increasingly authoritarian and unstable, exacerbating tensions between the leadership and membership of the union movement that contributed to declining union density and ultimately helped to drive Labor from office.

The policies that the unions advocated and accepted through the Accord shifted fundamentally over the latter's life (see Gardner, 1995, pp. 43, 45).[1] To justify union co-operation in economic stabilization through wage restraint, the first Accord committed the Government to implementing a range of policies supportive of unions' aims, in particular interventionist industry policy. Yet by the mid-1980s the ALP government had embraced an economic liberal approach to industrial adjustment that drove towards labour market deregulation. Given that the government reneged on the key industry policy provisions of the Accord, union leaders would have been justified in breaking out of the agreement. But they did not. Instead, the Accord and its associated 'corporatist' practices remained intact, locking the union movement into economic liberal policies it could not control, and which were opposed to its interests. These policies included the increasing 'flexibilization' of the labour market, leading to work intensification and increasing insecurity.

But the state and the ALP government did not simply imprint economic liberal policies on the union movement. Rather, elements of the union leadership helped to conceive and enforce them. This partly explains the 'paradox' in the experience of unions and economic restructuring under the Accord noted by Gardner (1995, pp. 47, 61–3) – that the unions accepted, and even drove the restructuring process, yet the latter worked against them – a paradox that bespeaks failures of strategic design. Union strategic documents had noted relatively early that dramatic declines in union membership coincided with unparalleled union influence on policy as a result of the Accord (Berry and Kitchener, 1989, p. 15). But the leadership failed to pose the question of whether this decline might be a *consequence* of the alleged 'influence' of union leaders over policy.

This chapter argues that the conjunction of economic liberal policies and the 'participation', even consent, of the labour movement in their implementation caused the nature of Australian corporatism to become increasingly exclusionary and authoritarian. The increasing concentration of decision-making power within the labour movement, not the latter's democratization, was the inevitable counterpart of the star-crossed marriage of economic liberal policies (with their inherent challenge to workers' interests) and corporatist politics. Making this argument necessitates drawing out clear categories from the voluminous and somewhat amorphous literature on 'corporatism'. This is the task of the first section. The chapter then charts a drift in the nature of Australian corporatism from inclusionary to exclusionary forms, by inquiring into the extent to which the interests and preferences of organized labour were incorporated in state policies, at least in the most crucial policy contests over restructuring policy. Section two sketches the historical roots of Australia's social settlement, highlighting how the latter was challenged by the changed economic environment to which the concept of globalization alludes. Section three describes the fundamental contest over industry policy, which organized labour had lost by the mid-1980s, testifying to the ascendancy of economic liberalism in policy-making. By choosing to stay in the Accord despite this labour leaders implicitly accepted that the burden of industrial adjustment policy would be borne by workers. Section four describes the contest over reforms to the industrial relations and training systems, which increasingly reflected business preferences. Section five discusses how the 'corporatism' necessarily assumed a more authoritarian quality, as ordinary unionists were denied influence over policies set at the top, and transmitted to the base of the movement.

Classifying Corporatism

If we can identify the major political possibilities inherent in 'corporatist' political formations, we will be better able to assess what variants fit Australia. At various times the following polities have been described as 'corporatist' – Austria, Switzerland, Sweden and Germany (Katzenstein, 1978, 1985), Japan

(Pempel and Tsunekawa, 1979; Hirst and Zeitlin, 1989) and Singapore (Deyo, 1989). Given such diversity, if the concept of 'corporatism' is to be illuminating, it must contain sub-variants that register differences in national political economic structures, in particular relations between the state, business and labour. This necessitates a typology of corporatisms. Writers like Archer (1992, p. 377) sidestep this by defining 'corporatism' as an *industrial relations system*, characterized by a high degree of centralization, public involvement and class co-operation. But the study of corporatism leads beyond industrial relations (job regulation) properly so-called (Valenzuela, 1992, p. 53), and one of its strengths is that it spans the sometimes artificial divide between industrial relations and politics.

As a starting point in developing a taxonomy of 'corporatisms', the work of Katzenstein (1985, chapter 1) is useful. Katzenstein classifies capitalist economies under three headings; liberal, statist and democratic corporatist. Despite the inevitable anomalies that such broadbrush categorizations generate, they are useful. Liberal economies prioritize market processes and macroeconomic approaches to economic management. Ideological preference and the state's inability to shape powerful interests in the polity minimize interventionist policies. The examples here are Britain and the USA. In statist political economies the state has taken a major role in driving late ('catch-up') industrialization through industry policy and various forms of labour exclusion. The best example here is Japan (Johnson, 1982), but Katzenstein also mentions France and there are many examples in Asia (Deyo, 1989).

In 'democratic corporatist' political economies, small size and a resulting sense of external vulnerability encourage the development of a sense of shared interests and a willingness to adopt inclusive political strategies, in particular tripartite negotiation over the terms of industrial adjustment. As Katzenstein acknowledges, the position of Germany is problematic here. Germany approximates the structure of the small, European states, despite its large size (Katzenstein, 1978). It is generally held to be characteristic of this type of corporatism that the labour movement is organized under powerful peak bodies, and in the Nordic countries has very high union density, and considerable clout in national politics. Reflecting this, strong, universalist welfare systems and a battery of institutions compensate the potential losers of industrial adjustment in a politics of 'domestic compensation' (Katzenstein, 1985, chapters 1, 2).

The nature of state–union relations is crucial to define the nature of 'corporatism', and these vary greatly within economies classified as 'corporatist'. Japan is categorized as 'corporatism without labour' (Pempel and Tsunekawa, 1979), because of the high degree of interconnectedness between state and business interests, and organized labour's political exclusion. There are several union peak bodies in Japan, but, unlike 'Euro/Scandinavian' peak union bodies, they have little influence over public policy. Other types of Asian corporatism are interesting because they combine the appearance of political inclusion with the reality of exclusion. Apparently tripartite and inclusive institutions, like Singapore's National Wages Council, mostly transmit the imperatives of economic development, as defined by the state, to the union movement. Indeed, the latter has been subject to extensive intervention into its very structures, even to the extent of choosing its leaders, and appointing them to Cabinet. (Leggett, 1988, p. 247; 1993; Deyo, 1989, pp. 107–8, 141). Joint incumbency of political and trade union office blurs the boundaries between the union movement and the state, a situation with certain similarities to Australian corporatism, as we will see.

In summary, it is useful to distinguish three models of state–union relations. First, as in the above example of Singapore, the state may control the unions. Secondly, unions may bargain autonomously with the state, influencing to greater or lesser degrees the latter's policies. This gives two broad variants of corporatism: state, or authoritarian corporatism; and societal, or liberal, or social corporatism (Schmitter, 1979, p. 20; Lehmbruch, 1979, p. 54; Deyo, 1989; Pekkarinen *et al.*, 1992a). In the former, organized labour is incorporated in the institutions and functions of the state, entailing loss of political autonomy. In the latter, organized labour retains the possibility of independent action, indeed of influencing the state to its advantage (Valenzuela, 1992, pp. 70–1). The third notional possibility is that the unions might control the state. But such a political economy would not really be 'capitalist', and this takes us into a well-worn debate between those who think unions may be agents of democratic and gradual socialist transformation, and those who, while desiring socialist transformation, believe unions are not up to the job. On the one hand, for writers known variously as 'power resource' or 'labour movement' theorists (Clement and Mahon, 1994; Fulcher, 1991), through well-shaped 'corporatist' institutions and practices the labour movement might 'capture' the state, and use it to drive socialist transformation (Korpi, 1983; Higgins, 1985; Stephens, 1979; Rueschmeyer and Evans, 1985, pp. 63–4). On the other hand, socialists to the left of this position insist that such a strategy is doomed to fail, since social democratic governments necessarily serve business interests structured into 'the capitalist state'. Panitch's classic definition of corporatism *qua* incorporation emphasizes 'representation and co-operative mutual interaction at the leadership level and mobilization and control at the mass level' (1981, p. 21). The Australian experience reveals a drift from democratic to authoritarian corporatism, and some resonances with

Panitch's 'labour incorporation' model. Before charting this drift it is necessary to identify key features of the Australian social settlement and say how they were challenged by 'globalization'.

The Breakdown of the Australian Social Settlement

The Australian social settlement is not well captured in the taxonomies developed by dominant analysts of comparative political economy. Francis Castles (1988) notes that Australia most resembles the 'small states' of Europe and Scandinavia (in terms of population if not land mass) and therefore, following Katzenstein, one would expect to find the capacity for flexible industrial adjustment and the politics of 'domestic compensation'. However, the accommodations between producer groups that underlie the Australian social settlement, which date to the turn of the century and earlier, were fundamentally different, and were based on shutting out external sources of change, rather than adapting to them. Developments in the world economy called them into question from the late 1960s, and by the early 1980s pressures for change were becoming acute (Castles, 1988; Fagan and Webber, 1994). The breakdown of the Australian social settlement, or at least the loss of its economic base, has occasioned the current period of policy instability, and the experiments with 'corporatism'. Castles suggests that Australia is 'between historic compromises'. Through the 1980s, the political accommodations between the state and major producer groups were recast. But instead of 'consensual industrial adjustment', there was sharp policy contest over the terms of Australia's social settlement.

Castles (1988) characterizes Australia's social settlement in the concept of 'domestic defence'. This formation arose essentially from a political accommodation between Protectionists (manufacturers) and the Labor Party, at the expense of Pastoralists who favoured free trade. Labor sought a compulsory arbitration system, to redress the imbalance of power (evident in major industrial defeats in the 1890s) between workers and employers. Manufacturers sought protection from cheap imports, and these forces agreed to support each other's interests. The conceptual expression of this accommodation was 'new protection'. Manufacturers were to have access to industry protection provided they paid wages determined in industrial tribunals with powers of compulsory arbitration, and expressed in legally enforceable 'awards'. Wage levels were to be determined, not according to market demand and productivity, but according to the 'needs' of a normal male, supporting a dependent woman and three children, in a condition of 'frugal comfort'

(Macintyre, 1986, pp. 107–9). Awards prescribed conditions of work, and regulated inter-union competition. The system defended, sheltered and shaped the pattern of unionism, in which the craft element was predominant (Macintyre, 1990). These arrangements, and the minimal welfare system with which they were associated, institutionalized women's dependence on men. Protection for the 'working man' also excluded Asians and Pacific Islanders through restrictive immigration, known (then) unashamedly as the 'White Australia policy'. 'Domestic defence' was therefore composed of the inter-locking policies of industry protection, compulsory arbitration, restrictive immigration and minimal welfare (Castles, 1988). To this Kelly (1994) adds 'imperial benevolence', emphasizing that the system depended on guaranteed markets for primary products. The Labor Party would champion the political interests of workers, and while its constitution held a commitment to socialism, the roots of social democracy did not strike deep into Australia.

Despite this unusual social settlement, the turn of the century saw Australia with the world's highest living standards, in terms of income per capita, based on wealth generated by primary exports (Castles, 1988; Fagan and Webber, 1994). To understand Australia's predicament in the 1980s, it is important to emphasize the role manufacturing industry and the industrial relations system played in these arrangements. This was to provide employment and to transfer wealth from the primary sector to the urban population (Capling and Galligan, 1992; Bell, 1993; Higgins, 1994). That is, the manufacturing sector was not a major source of wealth generation, certainly not on export markets, and was not designed to be 'internationally competitive'. Instead, it was an instrument of 'wage-earners' welfare' (Castles, 1988), doomed by increasing international competition and other developments. It became increasingly difficult for Australia to earn revenues on world markets by exporting primary products, in particular with Britain's entry to the EEC. The then Liberal administration sought markets for the expanding mining industry in Asia, particularly Japan. But the Japanese also encouraged other suppliers, giving rise to competition in the industry, and lowering prices. At the same time, the composition of world trade was shifting in favour of manufactured goods, and developments in the technologies of transport and communications were eroding the natural protection given to Australia by distance and isolation (Dicken, 1992). For these and other reasons, a consensus emerged among Australian policy-makers that the old ways would have to change (Fagan and Webber, 1994). Manufacturing industry would have to play a greater role in earning the nation's wealth, rather than simply redistributing it.

The Whitlam Labor Government struck the decisive blow against domestic defence in 1973, with a 25 per cent across-the-board reduction in industry protection. This reflected the emerging ascendancy in the state policy-making bureaucracy of the 'new' free traders, economists educated after neo-classical economic orthodoxy, many of them in the Chicago School (Warhurst, 1982; Stretton, 1986; Pusey, 1991). Their approach to industry development was captured in the simple (if logically questionable) proposition that if protection had led Australia into manufacturing decline, removing protection would boost manufacturing – or at least the latter's worthy sectors. This became known as the 'rationalization by competition' strategy, but was hardly a substitute for a comprehensive industrial restructuring policy (Ewer *et al.*, 1987). The tariff reduction programme commenced in a climate of near full employment. But soon, rising unemployment caused politicians to reconsider, as they faced a choice between the purity of economic 'rationality' and electoral survival. Industry policy for the next ten years oscillated between these two imperatives (Bell, 1994, p. 258; Warhurst, 1982). With decreasing protection came imperatives to reorganize work, and to recast the industrial relations system. But these developments would have to await the arrival of the Hawke Labor Government in 1983.

Corporatism and the Industry Policy Debate

Industry policy has special significance within corporatist politics as the point of intervention where the state seeks to shape industrial structure to ends deliberately chosen, and therefore potentially highly politicized. Industry policy may be the most significant trade-off to unions for co-operation in economic stabilization in a period of crisis, since union members are to be found in greater frequency within manufacturing than within the service sectors that characterize 'post-industrial' economies. Industry policy is also of major ideological significance, given that it signals a departure from economic liberalism. It is often seen, on both the Left and the Right, as the 'thin end of the socialist wedge', the harbinger of the subordination of economics to politics. All this was true in the heyday of Australian corporatism, the early- to mid-1980s, and it is why the staunch commitment to economic liberalism that characterized the Labor administration was bound to produce tensions within the 'corporatist' arrangements, and even provide clear rationale for the unions to end them.

The ascent to power of the Hawke-led ALP in February 1983 offered the unions special access to public policy-making since 'their' party was in government. This 'special access', and the alleged 'responsibility' with which it was used, led some to write of a new 'political unionism' in Australia. On this view,

Australian unionism was now embarked on a virtuous upward cycle of increasing political efficacy and influence which might even culminate in socialist transformation (Higgins, 1985, 1987). In the words of Mathews, the Accord was a 'powerful engine of socialist advance' (1986, p. 177). Appreciating this point is essential if one is to understand the dynamics of the early corporatist exchanges. The support of the industrial Left was crucial to the success of the incomes policy, since the Left had the industrial muscle to disable such a policy, and industry policy was the price of its support (Ewer *et al.*, 1991, p. 28). The 'mainstream' Left saw the Accord as a sophisticated form of class struggle, marking the latter's entry into the state arena. Although far from universally held throughout the union movement (and somewhat Quixotic from the vantage point of the 1990s), these ideas underpinned the first Accord, although they were conspicuously absent from its subsequent incarnations. Its alleged socialist potential caused many Leftists to persevere with it in face of a drift of policy that would have drawn strong opposition had it come from the other side of politics.[2]

As is common in 'corporatist' arrangements with a social democratic flavour, the central trade-off in the Accord included wage restraint on the unions' part, and on the government's part the implementation of favoured policies, and the institutionalization of various forms of participation in their formation and execution. The Accord was to provide for political resolution of competing income claims with less inflationary pressures at higher rates of economic growth. At the same time, directing investment into manufacturing industry would not only create jobs, but, by increasing domestic productive capacity, would help to overcome the tendency for increasing economic activity to be cut short by policy measures aimed at curtailing imports. Thus, arguably, the centrepiece of the Accord was its commitment to industry policy and interventions into the investment function, although the document itself contained a range of 'supportive' policies, including improvements to the 'social wage', in particular a national public health system. Significant and much publicized successes were achieved in this area, albeit against a general drift to selectivism in welfare policy. But backed by legislative reforms to industrial relations, and mandating industrial democracy, the package would provide for a significant erosion of managerial prerogative, and enhance the union movement's position in Australian politics (ALP/ACTU, 1983; Higgins, 1987; Stilwell, 1986; Castles, 1988). This more radical arm of strategy was less successful.

Despite stage-managed shows of consent, the strategy was not supported by the whole union movement, reflecting deep historical enmity between the Left and the Right (Turner, 1978, pp. 111–14; Rawson, 1986, chapter 5). Indeed, writers have cautioned against using the term 'movement' to refer to Australia's unions, since the term implies a degree of unity that is not actually present (Singleton, 1990, pp. 6–7; Rawson, 1986, p. 10). These divisions impeded Australian unions' participation in democratic corporatism, in particular their ability to mobilize around shared goals to pressure the government.

Just as the union movement's participation in the corporatist processes was enigmatic, so was that of Australia's employers. Their peak bodies, habitually divided between the interests of small business, manufacturing, agriculture, mining and finance, maintained an appearance of consent to the Accord in a carefully stage-managed 'National Economic Summit' in 1983. But big business was not organized under any peak body, and its support or acquiescence was important for any economic strategy. Therefore Prime Minister Hawke personally invited certain business leaders to attend the summit. Later in 1983 these elements organized themselves into the Business Council of Australia (BCA), representing Australia's largest 80 corporations, chiefly in the mining and finance sectors, and made a bid for policy leadership (Carney, 1988, pp. 69, 75; Wanna, 1992, pp. 66–7). That business lacked a single peak body that could speak in the national arena militated against claims that the Australian system was 'corporatist' in any tripartite sense.[3] Trevor Matthews (1994, pp. 204–9) therefore invented another variant of corporatism to capture the Australian situation – 'corporatism without business'.

For optimists like Kyloh and Archer, and other commentators like Bray and Walsh (1995, pp. 18–19), disunity prevented the employers foiling the 'corporatist' intentions of the unions. But this apparent exclusion did not mean that business lacked influence over policy outcomes, or derived no benefit from the agreement. As Matthews notes, following Streeck, this kind of political fragmentation can actually be a source of political power, as the lack of a single voice absolves the business sector as a whole from making any commitments, for instance to direct investment or to restrain prices or executive salaries (Matthews, 1994, pp. 209, 217). Business interests also influenced the course of government policy by other means, like lobbying and shaping media discussion. Supporting this analysis, Australia's Treasurer (i.e. finance minister) Dawkins claimed on the occasion of his retirement that the BCA was the dominant influence on Labor's reform agenda in the past decade, and even on the ACTU after the first few years of the Accord (*Australian Financial Review*, 15 July 1994).

The BCA joined forces with economic 'rationalists'[4] to defeat the Accord's industry policy, arguing that it 'would lead us back to the quagmire of the past' (BCA, 1986, p. 13). In the face of determined opposition from these business interests, combined with that of the economics profession and the financial press, whatever enthusiasm the government had for industry policy was short-lived. There was an initial surge of activity, as industry plans were put in place in the Textile, Clothing and Footware, Steel and Automotive sectors. But these plans were not linked into any *overall* industry development strategy. Nor were they orchestrated from a single national institution with a brief to co-ordinate and direct the diverse arms of policy that affected industry (Bell, 1991, p. 120; 1993, chapter 6; 1994, p. 251; Stewart, 1990, p. 105), even though the Accord committed the government to build such institutions.

The institutional embodiment of the industry policy agenda was to be the Economic Planning and Advisory Council (EPAC) (Ewer *et al.*, 1987, p. 120; Boreham, 1990, p. 46). As its name suggests, EPAC was to provide a conduit for labour influence on economic policy. However, Treasury resented the challenge to its monopoly. It therefore set out to undermine EPAC's status with the government, and to colonize it. This ensured that EPAC would become, not a forum for labour input to economic policy-making, but an instrument for 'locking both parties into support for government policies' (Boreham, 1990, p. 49; Capling and Galligan, 1992, p. 48). In other words, EPAC was to function like a classically authoritarian corporatist institution, and deny institutional carriage to ideas critical of economic liberalism.

The Fraser Government (1975–83) began the programme of financial deregulation, removing certain regulations on banking, finance and movements of foreign capital (Davidson, 1992, p. 222). But political opposition, especially by the unions, impeded full financial deregulation. It fell to the Hawke Labor Government to press ahead, with the unions locked in via the Accord. The Hawke Government's financial reform package assumed economic efficiency would result from minimal government intervention (Campbell *et al.*, 1981, p. 1; Daly, 1993, p. 74). Accordingly, the government 'floated' the Australian dollar in December 1983, permitted the entry of sixteen new fully or partly foreign-owned banks, and removed many controls on banking, interest rates and foreign investment in 1986 (Davidson, 1992).

In no small measure due to the Accord's wage restraint, the Australian corporate sector showed good profits from the very beginning of the Accord years (Ewer *et al.*, 1991, p. 30; Stegman, 1993, p. 89). Unfortunately, these were not wisely used in the climate of financial deregulation. Lifting exchange controls and the floating of the Australian dollar exposed the economy to large and volatile capital movements, facilitating a dramatic increase in overseas debt (Ravenhill, 1994, p. 90; Daly, 1993, p. 77). The Australian currency became a plaything of international speculators becoming the sixth most traded currency in the world, despite Australia's not being in the top 20 exporters. (Ravenhill, 1994, p. 90; Davidson, 1992, p. 222). The entry of foreign banks did indeed increase competition in the finance sector, but not with the anticipated results (lower interest rates). It drove down prudential lending standards and placed huge amounts of capital in the hands of 'entrepreneurs', some of dubious character and business acumen (Davidson, 1992, p. 224; Daly, 1993, p. 77; Sykes, 1994). A spate of corporate collapses and poor profit results followed – accompanied by renewed calls for wage restraint (Ewer *et al.*, 1991, pp. 66, 70; Stegman, 1993, p. 90; Bell, 1993, p. 163). The foregone wages had apparently gone into executive salaries, management buy-outs, conspicuous consumption, unproductive 'paper entrepreneurship' and asset speculation (McEachern, 1991, pp. 64, 80; Davidson, 1992, p. 223; Bell, 1993, p. 163; Capling and Galligan, 1992, p. 123). As Bell (1993, p. 162) notes, 'despite the Accord, the policy context of the 1980s did much to ensure that manufacturing industry was not a target for new investment'.

The unions' plans for industry policy were thus thwarted by the government's deregulatory drive, with disastrous results for the Australian economy. Further, the policies pursued actually decreased state autonomy, forcing the government to pander to financial interests, lest the financial markets judge their policies harshly and adversely (Stilwell, 1986). Against the optimistic corporatist theorists like Kyloh and Archer, this is hardly successful industrial adjustment.

The most obvious union response to the government's refusal to implement a comprehensive industry policy was to argue the case more fully via policy development – as if rationality, not political power, might recast the relationship between business and the state. The unions and segments of the bureaucracy undertook a 'Mission' to certain European countries, to uncover the secrets of their success. The report of the Mission, *Australia Reconstructed* (ACTU/TDC, 1987), admired the Swedish wage earner funds and solidarity wages policies, and the German training system. It also advocated an inquiry and significant interventions into the investment function. The proposed interventions included a 'National Development Fund', and a 'National Training Fund', to correct the shortfalls in manufacturing and training investment. But again the unions' proposals gained only lukewarm support, even embarrassment, from the incumbent political arm of the labour movement, and faced overwhelming employer opposition to the 'thin end of the socialist wedge' (CAI, 1987a, p. 30; also see CAI, 1987b, and McEachern, 1991, pp. 70–1; BCA, 1987a, p. 6).

Given the importance of industry policy to the integrity of the corporatist processes, especially for influential sections of the Left, it might be presumed that the rational course of action for the union movement (or at least the Left) in this situation was to rescind the Accord and pursue wage gains in the field.

Whatever strategic justification deferring wage rises might have had clearly no longer applied. As early as 1984 the Left expressed disquiet by convening a special conference to discuss areas where the government had departed from its obligations under the Accord (*Sydney Morning Herald*, 21 February 1984). Some Left leaders threatened to rescind the Accord (*Sydney Morning Herald*, 12 April and 11 October 1984). However, despite its public displays, the Left was apparently prepared to stay in the Accord, despite the government driving policy reform in exactly the opposite direction to that envisaged in the document. To be fair, the Left unions could not pursue the radical agenda on their own – the political capacities of the movement were limited by the above-mentioned lack of unity in the movement as a whole. Furthermore, what industrial muscle the Left had at the beginning of the 1980s atrophied rapidly with disuse (Ewer *et al.*, 1991; Lloyd, 1990). But by not rescinding the Accord and pursuing wage gains, despite the Accord's failure to live up to its inter-ventionist promises, the movement accepted that since industry policy could not be invoked in quest of international competitiveness, the latter would have to be achieved by means of contributions from workers on top of their already considerable wage restraint. Thus, while 'the Accord' remained intact, its failure to deliver industry policy was a major defeat for organized labour, and in particular the Left.

The situation gave rise to strategic dilemmas for all concerned. The government was uncomfortable in the crossfire of competing union and business interests, and seemed anxious to avoid deeply offending either constituency. The appearance of consensus was crucial to the ALP's electoral strategy, which could not withstand the Accord's breakdown. The ACTU would not call out the troops on behalf of industry policy, especially given the lack of support from the Right. And if the ACTU did end the Accord, the outcome would probably include the end of the ALP government, the loss of the ACTU's privileged position in Australian politics, and the postponement of certain political careers in transit from union leadership to political incumbency. (This course of action might, however, have preserved what was left of the union movement's militant potential.) On the other hand, if the ACTU maintained the Accord, continuing to police the government's wages policy, it would damage its relations with its constituency and the internal coherence of the movement. But this would at least postpone the inevitable day of reckoning when the corporatism would collapse, ushering in a Conservative government with distinct Thatcherite overtones. In the event the ACTU opted to maintain the Accord, support the ALP's political incumbency, and persist with a reform agenda that was set, at least in part, by *Australia Reconstructed*. The document was a turning point, in which the union movement accepted the need to recast its own structures and embark on wholesale skill formation and work reorganization in pursuit of international competitiveness. The Stock Market crash of 1987 made economic restructuring more urgent. But economic deregulation and the lack of a political constituency for industry policy dramatically restricted the policy options. As noted, the deregulatory climate encouraged business to invest in speculative and unproductive activity, and not in manufacturing industry. But if policies to guide investment were off the agenda, then extracting more profit from workers on the shop floor would have to underpin economic recovery. And if the guardians of Australia's economic surplus would not fund Australia's economic recovery, overseas investors would have to be enticed to do so. These imperatives converged on industrial relations reform, as Australian policy-makers attempted to encourage Japanese investment to fill the gaps left by Australian investors' reluctance to invest in manufacturing industry, and the failure of government policy to make such investment attractive. This was not just a matter of 'image engineering', although there were numerous such efforts by tripartite 'missions' aimed at explaining to the Japanese the new, congenial Australian industrial relations environment, that followed from the unions' new-found co-operativeness and 'flexibility'. It also entailed far-reaching changes to make Australian industrial relations a congenial home for 'best practice' work organization, the image of which was increasingly provided by 'lean production' and the 'Toyota production system' (Dertouzos et al., 1989, pp. 127–8; PCEK/T, 1990, pp. 58, 62).

Attracting Japanese investment implied a certain 'Japanization' of Australian industrial relations. The new Toyota plant at Altona, Victoria was something of a test case. In early February 1991 Toyota announced that it might build a new car plant in Australia, and flagged the site at Altona. It indicated that before it would give a firm commitment it wanted a single site agreement with the relevant unions to adopt 'flexible production arrangements and multi-skilling agreements', known increasingly as 'lean production' (Australian Financial Review, 25 January and 12 February 1991). The Federation of Vehicle Industry Unions (FVIU) eventually accepted these proposals (Australian, 27 July 1991, p. 39). Reflecting these imperatives, and despite the danger to workers' conditions well attested in the international literature (e.g. Dohse et al., 1985; Parker and Slaughter, 1988), Japanese forms of work organization became prominent exemplars of 'best practice' in Australia, even encouraged not only by a government programme that dispensed funds to encourage 'best practice' organization, but also by a new army of workplace change consultants, many of them with union backgrounds (e.g. Ogden, 1993). Thus increasingly the conventional wisdom was that the way to economic success was not to address the failures of investment and public policy for which corporate leaders and government were responsible, but through work reorganization along 'lean' lines. But to enforce these forms of work organization demanded considerable industrial relations reform, and deepened the authoritarian element in Australian corporatism.

Industrial Relations and Training Reform

Thus by 1987 there was little prospect of industry policy, and it was clear that union leaders would not destroy the ALP's incumbency of office by withdrawing from the Accord, since their own fortunes were so closely tied to those of the ALP. Thus elements of the union movement decided to concentrate on overhauling the industrial relations system and the training regime instead. These were clearly aspects of the Australian polity crucial to the interests of workers, but once the unions agreed to reform them, it proved impossible to insulate the course of that reform from business influence. Much of the jousting took place in the Industrial Relations Commission, which administered awards and wages as described above. Government, employers and unions argued their cases before it, and it made determinations that set the parameters for wages movements. But the tension between economic liberalism and centralized industrial relations meant that the Commission was called upon to oversee decentralization, and ultimately undercut its own role.

There was a clash between two visions of the future of Australian industrial relations. On the union side, *Australia Reconstructed* advocated major changes to Australia's skill formation and training system, in particular moving from 'front-end training' to 'lifetime learning'. In the former, training was completed prior to entry to the labour market proper, for instance in apprenticeships. The latter entails continual upskilling, increasingly a requirement of modern manufacturing processes. This required major changes to awards, in particular the construction of skill-based career paths, which would encourage upskilling and permit pay rises. Workers' abilities would be 'objectively' determined by competency testing, not time served, or employer fiat. Pay would correspond to the skills (or, in the new language, the 'competencies') with which workers were accredited. Recognition of Prior Learning (RPL) would acknowledge skills workers already possessed. This agenda became known as 'award restructuring', and its architects on the Left insisted that it take place within a nationally integrated framework (AMWU, 1988; Macken, 1989). The national framework was crucial to unionists and the national manufacturing effort alike. It would underpin skills portability, so improving workers' bargaining position and life-chances, and help retain, recognize and transfer skills otherwise potentially underutilized as industries restructured. National reference points for the content of training would help prevent workers being immersed in an organizational 'culture' controlled by their employer, at the expense of solidarity with their union (Ewer *et al.*, 1991, chapter 7). Linked to this was a programme of union rationalization and amalgamation, the aim of which was to reduce the number of unions from some 320 to between 17 and 20, and reorganize them along industry lines (ACTU, 1987).

The BCA's vision of the future of Australia's unions could not be more starkly different. The BCA argued that union structures and multi-employer awards impeded the competitiveness of Australian enterprises (BCA, 1990, pp. 8–9; Angwin and McLaughlin, 1990, pp. 11–12). The BCA also opposed the proposed national training system, which could underpin workers' mobility, increase their bargaining power, and undermine their loyalty to the firm by encouraging their own careers (BCA, 1990, p. 13). The BCA thus advocated enterprise-specific training, and 'human resource management' techniques, in particular performance-related payment systems beyond the reach of the Industrial Relations Commission. This would permit the creation of a unitarist culture of 'common purpose and caring', and ultimately deunionization (BCA, 1989, p. 96). All this entailed reshaping the power relations between capital and labour by redefining the bargaining structures of industrial rela-tions, in particular through decentralization and the development of a new system of 'enterprise bargaining' (Matthews, 1994, pp. 214–15; BCA, 1987b, p. 6; BCA, 1989). Enterprise bargaining units could effectively be detached from larger unions.

Initially the government expressed support for the unions' vision of award restructuring (Willis, 1988), but eventually accepted a version of industrial relations which resembled that of the BCA more than the initial union blue-prints. The debate became highly politicized, in part as a result of a campaign by the 'New Right' which publicized so-called inefficient work practices with the aim of calling into question the industrial relations system that permitted them. The campaign culminated in a stage-managed 'work practices summit', in September 1986. By now, the ACTU (or at least Secretary Kelty) appeared converted to the emerging right-wing version of labour-market 'flexibility', which became increas-ingly embodied in the wage systems set through the Industrial Relations Commission, supported by the Accord agreements.

Under Accord Mk 3, the government and the ACTU successfully argued before the Commission that a percentage of the still centrally determined wage rises had to be justified by 'productivity offsets', or changes in work practices that increased efficiency. Thus many previous gains were traded off for wage increases (McEachern, 1991, p. 46). The wages system sanctioned by Accord Mk 4 made wage rises conditional on union co-operation in award restructuring, such that in many cases work could be radically reorganized. The terms of this restructuring exercise were crucial and contested. The Industrial Relations Commission laid down a 'Structural Efficiency Principle' (SEP), according to which restructured awards should establish skill-based career paths, eliminate impediments to multi-skilling, and broaden the range of tasks a worker may be required to perform (Stilwell, 1991, pp. 37–8). The likely outcome of this was to be an increase in work intensity, as against the euphoric predictions of a new 'post-Fordist' era of work (Mathews, 1989).

One of the key goals of union reformers was training reform that put in place a national system that would permit skills portability. But this would require powerful interventions in workplace negotiations, in the face of employer opposition. The Industrial Relations Commission was ideally placed to perform this intervention, since it had to certify all agreements, but it did not accept the unions' arguments for training reform. In February 1989, the Commission reviewed the SEP. The ACTU argued that award restructuring should be restricted to measures designed to improve productivity via training and work reorganization, not giving away long-held entitlements. On the other hand, employers argued that award restructuring should make possible changes to working hours, penalty rates, manning levels, annual leave and sick leave (Stilwell, 1991, p. 39). The Commission agreed with the BCA (Ewer et al., 1991, pp. 42–3). Training was only a small part of such an agenda, and was easily marginalized in the face of the Commission's indifference.

The kind of training system envisaged by the union reformers required substantial institutional reform outside the industrial relations system. The initial blueprints envisaged that a National Training Board (NTB) would ensure that training made reference to an Australian Standards Framework (ASF) and therefore transferability between employers (see Ewer et al., 1991, chapter 7). But the NTB from the start lacked this capacity, as the government did not set up the body by statute, reflecting constitutional limitations on the Commonwealth's powers over education and training. Thus the NTB was formed under a memorandum of understanding between the State and Commonwealth Ministers of Vocational Training and Education (NTB Network, 1 June 1991, pp. 1, 10). It was understaffed, and lacked the statutory teeth to force firms to align their training programmes with national competency standards, and many firms chose not to co-operate with it. Such a lax supervisory infrastructure could not enforce national integration, and by 1993 it was clear that the system was not working (Allen Consulting Group, 1994).

Business interests were also, naturally enough, reluctant to pay for their employees' training, preferring to poach workers trained by someone else – a long-standing weakness in Australia's skill formation system that led to an under-investment in training. The government required large firms to expend a proportion of their payroll on accredited training, or forfeit the difference to the Tax Office. But, in part due to the lax supervisory infrastructure mentioned above, much of employers' expenditure was not directed to *bona fide* training, and the scheme was discontinued in the 1994 Budget. In its place, under the so-called 'Working Nation' set of policies, the government provided wage subsidies to employers to take on trainees, from the ranks of the long-term unemployed, already paid a below-award 'training wage' (Keating, 1994). Training reforms thus fulfilled the useful function of reducing long-term unemployment statistics and providing employers with cheap labour (Campbell, 1994). Thus the unions' aims to force employers to contribute more to the cost of training which served the interests of Australia's workers, and improve their labour market prospects, has been a failure.

Returning to industrial relations reform, it will be recalled how *Australia Reconstructed* outlined a robust image of the future of unions – amalgamated into large structures, supported by a centralized wage fixing system, and a centralized training system. This was anathema to the BCA, which increasingly influenced the public debate about industrial relations reform. When the BCA released its major report in July 1989, Treasurer Keating and ACTU Secretary Kelty came to accept the rhetoric of 'enterprise bargaining' as inevitable (Dabscheck, 1995, pp. 61–2). But they also sought to shape it to a form acceptable to both unions and employers. Thus the wages system associated with Accord Mk 6, negotiated near an election, was designed to emphasize collective ('enterprise') bargaining over the award system as a mechanism to gain wage increases (Stilwell, 1991, p. 41).

After the 1990 election, tensions within the industrial relations system increased, as the system of enterprise bargaining favoured by the BCA, and modified by the ALP–ACTU axis, was proving inconsistent with Australia's long-standing system of industrial awards and tribunals, and was straining the Accord. The ACTU saw enterprise bargaining as a way of attracting disenchanted workers back to unions (Evatt Foundation, 1995). Thus, from 1990 the wages systems were designed, in part, to force workers into enterprise bargaining and to improve profitability by workplace change. This enabled skilled or well-organized workers to gain wage rises. But it also exposed a major weakness in Australian unionism, revealing the difficulty of combining collective bargaining with the award system. Formerly, the wages and conditions of workers in non-unionized firms were set through the Industrial Relations Commission, the decisions of which, expressed in awards, covered non-union workers, even in non-union workplaces. But only unions could represent these workers before the Commission, and this ensured unions a privileged place in Australian industrial relations, as the automatic advocates of workers covered by awards (the vast majority). But the government, following economic liberalism, was inclined to further decentralization, even if that meant non-union enterprise bargaining.

Despite their differences, the parties closed ranks prior to the 1993 election, which the government looked likely to lose. Accord Mk 7, struck three weeks before the election, extolled the virtues of awards and the role of industrial tribunals. The unions' efforts in support of the ALP helped it win the election against expectations (*Sydney Morning Herald*, 30 July 1993). But the edge was taken off the euphoria created by the government's victory when Keating, now prime minister, immediately foreshadowed downgrading the award system and permitting the Commission to ratify enterprise agreements in which unions had no part. But this was a direct threat to the unions' institutional survival. Key union figures threatened to cut off funding to the ALP in retaliation, even turning to the tiny Democrat Party in the Senate to oppose aspects of the ALP's own legislative programme. The policy tensions between economic liberalism and the Accord thus expressed themselves in conflict over industrial relations policy between the ALP and the ACTU. Testifying to the strength of the 'corporatist' ties, and equally to their increasingly authoritarian nature, eventually the unions accepted the existence of non-unionized bargaining units. The Industrial Relations Reform Act 1993 (enacted in December, operative from March 1994) put all this in place.

On one view, the 1993 election was not won by Labor, but lost by Labor's opponents. The Liberals had chosen to run on a programme of extremely dry economic policies – to outflank Labor on the Right. This in a sense forced Labor to resurrect its social democratic pretensions, and increase government spending (Kelly, 1994). The success of this strategy, and the reluctance of voters to embrace hard-line policies articulated by a former economics professor, helped Labor limp across the line in 1993 (J. Edwards, 1996). But to call the strategy 'social democratic' somewhat strains the term. The contradiction between economic liberal (and therefore anti-union) policy, and the 'corporatist' practices and consultative mechanisms that enlisted labour behind it, was still the central dynamic of the relationship. This contradiction had intensified as the ALP rejected the Left's interventionist industry policy programme and pursued economic liberal reforms, like floating the dollar, liberalizing the foreign exchange and other financial markets, and ultimately moving down the path of labour-market deregulation. The latter is, by definition, opposed to unionism. It aims to make workers compete against each other for increasingly scarce jobs, and to break down the collectives workers form to protect themselves against the effects of that competition. Yet these collectives were the core of the Labor Party's own support. Attacking them was thus self-defeating for the ALP. And for the union leadership to acquiesce in such an attack was also and obviously self-defeating. Initially, the Left and the ACTU opposed deregulation, and criticized the failure to implement industry policies, which were the essential *quid pro quo* for the Accord. Over time, these criticisms became muted and less frequent, ultimately silent. For as yet unrevealed reasons, the ACTU and the union Left leadership stayed in the Accord, even though ALP policy was attacking its own constituency, and was bound to discredit both itself and the ACTU. The ACTU even acquiesced in a version of labour-market deregulation, albeit a weaker one than that advocated by Labor's opponents, in the absence of controls over investment that might have ensured that business interests carried a more substantial share of the burden of reform.

From Democratic to Authoritarian Corporatism

This sweep through the policy battles of the 1980s and 1990s reveals increasingly concentrated decision-making processes within the labour movement. The workings of it all remain shrouded in the close relations between the union movement and the ALP. While the latter is dependent on the former for electoral support and funding, the well-worn career path from union leadership to political incumbency can make union leaders vulnerable to promises of career advancement in return for support. It is also impossible to discount the impact of two powerful personalities, in particular Paul Keating (Treasurer 1983–92; Prime Minister 1992–96) and ACTU Secretary Kelty. Both were able to carry their respective constituencies, Keating in Cabinet, Kelty in the ACTU. Keating's biographer has recently thrown new light on the workings of their relationship. According to Edwards, Keating was cavalier about the Accord, which he regarded as 'just for the election', a view he made plain to the inner sanctum of the union leadership. This changed when Keating became convinced of the Accord's ability to enlist unions behind the government's policies (J. Edwards, 1996, pp. 161–2, 506). Edwards also shows how the workings of Australian corporatism were often not what they seemed. An important institution was the Australian Labour Advisory Council, which was composed of a small number of key officials from the ACTU and Cabinet ministers. As Edwards tells it,

> The explicit purpose of the meetings was to give the ACTU an opportunity to raise issues with the Cabinet. An implicit purpose was to give Kelty an

opportunity to denounce the government in the presence of his ACTU colleagues. This reassured his colleagues that Kelty was loyal to their interests rather than to those of the government, but not in a way that created a serious split (Edwards, 1996, p. 478).

Once again, Kelty planned what he called the 'choreography' – the form in which the public display of reaching agreement between the ACTU and the ALP government would be presented – and he wrote, even directed, the 'script' for important meetings between Keating and the ACTU executive (Edwards, 1996, pp. 473, 490). While too much should not be read into this, it does highlight an important ingredient of the dynamics of the 'corporatist' arrangements – the highly concentrated decision-making processes, and the role of private meetings between Kelty and Keating in cooking up key 'Accords', and selling them to their constituencies.

This was not fertile soil for democracy within the union movement. Enforcing wage restraint, then work reorganization and intensification, was bound to increase tensions in the corporatism, and discredit the union leadership. The government's own inquiries into the effects of enterprise bargaining revealed work intensification, increased stress, low levels of consultation in workplace change and high levels of dissatisfaction among workers (DIR, 1995, 1996). Survey evidence released in early May 1996 revealed considerable dissatisfaction with unions. Fewer than 40 per cent of traditional blue-collar workers believed unions were 'looking after them', a level of dissatisfaction 10 per cent higher than that of white-collar and professional workers (*Weekend Australian*, 11–12 May 1996; *Sydney Morning Herald*, 11 May 1996). This partly explains why the traditional blue-collar vote deserted Labor in the 1996 election. As the ALP report into the election loss put it:

> Despite the ACTU negotiating the Accord in the name of all Australian workers, there was not involvement or consultation with rank-and-file unionists. The shopfloor was not consulted in any meaningful way and only a handful of senior officials had any influence in many Accord outcomes. Most workers felt completely alienated by this process (Federal Campaign Consultative Panel, 1996, p. 7).

Such suppression of democratic process is hardly likely to build a politically robust union movement that can participate as a partner in 'bargained' democratic corporatist arrangements. The less responsive the union movement becomes to democratic participation within its ranks, the less effective it becomes as a political movement (Higgins, 1985). With the union leadership

apparently acquiescing in work intensification and wage restraint, the resulting dissatisfaction lacked institutional expression. Workers were unable to
influence, through their unions, policies opposed to their interests, making it
rational for them to leave the union movement and experiment with other
forms of interest representation – such as individual contracts and voting for
Labor's political opponents.

Conclusion

Australia's version of corporatism was from the outset impaled on the contradiction between an economic liberal approach to policy, and the interests of its
own constituency. That this was not fully appreciated is the central strategic
failure of the Accord. As the policy stance of the ACTU and the ALP became
increasingly dominated by economic liberalism, the logic of the situation
demanded silencing dissent within the union movement, to protect the
Accord and Labor Party incumbency. The union leadership did not resolve the
contradiction by ending the Accord, for reasons that remain to be fully
analysed. This necessarily caused the nature of the corporatism to become
increasingly less democratic and more authoritarian. The arrangements and
processes increasingly eroded the independence and legitimacy of the union
movement, to the point that many workers deserted their unions and ALP
voters deserted their party. The inevitable day of reckoning came in March of
1996 when the Conservatives came to power, leaving a formidable task of
rebuilding for both the ALP and the union movement.

Notes

1. The Accord actually went through eight 'versions' – Marks 1–8. Mk 3
   onward entailed varying degrees of industrial relations decentralization,
   and witnessed the increasing hold of economic liberalism on restructuring
   policy.
2. And indeed would do so after the electoral debacle of 1996, when the
   ACLU and the ALP retreated from their commitment to industrial relations decentralization.
3. It is a common misconception that the Accord is a 'tripartite' agreement.
   It never was, although it provided for setting up some tripartite institutions.
4. 'Economic rationalism' is the term used in Australia for the traditional
   politics of economic liberalism (Pusey, 1991).

7 GLOBALIZATION AND THE PURSUIT OF PAY EQUITY: CONTRADICTORY PRESSURES IN THE AUSTRALIAN CASE

Gillian Whitehouse and Di Zetlin

Globalization is one of the Alice in Wonderland terms of contemporary debate (Barnet and Cavanagh, 1994). It means almost anything the writer wishes. While claims about the scale of change are varied, proponents typically argue that the size of corporations, the internationalization of trade, the mobility of capital and the lesser but nevertheless significant mobility of labour, the capacity to shift production from one place to another and the effectiveness of modern communication, mean that governments and trade unions can do little to enforce protective labour standards. Most of the literature points to a weakening of national institutions in favour of supra-national and local institutions – a 'hollowing out' of the nation state which is frequently presented as inevitable and/or unproblematic. Even where globalization is seen not so much as a weakening of power and more as a replacement of one form of power by another, it is the nation state that is perceived to be the most displaced (Tickell and Peck, 1995; see also Hirst and Thompson, 1996).

There is considerable scope for disputing these contentions at a theoretical, empirical and normative level (see, for example, Weiss, 1997). Changes may represent not so much a hollowing out or weakening of the nation state, but deliberate strategies which might more properly be seen as aspects of an extension of the crisis of post-Keynesianism through a neo-liberal project of weakening politics in favour of markets. Typical of such strategies are the widespread reconfiguration of industrial relations systems, involving the devolution of negotiation processes to enterprise or workplace level and measures to facilitate greater flexibility of employment contracts. In spite of considerable variability among states, this type of reconfiguration is ubiquitous and is usually defended on the grounds of enterprise competitiveness in the global economy and in the interests of flexible production. Clearly, such changes may have significant implications for employment equity – risking fragmentation, the extension of peripheral labour markets and increases in the inequality of income distribution (Bennett, 1994; Howes and Singh, 1995; Whitehouse, 1992, 1995).

However, potentially balancing these risks are pressures to maintain a highly skilled workforce and to adopt regulatory standards established in supra-national forums. Even in industries where there is much to gain from the new flexibility, such as telecommunications, there is the need for stability and replenishment of a core workforce with high value-added labour (Sassen, 1991). An industrial relations system driven by employment practices associated with a peripheral labour market is unlikely to provide this. Moreover, within the labour movement and in women's organizations, there remains a strong rights-based approach to industrial regulation, which increasingly has turned to supra-national codes and agencies. Since the opening of the United Nations Decade for Women, considerable emphasis has been placed on advancing the status of women through such strategies. The establishment of human rights to equal treatment and social rights to equitable living standards have been pursued through a diverse range of international organizations such as the International Labour Organization (through conventions relating to employment equity) and regional level courts such as the European Court of Justice, as well as through various attempts to develop social charters as part of world trade agreements. Despite trade union reservations about the overall impact of supra-national structures, there is some evidence that rights-based international conventions can be used to modify disparities caused by labour-market deregulation in favour of employment equity (Howell, 1995/6).

This chapter is concerned with these potentially conflicting aspects of globalization, and the identification of their implications for women's conditions of employment. We argue, first, that a progressive decentralization of industrial relations systems does risk erosion of employment equity, particularly the pursuit of equal pay. We are not primarily concerned with arguments about the origin of industrial relations changes of this nature (for example, whether they are adopted as deliberate control strategies in the interests of assisting capital, or whether they represent the only options open to weakened nation states). Rather we seek to provide some empirical evidence of their effects on conditions of work for women. We then seek to investigate the extent to which the increased salience of international provisions on employment equity discussed above might counter the potentially negative influence of wage bargaining decentralization. Essentially, we argue that while a number of new opportunities may be opened up where there is political pressure to recognize international equity standards, these are unlikely to be able to be utilized to maximum effect in more decentralized industrial relations systems. Scenarios will, of course, differ between nations, with maximization of the positive potential of globalization most likely to occur where a strong judicial body (such as the European Court of Justice) is in place. Although the development of a reliance on supra-national regulation may be the best possible response to neo-liberal pressures in relation to globalization, this may represent a weaker strategy for labour market regulation than the more cohesive national social democratic strategies of the postwar years.

Our analysis proceeds in two stages, with the focus throughout on the specific issue of pay equity. The first stage involves statistical analysis of data from the OECD countries over the past two decades. The purpose of this analysis is to provide an empirical test of our first argument – that decentralization of industrial relations systems hinders the continued pursuit of pay equity. Our goal is to provide a direct assessment of the effects of globalization, through institutional and policy change, on pay equity. However, this type of analysis does not permit investigation of the contradictory pressures we are interested in, as the interaction between supra-national standards and national wage bargaining systems cannot be easily quantified for time-series statistical analysis. Hence the second stage of our analysis utilizes a more qualitative approach to investigate the interaction between increasing pressure to recognize international provisions relating to employment equity and changes in wage bargaining arrangements. Australia provides a useful case study for this purpose, with a recent series of test cases enabled through legislative recognition of international commitments, but fought out in an increasingly decentralized and deregulated environment. It reveals some of the dynamics which mitigate against effective equity measures in such an environment.

Wage Bargaining Systems and the Pursuit of Pay Equity: A Statistical Analysis

Our primary goal in this section of the chapter is to subject our expectation of a relationship between centralization of wage bargaining and pay equity to empirical investigation. There are several reasons why such a relationship might be anticipated. For example, centralized bargaining might produce a degree of wage compression through an enhanced ability to maintain minimum standards and/or control high wages, as well as permitting the spread of wage gains from stronger to weaker groups in the labour market.[1] Such systems may also extend the scope of comparison for pay equity/comparable worth purposes. Moreover, centralized industrial relations processes are typically co-ordinated by peak union organizations which in themselves may add to the capacity to prosecute pay equity cases and seek protections for the less well-paid sections of the labour market.

As our analytical focus is primarily on the effect of changes to wage bargaining arrangements in response to the pressures of globalization, we are not seeking in this instance to test all possible determinants of pay equity. Indicators of human capital, for example, are not included. In any event, suitable cross-nationally comparable, yearly data are not available to adequately represent this measure. Moreover, there is little reason to expect a high degree of explanatory utility in this case. Countries have been selected as examples of similarly advanced industrialized economies and differences in levels of education and training are unlikely to be of sufficient magnitude to explain the significant variation in pay equity outcomes.[2]

We do, however, include a range of control variables in the analyses to represent broader economic and labour-market trends that may affect pay equity outcomes. Overall economic and employment growth, for example, might be expected to provide a supportive environment for the pursuit of pay equity, with employers less prepared to concede wage gains for equity purposes when growth is limited. Increases in female labour-force participation may also affect outcomes, possibly negatively initially by increasing the number of women in entry level jobs, but potentially positively in the longer term by increasing the pressure for equity measures. Sectoral changes may be of significance, with a decline in manufacturing and an increase in service-sector employment possibly associated with the expansion of non-standard forms of employment and the concentration of women in poorly paid irregular work. Changes between public and private sectors could also have relevance – public-sector employment in many countries tends to be more closely regulated and co-ordinated, and to provide relatively high-skill welfare-type jobs for women. Thus a high level of public employment might assist overall equity outcomes, and may also have an indirect influence through a pace-setter effect.

If our hypothesis is to be supported, we require initial confirmation from the cross-national time-series data that measures of pay equity are positively associated with variables representing wage bargaining centralization. Our previous research has already provided some evidence to this effect (White-house, 1992, 1995), but the following analysis incorporates alternative measures of pay equity and an expanded data set including the period of the late 1980s and early 1990s, during which significant changes occurred in many countries as governments sought to adjust to increasing international pressures. Before reporting the results of our investigations, we provide a description of the variables and the statistical models applied.

The Data

The database utilized in this analysis includes variables representing economic, labour-market, institutional and political indicators for sixteen advanced, industrialized OECD countries and, in most cases, for each year from 1970 to 1992.[3] In the following analyses the number of countries and years included depends on the availability of cross-nationally comparable earnings data.

The dependent variable – earnings equity – is represented by measures of women's earnings as a percentage of men's. Although these data tend to be more widely available and reliable than other indicators of employment equity such as segregation,[4] earnings statistics are not without limitations. The most useful data are those based on hourly earnings, as these obviate the problem that men and women may have different hours of work per week, month or year. Where data are collected by the one agency there is also greater likelihood that some attempts at standardization across nations will have been made. The following analyses therefore rely primarily on hourly earnings data published by the ILO, although some interventions have been made (see details in the Appendix at the end of the chapter).

Two measures of pay equity are utilized in the analyses, the first based on the ILO category 'non-agricultural earnings', the second based on earnings in manufacturing. A significant drawback for cross-national analysis is that the most widely available figures are for earnings in manufacturing, and therefore exclude those areas of employment in which women tend to be concentrated. The non-agricultural earnings data provide a more inclusive measure and enable testing of a wider range of variables,[5] but these data are available for a much smaller number of countries and years.[6] The use of both measures therefore permits a more rigorous test of the relationship, although we emphasize that there are limitations in each case. Our approach is to use the non-agricultural earnings initially to test the hypothesized relationships, then to apply the same model to the manufacturing data (which has the advantage of being more comprehensive). To the extent that the relationships are similar between both equations, we argue that the more comprehensive manufacturing data provide some approximation of broader measures of cross-national, time-series variations in earnings equity.

The main independent variable was designed to represent centralization of wage bargaining. The variable takes the form of an index which rates countries on a scale from 1 to 10, depending on the balance between levels of wage bargaining and the co-ordinating influence of peak union organization. The highest values were accorded for those countries and years where there was a high degree of central union co-ordination of wage determination for all sectors at a national level, while the lowest scores represented bargaining at enterprise level only, with no confederation involvement.

Variables representing levels of, and growth in, GDP and employment, were selected as indicators of overall economic and employment growth. Other control variables included were female participation rates, measures of both industry and service-sector employment as a proportion of total employment, and a measure of government employment as a proportion of total employment.

Statistical Method

The analysis utilized pooled data for selected countries from 1970 to 1992, thus permitting analysis sensitive to changes over time as well as between countries. While there are some statistical difficulties in dealing with a data set of this nature which combines both space and time dimensions, there are significant advantages in terms of research design, enabling more effective examination of causal dynamics (see Stimson, 1985, pp. 915–16).

Ordinary Least Squares (OLS) regression was applied as it is among the most reliable techniques in dealing with pooled data (see Beck et al., 1993). However, we have also utilized a range of diagnostic tests,[7] and we apply stringent criteria for the acceptance of results as statistically significant, placing confidence mainly in results at the $p = 0.0001$ level. Models were constructed to test the determinants of earnings equity utilizing the variables outlined above, with all independent variables lagged one year.

Analyses and Findings

Our investigation involved modelling earnings equity as a function of centralized wage fixation, GDP growth, employment growth,[8] female labour-force participation, and sectoral (industry, service and government) shares of employment. Analysis A utilized hourly earnings in non-agricultural industries as the dependent variable and included eight countries over the time period 1971–1991.[9] Analysis B was designed to provide a check on the results produced by Analysis A, utilizing the more comprehensive hourly earnings in manufacturing as the dependent variable. It included fourteen countries over the time period 1971–1992.[10]

The results, shown in Table 7.1, provide clear support for the hypothesis,

Table 7.1 *Earnings equity: OLS regression coefficients*

	Analysis A* coefficients (significance)	Analysis B# coefficients (significance)
Independent variables		
Centralized wage bargaining	1.90 (0.0001)	1.65 (0.0001)
GDP growth	-0.60 (0.0019)	-0.18 (0.274)
Employment growth	0.33 (0.287)	-0.36 0.127
Female participation	-0.06 (0.257)	-0.006 (0.870)
Industry employment	-0.36 (0.019)	-0.03 (0.828)
Service-sector employment	-0.23 (0.102)	0.08 (0.450)
Government employment	0.69 (0.0001)	0.75 (0.0001)
Adjusted R^2	0.82	0.76

* Women's earnings as a percentage of men's – hourly earnings in non-agricultural industries (eight countries, 1970–1991, N = 168)
# Women's earnings as a percentage of men's – hourly earnings in manufacturing (fourteen countries, 1971–1992, N = 308)

with centralized wage bargaining highly significant and positive. This was the case for both measures of pay equity. The size of the coefficient is notable. Although this variable is represented on a different scale from the other variables included in the analysis (1–10 as opposed to 1–100), the scale is appropriate to what is being measured. The results imply that institutional changes of the order of a movement from the top of the scale (representing a system in which wages for a high proportion of the workforce are determined at national level) to a mid-point (for example, representing a system in which there is a mixture of industry-level and enterprise-level bargaining) correspond with a drop of around 8 to 10 percentage points in pay equity. While confidence cannot be placed in absolute numbers in an analysis of this nature, the example serves to reinforce the strength and size of the relationship suggested by the results.

The only control variable to show a highly significant relationship with the dependent variables was government employment. None of the other control variables reached the $p = 0.0001$ level of significance, although, by conventional measures, both GDP growth and industry employment appear to have a small negative association with the dependent variable in Analysis A. However, these relationships did not prove to be particularly stable through the diagnostic tests. In contrast, the centralized wage bargaining relationship proved remarkably stable throughout the diagnostic procedures. The models as a whole appear well specified, with an adjusted R^2 of 0.82 for Analysis A and 0.76 for Analysis B, emphasizing the importance of the main explanatory variable, centralized wage bargaining, to the understanding of pay equity.

While acknowledging the difficulties of this type of analysis, we emphasize the importance of establishing broad statistical confirmation of the hypothesized relationship as a basis for more detailed case study analysis. Having produced clear statistical support for our argument that a move towards decentralization of wage bargaining arrangements has potentially negative consequences for earnings equity outcomes,[11] we now turn to a case study analysis in order to provide a more complete understanding of this relationship, and to illuminate the conflicting influences that may be operating. The Australian case is particularly useful for these purposes.

An Australian Case Study

The Development of Equal Pay Principles in Australia

In this case study, we wish to explore the dynamics of an industrial relations system that is undergoing a transformation from a centralized and regulated system to a decentralized and deregulated system. In particular, we want to focus upon the use of international conventions as a mechanism for regulation in a decentralizing environment. Australia presents a particularly pertinent case study of these effects and may offer some plausible explanations for the positive effects between centralized systems and pay equity.

In Australia, wage rates and conditions of employment are determined by a system of industrial awards, generally covering a whole occupation, group of like occupations, or, less commonly, an industry. There have been two main types of awards regulating pay and conditions. Minimum rates awards traditionally operate in the private sector, prescribing minimum rates of pay and allowing over-award payments to be made, generally on a site-by-site basis. Paid rates awards, which represent the total rate of pay for ordinary hours of work, have predominated in the public sector. In addition to setting awards for particular groups of workers, the Australian Industrial Relations Commission has played a major role in individual disputes, through the phases of conciliation and, if necessary, arbitration. In addition to setting awards for particular groups of workers, the Industrial Relations Commission has determined national wage cases for minimum rates of pay to apply across the workforce.

Despite a long-standing acceptance of comparative wage justice (for men) that pay should be based on the same rate for the job, differential rates of male and female pay were explicitly justified by reference to a family wage until 1969. In a series of test cases between 1969 and 1974, the principle of equal pay was accepted. The landmark test case which still dominates the justification of equal pay in Australia was conducted in 1972. In this case, the Commission accepted that equal pay for equal work was too narrow: 'the time has come to enlarge the concept to equal pay for work of equal value. This means that award rates for all work should be considered without regard to the sex of the employee' (147 CAR 172, 1972, p. 178). The Commission was opposed to any automatic formula for the application of this principle, arguing for specific work value comparisons to be tested before its arbitral powers. The Commission was also of the view that such comparisons should be based upon comparators within the award under consideration and was clear that it would not extend its jurisdiction to over-award payments.

Nevertheless, these test cases had a dramatic effect on pay equity, raising the minimum award rate for women from 71 per cent of the male rate in 1968 to 92 per cent in 1975. Ordinary-time wage rates moved from 64 per cent to 83 per cent in the same period (Inquiry into Sex Discrimination in Overaward Payments, 1992, p. 25). Subsequent attempts to broaden the principles of the 1972 test case were largely unsuccessful. An attempt to introduce comparable worth through a case involving nurses failed, although ultimately the Commission accepted that nurses' rates of pay were anomalous by comparison with other health professionals, and that pay increases were warranted on the basis that this indicated that equal pay principles had not been implemented previously.

In short, the Australian Commission has technically never gone beyond the narrow interpretation of equal pay for like jobs to accept principles of measuring equal pay against dissimilar jobs or of accepting that gender wage disparity places an onus on the employer. Progress in narrowing the gender gap has been achieved primarily through the development of general wage principles in a centralized industrial relations system. The development of an Accord between the Australian Council of Trade Unions (ACTU) and the incoming 1983 Labor government led to a period of highly centralized wage fixation. During the 1980s, and particularly with the introduction of a major overhaul of

Table 7.2 *Mean average female wages as a percentage of male*

	Total earnings (Aug.)	Full-time adult (Aug.)	Full-time adult, non-managerial (Nov.)	Full-time adult, non-managerial, ordinary-time weekly earnings (May)	Full-time adult, non-managerial, award rates, weekly earnings (May)
1975	67.12	76.10	79.26	83.23	86.22
1980	66.26	79.69	80.77	85.67	88.33
1985	65.71	78.78	81.34	88.29	90.70
1990	66.35	79.93	82.69	89.58	91.50
1991	67.47	81.23	n.a.	90.14	91.74

Source: Adapted from Inquiry into Sex Discrimination in Overaward Payments (1992, p. 35) and various published and unpublished Australian Bureau of Statistics data prepared for the HREOC.

Note: n.a. indicates data not available.

all awards since 1987 (award restructuring), the Commission accepted a capacity to include skill levels as well as task performance in job evaluations. The 1989 National Wage Case established principles to enable a Minimum Rates Adjustment process to take place which facilitated the comparison of jobs across industries, using the metal industry classification scheme as a benchmark. These decisions, although not changing the 1972 equal pay principles, enabled women's jobs to be compared with male jobs in a broader sense than they were previously. The slender attrition in the gender gap in wages can be seen in Table 7.2.

The gender gap in total remuneration may be attributed to a range of factors, including the small numbers of women in the high-paid managerial sector, the prevalence of women in part-time employment, and the relatively smaller number of overtime hours worked by women. The narrower gap in ordinary-time award earnings has been associated with the concentration of women in low-paid occupations and the tendency for men rather than women to attract over-award payments. Closing this latter gap was more amenable to industrial principles and became the focus of the trade union movement.

The position of the Industrial Relations Commission on over-award payments on the minimum rates awards in the private sector has varied in response to the differing pressures of the external environment. Principles of wage compression and the minimizing of flow-on effects encouraged the Commission to absorb general wage increases in over-award payments, while flexibility and maintaining relativities exert pressure in the opposite direction. By the 1990s, over-award payments were made in three-quarters of the private sector (Morehead *et al.*, 1997, p. 216) although over-awards generally comprised less than 20 per cent of total pay (Gill, 1994, p. xi). The gender gap in over-award payments is significant. Women are less likely than men to be in workplaces that pay over-award payments and the rate of over-award payment, where women can access it, is lower than that of men (Gill, 1994, pp. 29–30). On average, women in full-time adult, non-managerial employment in manufacturing earn only 60 per cent of the over-award payments of men (Frizzell, 1992, p. 5). With the introduction of enterprise bargaining in 1993, it seems likely that over-award payments are being absorbed in enterprise agreements. The Australian Workplace Industrial Relations Survey (AWIRS) reports a drop in the number of firms with collective agreements paying over-awards (Morehead *et al.*, 1997, p. 216). Despite these changes, over-award payments remain more prevalent for men.

> Workplaces that paid over-awards tended to have a larger proportion of male employees than the population of all workplaces. Women made up 42 per cent of employees in private sector workplaces that paid over-awards, compared to 48 per cent at private sector workplaces without over-awards. As well, in private sector workplaces that paid over-awards, 36 per cent of employees receiving over-awards were women and 64 per cent were men. (Morehead *et al.*, 1997, p. 212).

Contradictory Trends in the 1990s

In the 1990s the Labor government and the ACTU became subject to calls for a more deregulated labour market to meet the demands of international competitiveness. Globalization, it was argued, demands greater flexibility. The strategy of the ACTU and the Labor government shifted from pursuing equity goals through broader principles achieved through a centralized system to a strategy in which decentralization would be accompanied by a regulatory framework of equity. The Labor government introduced a major overhaul of industrial legislation in 1993. Labor was defeated in 1996 and the incoming Liberal government introduced more radical decentralization later that year (Workplace Relations Act 1996). Thus, from 1993, Australia has seen an increasingly rapid movement away from its centralized wage fixing system to a system of enterprise bargaining.

Although some moves towards decentralization were made in the late 1980s, the first major move away from a centralized system was the Labor government's 1993 legislation. While this legislation espoused flexibility as a way of making the labour market perform more competitively in global markets and, therefore, introduced enterprise level bargaining as the major form of bargaining, it retained existing awards, allowed for 'safety net' increases, required specific tests of 'no disadvantage' and mandated consultation processes with disadvantaged groups of employees. It also introduced specific responsibilities for the Industrial Relations Commission in implementation of ILO and United Nations standards. Specifically, the Act incorporated the Convention Concerning Equal Remuneration for Men and Women Workers for Work of Equal Value (ILO, 1951), the Recommendation Concerning Equal Remuneration for Men and Women for Work of Equal Value (ILO, 1951), the Preamble and Parts II and III of the International Covenant on Economic, Social and Cultural Rights (United Nations), the Recommendation Concerning Discrimination in Respect of Employment and Occupation (ILO, 1958), the Convention Concerning Equal Opportunities and Equal Treatment for Men and Women Workers: Workers with Family Responsibilities (ILO, 1981), and the Recommendation Concerning Equal Opportunities and Equal Treatment for Men and Women Workers with Family Responsibilities (ILO, 1981).

In 1996, the newly elected Liberal government introduced legislation involving a radical shift towards bargaining either between employers and employees directly or through trade unions at the enterprise level, retaining only a minimal safety net role for the Commission. The legislation proposed to delete the division of the Act which had given effect to the ILO and United Nations Conventions and Recommendations and to remove these from the Act. Although the Bill maintained some references to equal pay in minimum wages, the government proposed that ILO Conventions should be dealt with by the much weaker body, the Human Rights and Equal Opportunity Commission. In order to have the Bill passed, the government needed the support of minor parties, and in particular, the Democrats, to secure a majority in the Senate, Australia's upper house. The legislation was, therefore, the subject of considerable scrutiny.

The Senate referred the legislation to its Economic References Committee (SERC) which reported substantial concerns with it (SERC, 1996), in part based upon the Human Rights and Equal Opportunities Commission's contention that the Bill substantially weakened the Australian government's commitment to international equity conventions. HREOC also pointed out that, unlike the AIRC, its decisions were not enforceable and that its remit is limited to redressing harm already done. The Committee concluded that there were a number of doubts about whether the Bill complied with Australia's international commitments, and noted specifically that the Bill would not be in compliance with the ILO's Equal Remuneration Convention (SERC, 1996).[12]

After extensive negotiations with the Democrats, sufficient amendments were made to achieve Democrat support in the Senate and thus allow passage of the Bill. Included in these amendments were changes to strengthen the pay equity provisions of the Bill. Of the Conventions and Recommendations referred to above, only the Convention Concerning Equal Opportunities and Equal Treatment for Men and Women Workers: Workers with Family Responsibilities and the relevant sections of the International Covenant on Economic, Social and Cultural Rights remain as Schedules to the Act. However, the definitions of the Convention on Equal Remuneration have been included in the reinstated Division of the 1993 legislation. Thus, although the general thrust of the legislation is to reduce the powers of the Commission to regulation of carefully prescribed minimum wages and conditions, the Commission has a broader ambit in relation to equal pay. In particular, its equity remit includes all aspects of remuneration, rather than being limited to award pay rates.

The history of these recent legislative changes in Australia is some indication that globalization might have contradictory effects. On the one hand, perceived demands for labour-market flexibility in response to globalization encourage a decentralized and deregulatory industrial relations environment. On the other hand, a global economy can focus attention on international obligations that can strengthen arguments for equity. However, it might be argued that the application of international labour standards will be highly influenced by the overall shape of the industrial relations regime. An examination of the attempts by the ACTU to utilize these provisions indicates some positive outcomes and some of the difficulties of applying international standards in a decentralized system.

Recent Equal Pay Cases

In the early stages of the move to decentralization in the 1990s, the Australian industrial relations system maintained several aspects of previous arrangements that were protective of pay equity. The move to enterprise bargaining has been reasonably gradual, although accelerating as the effects of the 1996 Act come into effect. The initial rounds of enterprise bargaining were seen as supplementary to awards and were marked by a high degree of pattern bargaining, which facilitated flow-ons across industries. Second- and third-generation enterprise agreements have weakened these industry-wide standards, thus diminishing the capacity to make comparisons across firms or between industries or distinct occupations and reducing the effect of flow-ons from pace-setter industries.

There have been two major opportunities to test the new capacities the Commission has to give specific consideration to Australia's international labour standards for women workers. The first arises out of a series of test cases initiated under the 1993 legislation in the manufacturing industry and continued under the 1996 legislation. These cases were designed to test the powers of the Commission in dealing with equal remuneration, including entitlements above the award. The second arose in the context of the ACTU's application for a living wage, which commenced under the 1996 legislation.

Example one: the company-by-company approach. In December 1995, the metal workers' union, supported by the ACTU, lodged an application for equal pay in three manufacturing enterprises. The cases involved arguments about whether the company total rate for the job, including over-award payments, was discriminatory. The Industrial Relations Commission was being asked to determine how it would exercise its new powers under ILO Conventions in order to assess gender implications of job evaluations and to extend its scrutiny to over-award payments. This involved a painstaking exercise of conciliation on a site-by-site basis, with one of the three companies, in particular, being recalcitrant and objecting to this process. Agreement was reached with two of the companies during 1996, but the case against the third company, HPM, has not been solved.

The difficulties in prosecuting cases of this kind are illustrated in the case against HPM. The 300 female workers on whose behalf the case was run by the metal workers' union and the ACTU are Process Workers and Packers whose claim for pay increases was based on a comparison with male General Hands and male Storepersons in the same factory. During the period between 1989 and 1991 the metal trades award had been rationalized from some 360 classifications into a 14-level classification structure linked strongly to competencies. The jobs under dispute were at the bottom level of the classification structure and concerned the actual rates paid within and between workers in the lowest two bands of the classification structure. In this unskilled area, competencies and qualifications were less developed.

The issues of principle canvassed in this case included the questions of which factors might be included in job evaluation, how discrimination is defined and where the onus of proof lies in establishing direct or indirect discrimination, and the extent to which an enterprise-based system of bargaining is compatible with a layer of decision-making by independent tribunals. Thus far, the

Commission has made conservative decisions (by comparison with decisions in other national and international jurisdictions) on each of these principles.

Quite early in the case, the Commission took the view that the onus to provide evidence of discrimination rested on the union being able to demonstrate this against comparators within the one workplace (Print N2367, 11 June 1996, p. 26). On this basis, consultants undertook an extensive evaluation of the competencies in the classifications under dispute at HPM. In arbitration of these matters more than twelve months later, HPM argued that, despite their participation in this exercise, they did not accept that competencies were the appropriate mechanism for determining a rate for the job, and suggested factors such as markets, responsibility and work environment needed to be included. In his decision in the case, Commissioner Simmonds, without making any final determination on whether the pay was discriminatory, agreed with HPM that competency standards were not a sufficient test:

> I am of the view that the competency standards, in the absence of agreement, are not an adequate tool for assessment for the purposes of this matter . . . They do not provide a means for assessing other attributes, such elements of responsibility that are not skill-related, the nature of the work and the conditions under which the work is performed. Nor are they the only means of providing an objective judgement of the factors which may have a place in an overaward system of remuneration (Print P9210, 4 March 1998).

Technically, this left it open for the unions to reapply on new grounds, which they did. Their application was accepted for hearing on the basis of evidence in May 1998. Justice Munro made it clear that the union would be required to provide evidence that the alleged discrimination is taking place in the present.

> [I]t would be reasonable to assume that *the Commission will need to be satisfied that there is not equal remuneration for work of equal value for a particular employee or class of employees* before making an order to provide prospectively for an increase in rates of remuneration appropriate to ensure there is equal remuneration (Print Q1002, 19 May 1988, emphasis added).

On 10 July, HPM sacked all its male employees, claiming they were redundant.

In practice, the incorporation of international conventions has been of little utility in prosecuting pay equity in these examples. While it may well have assisted in establishing consent in two of the three cases taken by the trade unions, the HPM case illustrates how an enterprise bargaining environment and an intransigent company can frustrate the weakened arbitral powers of the Australian Industrial Relations Commission.

Example two: Equity and low pay. The second example where the new powers of the Commission were tested was in the ACTU's living wage case. Past experience in Australia has been that pay equity has been advanced more through the effects of a national arbitral system which has kept minimum wages at a tolerable level in relation to living standards and overall wage dispersion. Despite the radical changes to the industrial relations system under the Workplace Relations Act 1996, the Commission retained a role in relation to maintaining awards as 'a safety net of fair minimum wages and conditions', having regard both to prevailing living standards and the needs of the low paid (S88B[2 {a} and {c}]). However, the exercise of this power is conditioned by the responsibility the Commission has to encourage 'the making of agreements between employers and employees at the workplace or enterprise level by maintaining an incentive to bargain' (Dec 457/98 M Print Q1998).

In June 1996, the ACTU lodged a claim for a living wage that has been the subject of Commission determinations in 1997 and 1998. In the 1997 case, the ACTU submitted that granting its claim would be an exercise of the Commission's equal pay powers. One-third of the female workforce would be affected by the full claim (ACIRRT, 1996, p. 5). The Commission rejected this argument on the grounds that equal pay cases should be brought under ss170BA to 170BI, the sections being utilized in the HPM case detailed above (Dec 335/97 S Print P1997, April 1997). This does not mean, of course, that increases to low- and medium-paid workers do not disproportionately benefit women. As the state government of New South Wales submitted to the Commission in its 1998 proceedings:

> New South Wales submitted that the ACTU's claims were of particular importance to low paid female employees and would, if granted, benefit female employees in a number of ways. The absorption of the minimum rates adjustment into overaward payments would help compensate for female employees' lesser access to overaward payments. This would assist markedly in minimising the discrepancy between the earnings of men and women. Due to a higher concentration of women in the non-bargaining sector the differential between enterprise bargaining outcomes and award safety net increases affects women disproportionately. Strengthening the safety net would partially redress the position (Dec 457/98 M Print Q1998).

In the event, the Commission followed a cautious increase in 1997 with a more generous one in 1998. In juggling their responsibilities to look after the interests of the low paid while maintaining the incentives to bargain at the enterprise level, the Commission noted in its 1998 decision that no particular priority attached to these potentially contradictory principles (Dec 457/98 M Print Q1998). Since the introduction of enterprise bargaining, greater wage increases through bargained outcomes have increased the discrepancy between AWOTE (Average Weekly Ordinary Time Earnings) and award increases and '[a]s a consequence income inequality in Australia is increasing' (Dec 457/98 M Print Q1998). In the Commission's view, this assisted their determination to award a more generous increase in 1998, although they were careful to make a decision that would still have a minimal impact on AWOTE. Thus, the living wage case has provided a vehicle for narrowing the growth of wage dispersion. Given the difficulty in establishing equal pay principles on a company-by-company basis, the utilization of safety net increases may continue to be the main avenue for the prosecution of pay equity outcomes (or perhaps more accurately, of minimizing the negative impact of wage dispersion on pay equity outcomes).

Conclusion

Our chapter as a whole has attempted to establish that centralization of wage bargaining – an institutional arrangement under some threat under globalization – is an extremely important factor for pay equity outcomes. On the basis of providing some statistical confirmation of this proposition, we have sought to use the Australian case to explain some of the ways in which such a relationship operates, and to examine the potential for recognition of international standards to offer avenues for the pursuit of pay equity in a decentralizing environment. As we have noted, globalization might provide some opportunities to develop and advance international obligations for just labour standards. In this context, it seemed plausible that honouring international obligations might encourage regulation despite other deregulatory changes.

However, despite the fact that in Australia a movement towards decentralization and deregulation of wage bargaining has been accompanied by attempts to provide a regulatory framework to pursue equity, the pursuit of pay equity appears fraught with difficulties in the current environment. Recent pay equity cases before the Australian Industrial Relations Commission demonstrate how the explicit recognition of international labour conventions may be a relatively weaker instrument for wage justice than a centralized wage fixing system. In the first place, the Commission has argued that its international treaty obligations must be dealt with only under the specific clauses of the legislation. The effect of this is to require specific cases to be brought before the Commission, with the broad-ranging capacity to introduce principles conducive to equity through cases at the national level significantly diminished.

Secondly, although the Commission now has the specific powers to examine total remuneration, and thus appears to have in some ways an expanded capacity to deal with pay equity matters, the basis for its judgement about appropriate relativities is weakened as actual wage rates devolve from a regulated award system to an enterprise-by-enterprise-based system. Thus it is unlikely that job evaluations which extend significantly beyond the enterprise will be easy to prosecute.

Finally, a centralized wage fixing system has much more scope through national wage cases to deliver timely decisions with broad flow-on effects. The lengthy proceedings against HPM and the usual judicial backlog of individual cases awaiting decisions will act as its own inhibition on closing the gender gap through these means. In short, while the introduction of international labour standards on equal remuneration is an appropriate response to the industrial pressures of globalization, it is difficult to see how such principles can be applied without a strong central arbitral body prepared to override the interests of workplace flexibility for the principles of equal remuneration. The living wage case has been of greater benefit to more women in this environment, despite the fact that its capacity to give effect to pay equity is an indirect product of the concentration of women workers among the low paid. This strategy has relied upon the remaining centralized elements of Australian wage fixing arrangements – the award system and minimum pay rates – rather than the incorporation of international labour standards. Its effect is limited by the principles enshrined in the Act to balance increases in awards against encouraging enterprise bargaining.

Appendix

Data Definitions and Sources

Earnings equity.   Women's hourly earnings in non-agricultural and manufacturing industries as a percentage of men's, based on ILO series.

ILO data for non-agricultural earnings were available only for eight countries and only to 1991, and variations were present in the number of industries included in different countries. Data for Japan were monthly rather than hourly. No modifications to the series were made.

Data for manufacturing industries were available for twelve countries up to 1992, with figures for Japan being monthly rather than hourly. The manufacturing series was extended with data from Canada and the USA. Full year full-time earnings for Canada were adjusted in line with the ratio of this series to data for earnings in manufacturing in the year that the latter were available. The adjustment involved an upward revision of the Canadian data by 2.5 percentage points. The figures used for the USA were for median weekly earnings for full-time workers in the occupational category 'Operators, fabricators and labourers'. For Japan, monthly earnings given in the ILO publications were modified in line with the ratio between these and hourly earnings (available up to 1986 in OECD, *Employment Outlook*, 1988) for 1986.

(*Sources:* ILO *Yearbooks;* Statistics Canada, *Earnings of Men and Women,* Cat. No. 13–217, Ottawa: Minister of Industry, Science and Technology (various years); United States Department of Commerce, *Statistical Abstract of the United States*).

Centralization of wage fixation.   Extent of centralization of the wage bargaining process and the extent to which this is co-ordinated by central union confederations. An index was constructed based on a 10-point scale which took into account the balance between levels of bargaining and ranged from official inclusion in national level wage determination, through formalized participation in industry-wide bargaining, consultative involvement in industry-wide bargaining, to enterprise level negotiations with no confederation involvement.

(Sources used to construct the index include: Baglioni and Crouch, 1990; Bamber and Lansbury, 1987, 1993; Western, 1995; Ferner and Hyman, 1992a; and various issues of the *European Industrial Relations Review*).

Growth in GDP.   Annual percentage growth in real GDP.

(*Source:* OECD, *Economic Outlook*, various years.)

Growth in employment.   Annual percentage growth in employment.

(*Source:* OECD, *Historical Statistics*, various years.)

Female participation.   Female labour force as a percentage of the female population aged 15–64 years.

(*Source:* OECD, *Historical Statistics* and *Labour Force Statistics*, various years.)

Industry employment.   Industry-sector employment as a percentage of total employment.

(*Source:* OECD, *Labour Force Statistics*, various years.)

Service-sector employment.   Service-sector employment as a percentage of total employment.

(*Source:* OECD, *Labour Force Statistics*, various years.)

Government employment.   Government employment as a percentage of total employment.

(*Source:* OECD, *Historical Statistics*, various years.)

Statistical Tests

Three potential risks in interpreting OLS regression results from the analysis of the pooled data were considered. These were: bias in the results due to the effect of outliers (exceptional countries or years); distortion of regression coefficients due to high levels of variation between countries; and autocorrelation and heteroscedasticity associated with the use of time-series data.

The first of these was addressed through the process of successive elimination of individual countries and years from the regression analysis (jackknifing). With the data applied here, the risk of individual countries having an inordinate effect on the results is always present, particularly given the extent of cross-national difference in the main variables. Jackknifing, therefore, provides a test of the stability of the results and allows identification of outliers. This test was also important where data from individual countries was in a different form or from a different source. Thus, the exclusion of Japan (with monthly rather than hourly non-agricultural earnings) and Canada and the USA (with yearly and weekly earnings respectively, and with data from different sources modified to approximate a match to the manufacturing series) were important tests. Findings were only accepted if the sign and statistical significance of coefficients were unaffected by the procedure.

The second potential risk was addressed through the introduction of country dummies into the equation – the Least Squares with Dummy Variables (LSDV) model (see Stimson, 1985, pp. 921ff; Dowrick, 1993, pp. 23–4). This procedure allows the identification of country-specific effects, and removes bias that between-country differences might be exerting on the regression coefficients. Country-specific effects are expected in the analyses, for while an ideal model would convert all country-specific factors into more general institutional, policy, cultural or other variables, our focus has been analysis of the variables relevant to our theoretical interest rather than provision of a 'total' explanation. The LSDV process therefore has some inherent problems for the analysis, most particularly by possibly explaining variation in the dependent variable with atheoretical dummy variables that may well be collinear with the explanatory variables of theoretical interest (Stimson, 1985, p. 922).[13] Nevertheless the use of the LSDV technique provides a check on the OLS coefficients for the theoretically important variables, and use of the procedure was limited to that purpose.

The third potential problem – autocorrelation associated with the use of time-series data – can be best addressed through the use of a Generalised Least Squares (GLS) procedure based on the work of Kmenta (1971, pp. 512–14; see also Stimson, 1985, pp. 926–93). This technique provides a means of controlling for autocorrelation and heteroscedasticity, thus helping to avoid the risk inherent in the use of large cross-national/time-series data sets that error terms will be biased, over-stating the significance of results. Although this risk has also been guarded against by an extremely conservative approach to the interpretation of significance levels and standard errors, checking crucial findings with a GLS procedure provides another safeguard. It is important to note, however, that this procedure also has limitations (see Beck *et al.*, 1993). While acknowledging that no analytical process is without inherent limitations, the combination of techniques adopted here provide a range of suitable safeguards, and ensure greater confidence than reliance on a single method.

Notes

1. Austria provides a notable exception – a high degree of centralization is accompanied by a high level of wage dispersion (see Rowthorn, 1992). However, there do not appear to be any clear examples of the opposite scenario – that is, combination of a highly decentralized system with compressed wages.
2. For example, a consistent difference between Sweden and the UK of around 20 percentage points in the female/male earnings ratio is unlikely to be the product of differences in human capital attributes between Swedish and British women.
3. The database has been constructed by researchers in the Labour and Industry Research Unit at the University of Queensland. It currently contains over 200 variables, most of which are based on OECD and ILO statistics. The sixteen countries included were chosen on the basis of their comparability and the availability of data. They are Australia, Austria, Belgium, Canada, Denmark, Finland, France, Germany, Italy, Japan, Netherlands, Norway, Sweden, Switzerland, the UK and the USA. Details on all variables are provided in the Appendix to this chapter (see above).
4. For a discussion of the difficulties of measuring segregation for the purposes of cross-national comparison see Blackburn, Jarman and Siltanen (1993) and the ensuing debates in *Work, Employment and Society*.
5. For example, variables unrelated to the manufacturing sector such as the extent of public-sector employment.
6. There is also some variation in the number of industries and types of workers included for different countries, hence the series has some limitations both for cross-national comparison and as an inclusive measure of earnings differentials.

7. Diagnostic procedures to test the reliability of the OLS results are described in the Appendix.

8. Growth in, as opposed to absolute measures of, GDP and employment are the more theoretically sound control variables as they would be more likely to stimulate movements in equity outcomes. Nevertheless, the absolute measures were also tested in analyses of the data. However, they did not add to the findings.

9. Limited availability of non-agricultural industry data meant that the analysis was restricted to Australia, Belgium, Denmark, Germany, Japan, Netherlands, Switzerland and the UK.

10. Of the sixteen countries in the data set, ILO manufacturing earnings data was not available for Austria, Italy, Canada and the USA. Alternative sources were used for Canada and the USA (see details in the Appendix), but no alternatives were found for Austria and Italy. The analysis therefore utilizes data from fourteen countries.

11. Our analyses also demonstrated a relationship between the level of government employment and pay equity. This finding also has potential ramifications for the globalization debate, as a high level of public employment is likely to be indicative of the type of intervention that is purported to be under threat with globalization. However, the difficulties of extrapolating from manufacturing data (even though we have also used a broader measure of earnings) mean some caution is required in interpretation. In this chapter, our central focus remains with the issue of wage bargaining centralization.

12. This was on matters additional to equal pay, such as sympathy strikes, rights of unions in collective bargaining and dismissal.

13. Furthermore, the coefficients of the country dummies are not clearly interpretable, representing differences between individual countries and the reference country omitted from the analysis. Coefficients will therefore vary depending on which country is omitted, and significance levels are similarly misleading (see Stimson, 1985, p. 936).

8 LABOUR CLAUSES, THE WORLD TRADE ORGANIZATION AND CHILD LABOUR IN INDIA

Robert Castle, D. P. Chaudhri, Chris Nyland and Trang Nguyen

The recent acceleration in the process of economic globalization has induced widespread concern that governments and labour organizations may no longer be able to preserve those 'core' labour standards the International Labour Office (ILO) deems fundamental to human dignity. In 1993 this concern led the International Confederation of Free Trade Unions (ICFTU) to call for the inclusion of a labour clause in the programme of the World Trade Organization (WTO) that would aid the preservation of these basic rights (ILO, 1994a; ICFTU, 1994). Though this demand was not endorsed by the WTO, it has won support from governments in North America and from the European Parliament and was debated at the WTO's first Ministerial Meeting in December 1996. The leaders of the many institutions promoting a labour clause argue that if international trade and the defence of labour standards are not linked there may occur a global devaluation of employment conditions with nations engaging in a competitive 'race to the bottom' (US Department of State, 1994).

This chapter examines the labour clause proposal by focusing on the issue of child labour, a problem that the ILO has addressed as a fundamental issue since its inception in 1919. The chapter begins by discussing the recent difficulties the ILO has experienced in maintaining respect for its standard-setting procedures and the consequent emergence of the demand for alternative instruments that can ensure these standards. It then proceeds to detail the recent history of child labour in India and argues that the policies being promoted by recent Indian governments may show a way forward for those seeking a solution to the trade-rights issue acceptable to both the developed and the developing nations. It examines the interaction between national and international regulation in tackling an issue that has supranational as well as national dimensions in an increasingly integrated world economy.

The ILO and the Demand for a Labour Clause

The main international body which regulates labour is the International Labour Office (ILO) which was established in 1919. Over the last 75 years it has formulated a series of voluntary conventions which its members are free to ratify or ignore as they choose (see Table 8.1 for a summary of ratification of conventions). The ILO's voluntarist approach and tripartite structure were developed as instruments for improving living standards and relieving the inequalities and injustices experienced by workers by way of gradual reform rather than revolution. As Emil Vandervelde, one of the founders of the ILO observed in 1919, 'there are two methods of making the revolution which we feel is happening throughout the world, the Russian and the British method. It is the British method which has triumphed in the Labour Commission' (cited in Butler, 1951, p. 175). The 1919 Preamble to the ILO's constitution states that 'the failure of any nation to adopt humane conditions of labour is an obstacle in the way of other nations which desire to improve the conditions in their own countries' (Hansenne, 1996). In other words, an aim of the ILO has always been to ensure that states which elect to introduce progressive social reforms in the process of economic development are not disadvantaged in international competition as a consequence.

The voluntary nature of the ILO's system of ratification has been a major factor contributing to the organization's survival and success, for it has meant that its conventions have not been imposed on nations that could not accept all their provisions and hence would feel forced to resign should they be compelled to do so. Also important in the ILO's survival were the seven decades of the cold war, a struggle that led employers in the capitalist world to accept important parts of the ILO's reform agenda much more readily than would otherwise have been the case (Creighton, 1996). At the same time the fact that nations can ignore the ILO's conventions by simply refusing to grant ratification limits the organization's capacity to act as an agent of progressive social reform, a weakness that has become more apparent in recent years with the acceleration of the globalization process and the demise of the Soviet Union.

One important measure of the inability of the ILO to ensure respect for its standards is the fact (noted in Table 8.1) that no more than 70 per cent of its

Table 8.1 *ILO conventions by sub-periods and regions*

	The Americas	Africa	Asia and the Pacific	Europe	Total	Total no. of ratifications	Total no. of conventions[1]
Situation on 31 December 1942[2]							
Total no. of ratifications	237	11	87	521	856	856	
No. of member states	22	4	9	26	61		67
Average rate of ratification	10.8	2.8	9.7	20.0	14.0		
1945–54							
New ratifications	156	7	112	331	606	1462	
No. of member states	22	5	17	30	74		103
Average rate of ratification	17.9	3.6	11.7	28.4	19.8		
1955–64							
New ratifications	258	690	190	377	1515	2977	
No. of member states	24	34	23	31	112		122
Average rate of ratification	27.1	20.8	16.8	39.6	26.6		
1965–74							
New ratifications	285	253	171	367	1076	4053	
No. of member states	26	37	33	33	129		140
Average rate of ratification	36.0	26.0	17.0	48.4	31.4		

Table 8.1 *Continued*

1975–84						
New ratifications	338	281	149	346	1114	5167
No. of member states	33	49	36	34	152	
Average rate of ratification	38.6	25.3	19.7	57.1	34.0	159
1985–94						
New ratifications	130	92	71	700	993	6160
No. of member states	33	51	37	50	171	
Average rate of ratification	42.5	26.2	21.1	52.8	36.0	175
Whole period 1945–94						
New ratifications	1167	1323	693	2121	5304	
Increase in no. of member states	11	47	28	24	110	
Total number of ratifications 1919–94	1404	1334	780	2642	6160	

Notes:

[1] Total number of conventions adopted by the ILO at the end of the respective period.

[2] The number of ratifications and the number of member states do not reflect fluctuations due to the withdrawal and readmission of several member states.

Source: Submission by the Department of Industrial Relations to the Tripartite Working Party on Labour Standards, June 1995.

member states have ratified its core conventions. The Conventions that make up this core are as follows:

- freedom of association – workers and employers have the right to establish and join organizations of their own choosing without prior authorization (ILO Conventions 87 & 98),
- freedom from forced labour (ILO Conventions 29 & 105),
- freedom from discrimination (ILO Conventions 100 & 111),
- minimum age for the employment of children (ILO Convention 138).

The fact that not even these basic standards have been ratified by all member states has been compounded in recent years by the fact that the whole pace of ratification has slowed considerably with this trend being particularly noticeable among the Asian nations. No convention adopted since 1976 has attracted as many as 50 ratifications; none adopted in the last ten years has attracted 25; and none adopted since 1987 has reached double figures. This decline in the significance of the ILO's standard-setting procedures was brought to crisis point in the late 1980s by the collapse of the USSR, a development that convinced many Western employers and the governments of developing nations that it was no longer necessary to pander to the ILO's tripartism and what was seen as its overly enthusiastic and prescriptive approach to human/ labour rights. Reflecting their dissatisfaction with the ILO's means of establishing standards and the prescriptive nature of these standards, governments turned increasingly to alternative forums when they found it necessary to express their humanity.

As a consequence, over the last decade other UN organizations, such as UNICEF, have been much more successful in obtaining ratification of conventions relating to rights. Child labour, for example, is an area of reform that was among the earliest subjects of ILO conventions (Conventions 5 & 6, 1919) and its elimination is one of the organization's 'core' goals. In 1973 the ILO codified its previous conventions on child labour into a single convention (Convention 138) but because the new standard was so prescriptive it received only 46 ratifications over the following two decades with no country in the Asia-Pacific region, including Australia, electing to ratify. By contrast, the Convention on the Rights of the Child (1989) for which UNICEF has responsibility, and which is much less prescriptive, has already attracted ratification from 156 countries.

One result of the ILO's declining relevance has been that the United States, a leader among those states now promoting the multilateral regulation of labour standards, has become increasingly active in the promotion of unilateral action to defend labour rights. This development is somewhat ironic, for a significant factor inducing the undermining of the ILO was the lack of support it received from the USA through the 1980s. Thus the US government has enacted measures such as the Child Labour Deterrence Act (1993), the Super 301 provisions of the Omnibus Trade Act (1988) which retaliates against countries deemed to be unfair traders, and recent laws which penalize companies from third countries as well as American firms which invest in nations deemed by the USA to support terrorism. Such measures appear *prima facie* to be illegal under GATT and WTO rules but are nevertheless being promoted vigorously by the Americans because of the increasing anxiety among the US population at what it perceives to be a serious threat to their well-being posed by those nations which do not respect even the most fundamental rights of labour. Increasing impatience with the level of protection that multilateral organizations can provide to developed countries that respect core labour standards has also been voiced by the European Union, Canada and Japan through the 1990s. As a consequence, while Japan has yet to take any decided action, the European Union has joined the USA in enacting unilateral bulwarks aimed at preserving labour rights while concomitantly calling for a strengthening of the multilateral system. Child labour has been specially targeted.

It is pressure from these nations that has made the demand for a labour clause an issue that developing nations are finding increasingly difficult to dismiss. The governments of these nations are well aware that the developed states have the capacity to impose a labour clause on them. That this is the case was shown by the fact that it was pressure from the USA and EU that induced the adoption of changes to the GATT dispute settlement procedures which now give the WTO the power to enforce whatever provisions its members choose to adopt. Whereas the GATT procedures only operated if the parties to the dispute consented, it is a condition of membership of the WTO that members automatically accept the jurisdiction of WTO panels. A country can no longer veto a panel decision which goes against it, and if the parties do not apply the recommendations set out in the panels' report within 60 days (Article 16), then the injured state may seek compensation or the suspension of concessions (Article 22). Penalties under Article 22 could include sanctions on other products or areas of trade from the offending country (Nguyen, 1995).

The possibility that the WTO would embrace a labour clause backed by these powers has raised great dismay among the developing countries, with the ASEAN states being particularly vehement in their opposition. At the Marrakesh meeting in 1994, this response prevented a labour clause from being included in the WTO programme. Nevertheless, the issue was kept very much alive by the North Americans and the Europeans who insisted on having the clause referred to the WTO's preparatory committee and subsequently insisted that labour standards be debated at the first Ministerial Meeting held in Singapore in December 1996. As a result the Ministerial declaration which concluded the meeting included an endorsement of the ILO as the main body responsible for labour standards, but with the ILO working closely with the WTO.

The possibility of linking an enforceable labour clause to WTO membership poses severe problems for many developing countries. In recent years most of these nations have adopted an outward-oriented development strategy based on the successful model pioneered by the Asian newly-industrializing economies in the 1970s, which has been promoted by agencies like the World Bank and by economists such as Bhagwati and Hudec (1996). This has replaced the post-colonial emphasis on import substitution championed in the 1960s by Prebisch and UNCTAD. A fundamental element of the outward-oriented strategy is access to both the consumer and capital markets of the developed countries, and this is a requirement that for many would be threatened should this access be tied to respect for basic labour standards. For this reason most developing nations have joined the Western employers in opposing all attempts to extend the scope of international labour regulation.

The hope of the developing nations is that competition between the investors of the developed states will undermine their governments' attempts to compel respect for basic labour rights. This strategy, however, is being countered by the fact that the North Americans, the EU and at times the Japanese are acting in concert. The developing nations cannot, therefore, simply ignore the demands of the developed states and hence there has been considerable negotiation over the last two years to find a formula on core labour standards acceptable to all present and potential signatories to the WTO agreement. This process led to the developing nations and the employers of the developed states re-evaluating their earlier antagonism to the ILO. This is a trend that has accelerated since 1994 when the ILO was first given an opportunity to play a major role in the labour–trade debate by US Labor Secretary Robert Reich. At a US-sponsored symposium to honour the seventy-fifth anniversary of the ILO, the USA offered the developing nations a middle way between an ineffectual ILO and a rigorously dominant WTO. Reich proposed that strengthened ILO conventions should be the basis of appropriate labour standards for civilized nations. He accepted that not every country could be expected to meet all standards immediately. Instead the international community should specify a core list of human rights that must be enjoyed by all workers irrespective of a nation's level of economic development together with a second more nuanced list of standards linked to a country's level of economic development (Reich, 1994).

Reich's offer has received support from the ILO Secretariat, and at the 1994 ILO Conference they presented a report entitled *The Social Dimensions of the Liberalisation of World Trade* which examined ways in which the ILO could reconcile its reliance on co-operation with its need to defend basic labour standards. The report proposed the development of a multilateral approach to labour standards, centred on the notion that ILO member states would guarantee to honour its core standards, with this promise backed by the ILO's regulatory mechanisms which would have the role of monitoring individual economies to ensure that measurable results were delivered. Alternatively, it was suggested, it might be necessary to investigate the possibility of drawing on support from the WTO (ILO, 1994b).

The Secretariat's proposals were applauded by most of the developed states, a minority of radical developing nations such as Nicaragua, and the Workers' Group at the International Labour Conference. The latter body subsequently accepted that a strengthened ILO may be a more viable way of securing international co-operation on labour standards than an enforceable WTO clause. In doing so, however, the Workers' Group have made it clear that if respect for ILO instruments is not forthcoming they would be compelled to conclude they had no choice but to insist on the direct linking of trade and labour rights (ICFTU, 1994).

Many developing countries are also examining the implications of these alternatives and in the period since 1994 these nations have become increasingly enthusiastic, indeed insistent, that the ILO is the correct and the only place to debate the labour standards issue, a stance reflected in the WTO Singapore declaration.

Irrespective of which forum eventually becomes the centre of debate, it is imperative that discussion move beyond the level of generality and abstraction that has thus far predominated at an international level. In short we need detailed empirical evidence of which sectors of society are likely to be affected by the various forms of regulation that have been proposed. In the case of child labour, for example, a WTO clause would only directly influence a small proportion of the child labour force in many countries even though it would target the high-profile areas of children in manufacturing, producing goods such as footballs and sports shoes for leading multinational companies. The informal and family sectors, in particular, would remain untouched. However, the international community needs an approach that will reach child labourers in all areas of developing economies. To look at how a mixture of national and multilateral measures could affect labour standards, we now turn to the recent history of child labour reform in India.

Child-focused Policy Initiatives in India, 1986–96

Recognition that the alternatives on offer from the governments of the developed nations, the ILO and organized labour require more than just debate has induced many individual governments to reassess their situation. In the case of India this new difficulty has added to the determination of recent governments to eradicate child labour. In putting forward this latter sugges-tion it is important to stress that the trade issue is far from being the only factor that has motivated Indian governments to strive to eliminate this scourge. At least three other fundamental determinants have contributed to the emphasis the Indian state now places on this area of labour reform. First, most analysts now emphasize the role of human resource development in the promotion of industrial productivity and this especially in relation to basic education. The experience of East Asia has shown that this factor is particularly important to states that embrace export-oriented development. For this strategy to be sustained it would appear to be vital that the state accelerate the creation of a skilled labour force capable of producing high value-added products (IBRD, 1994). Second, through the 1990s Indian governments placed greater empha-sis on the need to fulfill their obligations, enshrined in 'The Directive Principles of State Policy' of the Constitution of India, and also as citizens of the world by promoting respect for standards like those encapsulated in universal declarations such as the Convention on the Rights of the Child.

A third factor, and one that will be sketched in greater detail, is the fact that the recent history of India has highlighted the point that the child labour and school education policies of the different states of India have produced widely divergent results. This factor is of particular importance to the trade–labour rights debate because much of this discussion has been either assertive or deductive in character with a meagre empirical basis. What relevant empirical research exists primarily relates to shifts in relative wages and prices (e.g. Wood, 1994). However, if effective means of preserving and/or advancing basic labour rights are to be created, it is important that we have a detailed knowledge of the problems we are seeking to resolve. In the case of child labour this requires a detailed understanding of the present scale and dynam-ics of the problem.

Estimates of the size and composition of child labour in India (1961–96), computed from Census and other sources, are reported in Tables 8.2 and 8.3.

The estimated magnitudes for 1991, compared to a child population aged 5 to 14 years of 203 million are: full-time child workers (0–14 years), 12.7 million; full-time plus marginal child workers, 23.3 million; and non-students and non-workers, 97.6 million. *Child labour* is a sub-set of the *child population* and is directly linked to another related sub-set, namely *non-working* children whose number is at least three times larger than child labourers. Details pertaining to growth rates and sectoral shares, including projections to 2001, are reported in Tables 8.2 and 8.3.

The traditional agricultural sector employed 76 per cent of child labour in 1991. Comparable figures for 1981 are 77 per cent and 69 per cent in 1961. The share of manufacturing in the employment of child labour increased from 3.1 in 1971 to 5.7 per cent in 1991. The major part of the efforts of those who advocate a labour clause has targeted this latter segment which consists of about 0.65 million child workers. In absolute size in 1991, the number of full-time wage-based (excluding children working on their own family farms) child agricultural labourers was 5.4 million. However, it is the plight of children working in factories that has attracted most attention in the West and is the main focus of attempts by Western governments, trade unions and human-itarian groups to eliminate child labour.

A wide diversity in the pace and pattern of child labour use, its growth and subsequent decline can be seen in the different regions of India. In half of its states child labour is declining fast while in others it is declining slowly. Variations across states in labour-participation rates of children are also enormous with Kerala at 1 per cent and Andra Pradesh at 17 per cent for male children in 1981. Diversity can also be perceived between urban and rural development with the employment of child workers in the urban sector growing fast while concomitantly declining slowly in rural India. Interstate variations in these outcomes are very large, with Kerala reporting the lowest incidence and Uttar Pradesh the highest increase of urban child labour. Four activities registering fast growth in the use of child labour between 1961 and 1991 are manufacturing, transport, storage and communication, trade and commerce, and agricultural labourers.

The bimodal grouping of the states in terms of economic development, structural change and the incidence of child labour is unmistakable. The leaders and laggards in 1961 retained their relative positions in 1991 suggest-ing the presence of mutually reinforcing virtuous and vicious circles. The incidence of child labour was negatively correlated with per capita income, infrastructure development, school enrolment ratios and female participation rates in non-agricultural work. It was positively correlated with incidence of poverty, illiteracy and the percentage of the labour force in agriculture.

Table 8.2 *All-India: child population and child labour, 1961–2001 (in thousands)*

	1961	1971	1981	1991*	1996*	2001*	1961–71	1971–81	1981–91	1991–96	1996–2001
Total child population (5–14 yrs)	113,980	150,778	179,597	203,300	192,228	189,826	2.84	1.76	1.25	-0.56	-0.13
Total child workers #	14,470	10,754	11,196	12,622	12,720	10,984	-2.92	0.40	1.24	0.05	-1.46
Male child population	59,349	78,708	93,532	105,559	99,952	98,856	2.84	1.74	1.22	-0.54	-0.11
Non-workers	50,658	70,815	86,095	97,234	91,575	91,609	3.41	1.97	1.22	-0.60	0.00
Students (full-time)	23,641	32,510	49,086	57,384	54,537	52,748	3.24	4.21	1.57	-0.51	-0.33
Not workers or students	27,017	38,305	37,008	39,849	37,037	38,860	3.55	-0.34	0.74	-0.73	0.48
Male child worker total #	8,690	7,892	7,438	8,325	8,377	7,247	-0.96	-0.59	1.13	0.06	-1.44
Cultivators	4,225	3,042	2,903	3,213	3,192	2,754	-3.23	-0.46	1.02	-0.07	-1.46
Agricultural labourers	1,752	3,004	2,801	3,109	3,097	2,673	5.54	0.70	1.05	-0.04	-1.46
Mining, quarrying, etc.	837	758	586	652	651	562	-0.99	-2.54	1.08	-0.02	-1.45
Household industry	927	199	234	267	274	238	-14.26	1.64	1.30	0.29	-1.40
Manufacturing (not household industry)	185	240	396	471	506	443	2.63	5.12	1.75	0.71	-1.32
Construction	44	42	54	64	68	59	-0.39	2.54	1.70	0.55	-1.35
Trade and commerce	129	197	228	273	295	259	4.34	1.47	1.80	0.80	-1.30
Transport, storage and communications	21	35	32	39	42	37	5.34	-0.95	1.91	0.86	-1.29
Other services	567	282	200	237	251	219	-6.75	-3.39	1.71	0.59	-1.34

Table 8.2 *Continued*

Female child population	54,631	72,070	86,064	97,740	92,275	90,969	2.81	1.79	1.28	-0.57	-0.14
Non-workers	48,851	69,208	82,306	93,403	87,932	87,232	3.54	1.75	1.27	-0.60	-0.08
Students (full-time)	10,954	18,181	29,773	35,586	33,999	31,937	5.20	5.06	1.80	-0.46	-0.62
Not workers or students	37,897	51,026	52,533	57,817	53,933	55,295	3.02	0.29	0.96	-0.69	0.25
Female child worker total #	5,779	2,861	3,757	4,337	4,342	3,737	-6.79	2.76	1.44	0.01	-1.49
Cultivators	3,170	754	1,095	1,251	1,241	1,067	-13.38	3.81	1.34	-0.08	-1.51
Agricultural labourers	1,438	1,582	1,986	2,277	2,266	1,948	0.96	2.30	1.38	-0.05	-1.50
Mining, quarrying, etc.	202	151	153	178	177	153	-2.89	0.17	1.49	-0.04	-1.50
Household industry	555	139	198	233	239	207	-12.93	3.63	1.65	0.25	-1.44
Manufacturing (not household industry)	55	74	147	183	187	162	3.02	7.10	2.20	0.17	-1.40
Construction	22	17	31	36	37	32	-2.56	5.97	1.52	0.33	-1.43
Trade and commerce	24	13	20	24	25	22	-5.49	4.06	1.52	0.46	-1.40
Transport, storage and communications	2	6	3	6	6	5	10.30	-6.30	6.82	0.46	-1.40
Other services	307	123	120	149	182	140	-8.71	-0.23	2.17	2.01	-2.66

Notes:

* Projections using Metagraphics Software Corporation's PEOPLE and WORKERS projection modules 1987–88 (1981 participation rates assumed).

Census does not give breakdown for age group 0–14. National Sample Survey estimates suggest that the core of labour is in age group 10–14. Hence projections for 1996 and 2001 are for 10–14.

Sources: Census of India 1961, 1971, 1981 and 1991 and the Centre for Monitoring of the Indian Economy *Basic Statistics Relating to the Indian Economy*, Vol. 2, *States*, September 1984.

Table 8.3 *Growth rate of child population, labour and 'nowhere' children in the major states of India, 1961–91*

States	Child population 0–14 years			Child labour 0–14 years			'Nowhere' children 0–14 years		
	1961–71	1971–81	1981–91	1961–71	1971–81	1981–91	1961–71	1971–81	1981–91
Andhra Pradesh	2.2	1.6	0.5	-1.6	0.8	0.3	3.6	-0.2	0.5
Bihar	2.0	2.0	1.4	-3.7	-1.7	1.8	3.7	0.5	1.3
Gujarat	2.7	1.4	0.1	-1.7	-1.1	0.0	3.3	-0.5	0.3
Haryana	2.8	1.5	1.9	-4.2	0.3	1.4	3.1	2.0	2.1
Himachal Pradesh	2.8	1.7	0.0	-0.8	-1.7	0.7	1.0	-0.6	-0.4
Harnataka	2.3	1.7	0.5	-2.1	1.8	0.7	3.2	0.2	0.0
Kerala	1.8	0.3	-0.9	-2.8	-4.8	-0.2	0.1	-3.7	-0.5
Madhya Pradesh	3.3	1.7	1.1	-2.9	2.1	1.3	5.3	0.4	0.8
Maharashtra	2.6	1.5	1.1	-3.4	2.5	0.4	3.1	-1.1	0.3
Orissa	3.1	1.2	-0.3	-2.7	0.5	0.1	5.2	-0.4	-0.4
Punjab	2.8	1.0	1.3	-3.0	-2.6	0.7	3.0	-2.0	0.5
Rajasthan	2.9	2.5	1.2	-6.1	0.0	2.3	5.0	1.5	1.4
Tamil Nadu	2.1	0.9	-0.3	-3.5	2.0	-0.7	2.0	-0.2	-0.1
Uttar Pradesh	2.2	2.3	1.6	-3.7	-0.5	7.5	2.0	1.9	0.5
West Bengal	2.9	1.1	0.7	1.3	0.3	0.8	3.6	-0.3	0.2
All India	2.5	1.3	1.2	-2.9	0.4	1.2	3.2	0.0	0.9

Sources: Census of India 1961, 1971, 1981 and our estimates for 1991. Data for 1991 is our estimate based on population shares of Sample Registration Scheme and projections from 1981 with optimistic assumptions of declining Total Fertility Rate. The 1961–71, 1971–81 rates are based on Actual Census.

It is states with the slower pace of demographic transition (i.e. high total fertility rates and declining child mortality rates), static/inferior technology (reflected in low investment and low productivity per worker) and an absence of child-focused effective public policy which face a perpetuation of the vicious circle where demand for and supply of child labour grow through a mutually reinforcing process. Five of India's 22 states are still caught in this cycle, while eight have definitely broken out of it, with child labour declining rapidly in these states.

The liberalization programme followed by Indian governments in recent years has increased the openness of the economy. This has exposed old industries to global competition triggering technological change. Initially, this may increase the demand for child labour as these industries strive to cut costs to compete against better capitalized, more technologically advanced competitors, both national and international. This process is identical to that noted by Marx (1974, p. 394) in the first industrial revolution. Machinery enabled weaker women and children to be substituted for men. Many of the newer processes require skills and training more than muscle power so that new processes require better trained and educated labour. Numerous authors (e.g. Krishna, 1996, pp. 56–8) have noted the heavy use of child labour in old industries and this has also been confirmed by a number of recent reports on the incidence of child labour in South Asia (National Labour Institute, 1992a, 1993; Vijayagopalan, 1993; Juyal, 1993). These industries, with the exception of carpet making and some handicrafts, are mainly aimed at the domestic market (e.g. brick and tile making) rather than the international market. However, there are increasing signs that unscrupulous employers are continuing to use child labour even with new technology in areas such as packing, checking and some remaining intricate labour-intensive tasks in the production of clothing, footware and toys for the international market. Despite these cases, as inferior technology is phased out, the globalization process is expected to reduce the demand for child labour as the economy embraces new processes requiring more highly skilled workers. How long this process will take is dependent to a significant extent on the national policies embraced by national and state governments (as Marx, 1974, p. 371, again noted).

Awareness of the recent history of child labour in India, and the significant effects that widely divergent state policies have had on its prevalence, have been important influences motivating the nation's politicians, press and NGOs to intensify their demands for effective national reform. This is a demand that was taken up with some vigour by the Congress Party following the 1991 elections and with much greater enthusiasm by the left coalition that came to office in 1996. Indeed it is possible to date the present campaign to eradicate child labour in India from the mid-1980s. In 1986 the Federal Government enacted a Child Labour Employment Prohibition and Regulation Act that had been two years in preparation. The Act incorporated major features of earlier legislation pertaining to prohibition of employment of child workers (age group 0–14 years) in hazardous industries and activities. However, while it included clear and adequate deterrents aimed at the prohibition of child labour in these areas, it exempted family, non-wage-based enterprises and the agricultural sector. As these were the areas where most children are employed, this legislation was a far from adequate response to the child labour problem, an inadequacy compounded by the fact that the law was thin as regards regulation and enforcement. In short the new law retained many of the weaknesses inherent in earlier legislation. A National Policy on Child Labour was announced in 1987 and rules relating to child labour were further strengthened in 1988 (National Labour Institute, 1992b).

Following the elections of 1991, the Congress Party made it clear that it was determined to remedy this situation. Its resolve was highlighted in 1992 by its decision to ratify the UN Convention on the Rights of the Child. Ratification requires a state to institutionalize the enforcement of its provisions. One manifestation of this requirement was the 1994 creation of a National Authority on the Elimination of Child Labour (NAECL). This body is chaired by the Federal Minister of Labour, has nine secretaries of various ministries as ex-officio members and must report to the Parliament at least once a year. In 1995, at the behest of the NAECL, reform was further advanced by the creation of Child Labour cells in each state with some states also establishing a Task Force for the Elimination of Child Labour. The NAECL also identified 137 administrative Districts (out of a total of 362) in 11 states which had a high incidence of child labour and established District Committees in each of these areas to promote the campaign with their membership including NGOs, members of parliament and local officials. These committees have a mandatory obligation to report to the NAECL.

Carrying forward the reform programme in early 1996 the Congress government upgraded the Child Labour Cell of the National Labour Institute to the V. V. Giri Centre for Child Labour Studies. This body has also received substantial support from both UNICEF and the ILO, the latter being able to launch a 'Global Offensive' against child labour in 1991 as a consequence of having received a contribution from the German government of DM50 million for a period of five years to fund the campaign. This assistance also made possible the creation of the ILO's International Programme on the Elimination of Child Labour (IPEC), a body which has given new impetus to the ILO's operational activities in the field.

In seeking to combat child labour in the first half of the 1990s the government also strove to develop effective instruments that would enhance other aspects of children's quality of life. In so doing it was assisted by the technical and financial support the UN has promised all nations that promote respect for basic human rights. Thus along with the ILO's support (ILO's Child Labour Action Support Programme and IPEC), India received assistance from UNICEF in its campaign to overcome infant mortality and improve child welfare and from UNESCO and UNICEF it received help with school enrolments and retention rates. Moreover, technical and financial inputs from these UN agencies were augmented by the Indian government's adoption of time-bound targets in the areas of health, nutrition, water and sanitation, education, child labour and the creation of enabling legislation in relation to the Convention on the Rights of the Child.

The campaign to combat child labour was promised a further catalyst in 1995 when the Congress government announced it would introduce amendments to the Child Labour Employment Prohibition and Regulation Act that would plug the loopholes in the 1986 law. This was a promise the Congress Party was subsequently to prove unable to deliver because in the elections of 1996 it was replaced in government by the United Front minority coalition. This latter development, however, far from stalling the reform movement, promised greatly to accelerate the campaign to eliminate child labour. In its first national budget, produced in July 1996, the new administration dramatically increased the reform targets set by the former government. The allocation to school education was increased by 40 per cent and that of the Ministry of Labour's Child Labour cell was increased by 50 per cent. These increases, at a time of overall fiscal tightening, indicate the political and social will being applied to this core area of labour rights within India.

Further evidence of the resolve of the new government was provided in August 1996 at a conference of Education Ministers held in New Delhi at which the Union Human Resource Development Minister, Mr S. R. Bommai, announced that 'India would universalise primary education by the turn of the century, a year earlier than that already declared by UNESCO as being unattainable'. When making his announcement Bommai declared that 'what could not be achieved in 40 years can be achieved in three years if there is a political will'. Details of how this goal is to be achieved were to be worked out by a committee chaired by the Minister of State for Human Resource Development. This committee is comprised of twelve State Education Ministers, a member of the Planning Commission and the Adviser to the Jammu and Kashmir Government. It was instructed to report in two months and advised that when seeking to 'identify' the resources needed to attain universal basic education it should remember that the state of Kerala achieved this goal by electing to spend 40 per cent of its budget resources on education. Further, it should be remembered that the universalizing of elementary education cannot be accomplished unless the focus is turned on the education of girls, children from weaker sections of society and women. Finally, Bommai reminded all at the conference that the United Front's common minimum programme 'envisaged amendment of the Constitution to make universal elementary education a justiciable fundamental right'.

The Commission on Labour Standards and International Trade submitted its three-volume report to the Government of India in February 1996. The Chairman, Dr Subramanian Swami, emphasizing the potential role of the ILO in enforcing labour standards, made a pointed reference to the issue of child labour in his press release on the report. It states 'that the government should not brook any defence of child labour at any forum on any ground'. There should be a strict moral determination of the state that children have to be in schools, irrespective of their economic plight, environment or background, and not in factories. According to the Commission's consultants, the child labour force at the time was estimated at 25 million, was growing at 4 per cent per year and required a plan outlay of Rs15,000 crores (US$500 million) to abolish it in reality. Chaudhri's (1996) estimate of full-time child labour is about 14 million with another 10 million children as marginal workers. Growth of child labour in different states of India according to Chaudhri (1996) varies from 7 per cent in Uttar Pradesh to minus 0.7 per cent in Tamil Nadu. Nationally growth during 1981–91 was 1.2 per cent. Projections to 2001 suggest an annual decline of 1.44 per cent. A large financial outlay is required but, in itself, given the inefficiency of the primary school system in states with child labour growth, would achieve very little. A reformulated national strategy of the type promised recently is needed. However, the reality on the ground in different states of India provides a cause for optimism in some regions and alarm in the rest of India.

Policy Implications

India's campaign to eradicate child labour is a development that is of enormous significance for the trade–labour standards debate. If the campaign proves successful in both reducing child labour and overcoming systemic discrimination it will constitute a dramatic reply, even if this has not been its primary objective, to those who have offered the developing nations access to their economies in return for ensuring the basic rights of labour. Only 6 per cent of Indian child workers can be directly targeted through a WTO labour clause but the goal embraced by the Federal Government has been the complete elimination of this scourge. If successful, India's response will place an onus on the developed nations that have promised to deliver substantial assistance to nations that guarantee basic labour rights to deliver on these promises. This means increased direct support to both the nations involved and multilateral organizations such as the ILO. Were this approach to reform to be widely adopted by other developing nations, moreover, it would render the present trade–labour standards policy promoted by the developed nations largely redundant. This would place greater pressure on the governments of the developed states to create alternative policies that can deal effectively with those sectors of their societies that are highly vulnerable to competition from the developing states.

At the same time India's campaign to combat child labour and discrimination also poses critical policy difficulties for many developing nations. Coming from a regime that already guarantees the right of association and freedom from forced labour, India's policies challenge those developing states that insist it is unreasonable to expect them to respect the basic rights of labour. If India can deliver these rights to its people, what of the claims of other nations that their poverty makes it impossible for them to do so or who insist that ILO standards are not appropriate for developing societies? And if the ILO's standards do have relevance, what becomes of the demand that the ILO should become merely a specialist funding and technical support agency strengthened only in that it should be given more funds by the developed nations to extend its technical assistance?

In short, if India perseveres with its present programme it will carry the trade–labour standards debate to a new level. Its policy of reform is demonstrating that very significant gains can be achieved in the area of basic labour rights without the enactment of a WTO labour clause. As a consequence of the pressure already applied by the developed states, the major employer organizations and the governments of the developing states are now in agreement that the ILO is the correct instrument to ensure the attainment and/or the preservation of labour's rights (Hansenne, 1996). If these sectors are in fact willing to accept the compromise of a strengthened ILO, already partially urged by organized labour, we suggest this option should be taken up by the international community. We would also observe that, though it may prove to be the case that the challenge to basic labour standards presently being mounted by employers in the developing nations and their allies in the developed states is only transitory, this is a possibility which the governments of the advanced capitalist democracies cannot afford to take on faith. It is for this reason that the continuing possibility of a WTO clause and/or unified action by the USA and the EU is needed to ensure that real progress is attained. If this possibility is not sustained it is all too probable that the claim of the developing nations that the ILO is the proper forum for debating labour issues will simply prove to be a means of ensuring reform does not move beyond debate. Pressure from the international community is leading to national and regional policy action on child labour in India which can extend far beyond the formal factory sector to capture the majority of children in employment. Policy actions, legislation and effective regulation have had an effect on hastening the elimination of full-time child labour in developed countries. If this is to occur in poorer developing countries, it needs not only regulation but resources for enforcement and a range of other policies such as education and family support which the developed nations will have to sustain if they are to achieve a genuine reduction in child labour. Globalization may in the long run hasten this process.

The willingness of countries to adopt UN Conventions, such as that on the Rights of the Child, the attraction of the benefits of joining the WTO and the threat to their development strategies, should they lose access to markets in developed countries, mean that there is a more receptive climate for measures to improve the ILO's labour standards than at any time in recent years. An increased and strengthened role for the ILO's standard-setting procedures may be the best way to achieve multilateral and national progress on labour rights at this time rather than by forcing a labour standard through the WTO. Many developing nations are as yet still unwilling to cede powers over issues such as labour standards to multilateral organizations. A gradualist approach through greater ILO powers may well yield better results in the medium term than the development of untried new areas for international law. But if this approach fails, the USA and the EU will invariably insist upon the adoption of a labour standards clause by the WTO.

Such an outcome is likely to hurt the cause of child labour by concentrating on children in the traded goods sector which is a small fraction of total child labour (i.e. about 6 per cent for India) and hence fail to provide for the needs of child labourers who produce for the domestic economy and those 75 million 'nowhere' children who in India labour as producers of use-value in the homes of their parents. A strengthened ILO with an invigorated international programme for the elimination of child labour, on the other hand, has a great chance of achieving much wider goals. The outcome is largely in the hands of the developing countries who have been given room to manoeuvre by Robert Reich, the EU and trade unions in the developed countries. However, despite greater flexibility on means, there seems little doubt as to the resolve of the major OECD countries to achieve international action on labour standards before the new millennium. Indeed in September 1997 the US Congress made clear its determination to oppose social dumping and promote respect for worker rights by low-wage nations by passing a law that prohibits the import of products made with forced child labour. This legislation, which aims to end such child labour around the world, extends the 1930 tariff law that bars goods made with convict labour, and is specifically aimed at the producers of products such as carpets, toys and clothing. Following its passage a spokeswoman for the US National Consumers' League observed, 'now, hopefully, our Government can do the job of keeping these products out of the United States'. Likewise, Vulliamy (1997, p. 13) reports that upon hearing that the legislation had been passed, Terry Collingsworth of the International Labor Rights Fund, who toured India and Nepal for four years, exclaimed: 'You could walk into the factories at will and see children looking like they could fall over at any moment. Supervisors used hot irons to sear shut cuts on the children's fingers from endless stitching so they would not bleed on the fabrics.' The legislation was 'an incredible breakthrough'. This is the perspective on child labour at present prevalent in the developed nations. It is a perspective that the developing counties must try to counter by means other than bluster. Via a strengthened ILO they have an alternative to the compulsion inherent in a WTO labour clause and in unilateralism. There are choices that have to be made.

9 TALES OF TWO WORLDS: GLOBALIZATION AND SEXUAL EXPLOITATION

Julia O'Connell Davidson and Jacqueline Sanchez Taylor

The 1990s have witnessed increased global awareness of child abuse and concern about the commercial sexual exploitation of children, including the phenomenon of 'child sex tourism'. Although nation states have long played a key role in the regulation of commercial sexual exploitation through their responses to prostitution and pornography at national and local levels, groups campaigning against 'child sex tourism' and child pornography hold that the globalization of child sexual exploitation calls for an international response. Thus, one of the main objectives of the World Congress Against the Commercial Sexual Exploitation of Children held in Stockholm in 1996 was to 'raise the commercial sexual exploitation of children from being a concern of NGOs to a concern on the international agenda and to ensure that international action is taken against it' (Coalition on Child Prostitution and Tourism, 1996).

Given that a consistent legal definition of childhood is not employed around the globe and that legal codes governing sexual behaviour also vary from country to country, calls for international efforts to prevent and police sexual crimes committed against children are far from straightforward. In pursuit of international co-operation, the Congress therefore employed the United Nations definition of a child as a person under the age of 18, and defined the commercial sexual exploitation of children (CSEC) as:

> sexual abuse by the adult and remuneration in cash or kind to the child or a third party person or persons ... [it] constitutes a form of coercion and violence against children and amounts to forced labour and a contemporary form of slavery.

Drawing on Article 34 of the United Nations Convention on the Rights of the Child which forbids anyone using the sexual services of a child under 18, Congress further held that age of sexual consent legislation in any given country had no meaning in the context of child prostitution. The Congress Declaration, which included an Agenda for Action, called for states to give high priority to CSEC, and to focus on both the protection of children (through law enforcement, criminalization of CSEC and ensuring that offenders, not children are penalized) and the prevention of CSEC (through child-friendly, gender-sensitive programmes and other measures). That this Declaration was signed by all 119 governments attending the Congress, and that a number of these governments have subsequently been involved in joint initiatives to promote international co-operation on child welfare and the policing of CSEC, is a measure of how successful its organizers were in circumnavigating the innumerable political and legal difficulties associated with achieving a unified international response to a human rights issue.

Our own involvement with the Congress came about as a result of having been commissioned by ECPAT (End Child Prostitution in Asian Tourism) to undertake research on the identity, motivations and attitudes of tourists who use child prostitutes while travelling abroad. We conducted field research in seven countries and interviewed over 200 sex tourists, and our research informed one of the eight background papers for the Congress (O'Connell Davidson, 1996). Though we supported the Congress's aims and celebrated its achievements, we are conscious of the limitations of approaches to the issue of CSEC which do not address the fact that it is an international problem in a world in which nations are vastly unequal. Unless steps are taken to redress these fundamental inequalities, measures to regulate and control their consequences necessarily represent partial and inadequate solutions. This is particularly striking in relation to the problem of 'child sex tourism', which, as this chapter hopes to show, is a phenomenon embedded in, and inseparable from, extremely broad and general processes of globalization.

Tourism, Sex Tourism and 'Child Sex Tourism'

As a feature of the world system, international tourism rests upon and reproduces relations of dependence between nations. Though such relations do not always involve asymmetries of power (in fact, 'most tourism actually occurs within and between the developed world', Burns and Holden, 1995, p. 82), the extent to which 'developing' nations are now dependent upon tourism is a measure of their highly unequal position in the economic and political world order. Tourist development in poor and 'developing' countries since the 1970s has generally taken place as a response to declining terms of trade for main export commodities, massive international debt and the decline of import-substitution industries in many former colonies. Tourism promises a means of obtaining urgently needed foreign exchange and, in many cases, it has answered some of governments' immediate economic problems. Over the past two decades in the Caribbean, for instance, 'tourism has distinguished itself as the *only* steady growth sector for the region ... without tourism the region's current account deficit during the 1980s would have been nearly four times higher than its reported US$11 billion', and 'six Caribbean countries earned more from tourism in 1992 as a share of exports ... than they did from all other sectors' (Pattullo, 1996, p. 12, emphasis in the original). It is widely acknowledged, however, that tourist development in poor countries is associated with certain economic costs, as well as benefits. Lea (1988, p. 50) summarizes the potential dangers as follows:

> increased inflation and land values, increased pressure to import, seasonality of production, problems connected with over-dependence on one product, unfavourable impact on the balance of payments, heavy infrastructure costs, and the effect on growth of having much of the labour-force employed in a service industry with poor productivity prospects.

The problem is not simply that tourists demand Western-style amenities (which means government spending on 'airports, roads, water supply, sewerage disposal, electricity and telephones', Pattullo, 1996), and Western-style food and luxury goods (which involves using an often very large percentage of the revenues from tourism to pay for imported goods), but also that it is extremely difficult for locally owned small businesses and national companies to retain control over the developing tourist industry. International tourism is dominated by transnational corporations which operate at all levels of the industry, as travel agents, tour operators, hoteliers and airline operators, and which have frequently vertically integrated these different levels of the tourist industry (Burns and Holden, 1995). Locally owned hotels, guesthouses and restaurants are squeezed out and/or unable to expand and compete, and where they forge franchise or supplier relationships with transnational companies, local businesses are not usually in a position to negotiate especially profitable contracts. Conversely, profit opportunities for transnational companies and other foreign investors in tourism in heavily indebted countries are enhanced by the fact that those countries' governments often provide them with generous tax incentives in the form of exemptions on income, corporate and local tax, and sometimes also duty-free imports of goods not locally available (see Ferguson, 1992).

Tourist development is often urged on grounds that it will create employment, yet tourism is a low-wage and highly gendered industry, and while it undoubtedly generates lucrative jobs opportunities, such employment creation does not necessarily benefit local people. Foreign-owned companies operating in economically under-developed countries frequently bring in managers and staff from Europe, Australia and North America. Indeed, in many parts of Africa, Latin America, the Caribbean and Asia, 'expatriates hold virtually every position of importance, from general manager of a resort to assistant pastry cook' (Burns and Holden, 1995, p. 133). Thus, for local people, 'much of the earning associated with [tourism] happens – as it always has – outside the organised economy' (Black, 1995, p. 1). The informal tourist economy includes women, men and children working as unregistered taxi drivers, guides, souvenir sellers, fruit sellers, shoe-shine boys, masseuses, manicurists, hairdressers, cleaners in private apartments, even small children who, for a few coins, wash the sand off tourists' feet as they lie sunning themselves on sun loungers. It also often includes prostitution, and the phenomenon of 'sex tourism' is increasingly widespread in economically under-developed countries which are sites of mass tourism.

Sex tourism to Thailand, the Philippines and Indonesia is fairly well documented (Truong, 1990; Lee, 1991; Sturdevant and Stoltzfus, 1992; Kruhse-Mount Burton, 1995; Chant and McIlwaine, 1995; Bishop and Robinson, 1998), but sex tourists also travel to other parts of South East Asia and to a number of Latin American and Caribbean, African and Eastern European countries. There are differences between countries affected by sex tourism in terms of the structure of their 'sex industries' and the relationship between tourism and prostitution. In some cases (Thailand, the Philippines, South Korea and Taiwan, for example) sex tourism has involved the maintenance and development of existing large-scale, highly commoditized sex industries serving foreign military personnel. But it has also emerged in locations where no such sex industry existed, for instance, the Gambia, Cuba and Brazil, and even in countries like Thailand and the Philippines, tourist development has been associated with the emergence of an informal prostitution sector (in which independent and pimped prostitutes solicit in public places such as tourist bars and discos, on streets and beaches, etc.) *as well as* the reproduction of an existing, formally organized sector.

All of this means that, in terms of its social organization, tourist-related prostitution is just as diverse a phenomenon as prostitution is in general (O'Connell Davidson, 1998). The factors that underpin the supply of labour for tourist-related prostitution are remarkably similar in all those countries affected, however. On the whole, sex tourism flourishes in countries where a large percentage of the population lives in poverty, where there is high unemployment and no welfare system to support those who are excluded from the formal economy. In these countries, the annexation of subsistence land and/or promotion of cash-crop farming is often having a devastating impact on rural economies and creating powerful pressure on young people, especially young women, to migrate to urban areas or tourist resorts in search of work (see, for example, Crummett, 1987; Ekachai, 1990; Lee, 1991; Chant and McIlwaine, 1995; Black, 1995). Those working in tourist-related prostitution are thus very often migrants from rural areas or urban conurbations, and may be attempting to support several dependants as well as themselves through their prostitution. The 'pull' factor is quite simply that the economic rewards of tourist-related prostitution are generally higher than those associated with other alternatives (unskilled work in factories or the hotel or catering industries, domestic service, prostitution serving local demand, beach vending, or other forms of tourist 'hustling').

Tourist industry spokespersons in the countries that send and those that receive sex tourists generally insist that tourism and sex tourism are two quite distinct phenomena. Though we recognize that there are forms of tourism to 'developing' countries that are unlikely or less likely to involve the sexual exploitation of local persons (for instance, family holidays, honeymoon holidays, ecotours), and that single, long-haul tourists do not all practise sex tourism, we would none-the-less argue that the overlap between 'ordinary' tourism to poor countries and sex tourism is greater than most people care to recognize, and that sex tourism is entirely dependent upon mass tourism more generally. Very few sex tourists take organized 'sex tours' – the vast majority either make independent travel arrangements or take cheap package deals, booked through ordinary, 'respectable' travel agents. They are transported by ordinary airlines, they stay in ordinary hotels, eat in ordinary restaurants, and generally make use of the ordinary, tourist infrastructure. The relationship between the sex tourist and the international travel industry is a mutually advantageous one – on the one hand, mass tourism makes sex tourism an affordable and safe practice, on the other, the bulk of the money that sex tourists spend on their holiday goes to swell the profits of ordinary, 'respectable' travel and tourism companies and conglomerates. Furthermore, the way in which 'Third World' destinations are marketed to 'ordinary' holidaymakers in the West taps directly into highly sexualized forms of racism (the Orient as 'exotic' and 'mysterious', the Caribbean as 'relaxed' and 'sensual', and so on), so that it does nothing to deter, and if anything actually encourages, the phenomenon of sex tourism. Meanwhile, 'respectable' tour operators sell package holidays to known sex tourist resorts, describing them in advertising brochures as 'suitable for single travellers', as having 'a party atmosphere' and 'exciting nightlife'.

If tourism and sex tourism intersect in these ways, what is the relationship between sex tourism and 'child sex tourism'? It is extremely difficult to obtain accurate information about the extent of child prostitution in the contemporary world, but the more general body of empirical evidence on prostitution around the world allows us to argue that child prostitution cannot be neatly separated from adult prostitution. Academic and journalistic research suggests that most child prostitutes are integrated into the mainstream prostitution market serving *all* prostitute users, rather than working in some discrete 'market niche' that caters solely to the desires of 'paedophiles' or child molesters. Thus, for example, girls between 10 and 14 are variously reported to be prostituting alongside older teenagers and young women in mining encampments in Brazil and Surinam (Sutton, 1994; Antonius-Smits and the Maxi Linder Association, 1998), in brothel districts in Bombay and Bangladesh (INSAF, 1995; Rozario, 1988; Radda Barnen, 1996), in tourist areas in the Dominican Republic (Silvestre *et al.*, 1994), in brothels in Thailand (O'Grady, 1994), as well as on the streets in red light areas in affluent Western countries (Kelly *et al.*, 1995; Silbert and Pines, 1981). It is therefore reasonable to assume that a majority of the clients of child prostitutes are first and foremost *prostitute users* who become child sexual abusers through their prostitute use, rather than first and foremost 'paedophiles' using prostitution as a means of obtaining sexual access to children, and we have certainly found this to be the case in our research on sex tourists' use of child prostitutes.[1]

While there are people who conform to clinical definitions of 'paedophilia' who travel to poor countries in order to obtain cheap and easy sexual access to children, many sex tourists become child sexual abusers simply because they are willing to use prostitutes in settings where significant numbers of children, as well as adults, are driven to prostitution through economic compulsion and/or third-party coercion. Children's presence in tourist-related prostitution is largely predicated on exactly the same structural factors which encourage adult prostitution, i.e. poverty, the absence of welfare support for the economically inactive, and the immiseration of rural areas (see Bishop and Robinson, 1998, p. 94). For children, as well as adults, prostitution frequently offers greater financial rewards than any alternative means of economic survival (Black, 1995, p. 36).

Though adult prostitution is either legal or tolerated in some of the countries that receive sex tourists, there are no sex tourist destinations in which children can legally work in the formal prostitution sector. Children therefore tend to become involved in tourist-related prostitution in one of three ways: through a pimp or other third-party adult who illegally enslaves or employs them and/or touts for business 'on their behalf'; by lying about their age to a brothel or bar-brothel owner; by soliciting in public places such as beaches, streets, restaurants, hotel-foyers, or tourist bars and discos. The 'ordinary' sex tourist, as well as the 'paedophile', is thus highly likely to be approached by child prostitutes, and it is frequently a matter of indifference to sex tourists whether the prostitutes they pick up are 14 or 24, providing they fancy the look of them. And since sexual value is attached to youth by most cultures, the prostitutes that sex tourists fancy the look of very often are under the age of 18.

The real point is that children under the age of 18 are to be found servicing 'ordinary' sex tourists, as well as 'paedophiles' who travel abroad, and the distinction between sex tourism and 'child sex tourism' which has been so important to achieving international political co-operation is therefore largely fictional. Tourism, sex tourism, and child sex tourism are not discrete phenomena. Before looking at what this means for the regulation of sexual exploitation at both national and international levels, we want to use the Dominican Republic as a case study to highlight linkages between processes of globalization and sexual exploitation.

'One Night in Heaven'

Late one evening in November 1995, we were out conducting observational and interview work on sex tourism in Boca Chica, a small resort town in the Dominican Republic. We sat down in a bar, and after a while managed to strike up a conversation with a group of people sitting at the next table. Two of them were Americans, a father and his 19-year-old son, 'Alan'. The father owned a six-bedroomed house in Boca Chica, and let some of the rooms to tourists. He also owned a shipping firm, which was involved in the export of fruit and vegetables to other tourist-receiving Caribbean islands and to the USA. Alan explained to us that since dropping out of high school, he had tried working in the hotel trade in Florida, but did not like it, and so had recently emigrated to the Dominican Republic to help his father with his shipping business. We asked him what exactly he did. 'Mostly I just watch the Blacks that work for Dad', he told us. Alan then proceeded to enthuse about his new life in Boca Chica, expressing particular delight with his father's domestic arrangements:

Dad was married three times back home, so he's not going to marry again. He's got a kind of live-in girlfriend, she's called Lola, and she keeps house for Dad and me and the guys that come and stay in the house. She's great ... She's the best mom I ever had. When I get back to the house ... after I've been out and had a few beers, she'll take my shoes off for me and massage my feet and put me to bed ... She makes breakfast, she cooks, she cleans, she does all the laundry for all of us ... She's fantastic. If you just say you're thirsty, or say you want a coke, she just goes and gets it for you, *rapido* ... She's like a maid.

Sitting with Alan and 'Dad' were two German men, one of whom was staying at their house, the other a package tourist staying at Boca Chica's newest and largest all-inclusive hotel. Both of them were in their forties, and were accompanied by a young Dominican woman and a teenage Dominican girl who sat talking to each other while their 'boyfriends' conducted a conversation in English with the Americans and with us about the pleasures a 'single male' can find in the Dominican Republic. One of them explained to us that prostitutes were far cheaper here than in Europe, and that unlike Western prostitutes who are 'cold' and 'professional', Dominican prostitutes spend the entire night with their tourist clients, kiss and cuddle them and perform a range of non-sexual tasks such as tidying their hotel room, rinsing out their socks and shirts, acting as guide and interpreter for them. 'It's paradise here. It's heaven', the other man told us. 'Latin American girls are hot. It's the African and Spanish mix, it makes fire.' As we talked, two Dominican shoeshine boys, aged perhaps 8 and 10, approached the men's table. One of the Germans beckoned them over and proceeded to haggle over the cost of the service. He then sat drinking his beer while the child knelt at his feet, polishing his shoes.

Such scenes, which are commonplace in tourist resorts in the Dominican Republic and other economically under-developed countries we have visited in the course of research on sex tourism, are enacted against a backcloth of global economic, social and political inequality, and the powers and freedoms enjoyed by men like Alan, 'Dad' and the German tourists are incomprehensible except in relation to these broader structural inequalities. To begin with, these men are empowered by the very weak position that the Dominican Republic occupies in a specific political and economic world order:

For much of the last century, the Dominican Republic relied on the export of sugar, coffee, cacao and tobacco. Since the mid-1970s, however, in a move to protect domestic sugar producers, the United States has drastically reduced the Dominican sugar quota ... exports plummeted and agriculture

entered into a crisis which continues today. This crisis forced thousands of
farmers out of business and led many to migrate to the cities or abroad
(Betances and Spalding, 1997, p. 16).

By the early 1980s, the country was in debt to the tune of some US$2,400
million, a debt which may appear small by Latin American standards, but was
'disturbingly high for a small country with limited political influence' (Plant,
1987, p. 141). By May 1982, 'the country was running a deficit of over $550
million, and the Central Bank had fallen some $400 million in arrears in its
international payments, while overdue debt repayments were in excess of $200
million. Incoming President Salvador Jorge Blanco was compelled to go to the
International Monetary Fund' (Plant 1987, p. 143). One outcome of negotiations with the IMF was a currency devaluation in 1983, which

> lowered the cost of doing business on the island for firms earning other
> currencies, and therefore attracted foreign investors who wished to take
> advantage of low wages. This led to a rapid expansion of zonas francas, or
> free-trade zones (FTZs) – areas in which foreign, export-oriented firms were
> granted tax and tariff breaks (Betances and Spalding, 1997, p. 16).

Structural adjustment measures adopted in the 1980s 'forced the basic cost of
labour in the free-trade zones down from $1.33 an hour in 1984 to $.56 an hour
in 1990' and today, 180,000 Dominicans work in this sector (Safa, 1997, p. 32).
They also had a profound impact on the gender composition of the Dominican
labour force, since they involved a shift from import-substitution manufacturing, which was male dominated, to export promotion, which 'has favoured the
employment of women – the preferred labor force in garment production, the
predominant industry in the free-trade zones' (Safa, 1997, p. 32). Despite a
rapid increase in female employment, however, female unemployment
remains much higher than for men, and the wages of those employed in the
free trade zones are insufficient to live on: 'In 1992, a family of five needed an
estimated 7,580 pesos, about $600, to cover monthly expenses for basic necessi-
ties, but free-trade zone workers at that time were earning a monthly minimum
wage of 1,269 pesos, about $100' (Safa, 1997, p. 34). Safa further observes that
'Structural adjustment, by forcing women to assume more economic responsibility and reducing employment opportunities for men, seems to be
contributing to [an] increase in female-headed households' (Safa, 1997, p. 35).
In 1991, it was estimated that some half a million women in the Dominican
Republic were bringing up families on their own, and that of these, almost 27
per cent were under 35, and 25 per cent of woman-headed households were

dependent on a single wage earner. In this context, it is clearly children, as well as women, who are made economically vulnerable, and child workers are highly visible in the informal economy as a consequence.

The 1983 currency devaluation also stimulated the expansion of tourism, a sector which the Dominican government had been promoting since the mid-1970s. More than 35 per cent of tourism growth in the Caribbean over the past two decades 'directly reflects the industry's growth in the Dominican Republic', which now receives over 1.5 million tourists annually (Latinfinance, 1995). This has undoubtedly created jobs (an estimated 149,561 jobs in the country are related to tourism, Latinfinance, 1995), but most of these are extremely low waged and as Safa (1997, p. 36) has remarked more generally, 'The need for alternative sources of income to supplement or substitute for wages under structural adjustment has contributed to the growth of the informal sector in the Dominican Republic.' Certainly, the tourist industry, and the entertainment industry which operates alongside it, provide a range of opportunities for informal economic activity, and while many of these activities may be illegal or conducted illegally, it is worth noting the Dominican State is actually dependent on certain types of informal activity to support the rapid expansion of the formal tourist sector. The country can ill afford, for example, to provide municipal services such as rubbish collection on a scale that could match the need for waste disposal generated by 1.5 million tourists. The fact that children, some as young as 4 years of age, will collect bottles and tin cans tossed aside on beaches and streets by affluent visitors, in order to sell them on for a few pesos, is thus of benefit to the state and the tourist industry. This form of child labour provides a service (maintaining beautiful, litter-free beaches that are demanded by tourists) that the State would otherwise have to fund itself.

It is also important to note that tourist development has diverted public money from the kinds of projects and spending which might alleviate existing social and economic problems: 'Government spending on infrastructure . . . has been aimed at tourist areas and facilities . . . neglecting basic services such as water supply and access in poor rural and urban areas. As a result, tourist zones operate as enclaves within wider areas of deprivation' (Ferguson, 1992, p. 71). Coupled with the fact that tourist resorts are enclaves of plenty in a country otherwise hallmarked by its poverty, this encourages large numbers of adults and children, especially women and girls, to migrate to tourist zones from both rural and urban areas in search of work in either the formal or the informal tourist sector, and/or to spend weekends in resort towns attempting to supplement low wages from jobs in free trade zones through informal economic activities.

However, labour-market conditions in the informal economy are no more favourable to these economically desperate migrants than those in the formal tourist industry are, and one reason for this is that Western tourists (including one of the Germans at 'Dad''s table) are increasingly buying cheap, 'all-inclusive' package holidays provided by foreign-owned travel conglomerates. The 'all-inclusive package holiday' is a relatively new phenomenon, and involves the tourist paying in advance not just for flights, transfer, accommodation and full board, but also for 'extras' that would normally be purchased during the course of a holiday such as drinks, the use of sun loungers, and sport and leisure facilities. These holidays are marketed on the basis that they eradicate the need for cash (and therefore for onerous tasks like dealing with foreign currency, budgeting and so on). As the brochures put it, 'All you'll need cash for is to buy your souvenirs', and the all-inclusive package holiday thus represents another stage in international tourism's push toward vertical integration, allowing transnational companies control over virtually every single aspect of 'the tourist experience'. The only things that the German all-inclusive package tourist at 'Dad''s table had bought from locally owned businesses and local people in the course of his two-week stay in the Dominican Republic were drinks from local bars after the hotel bar had closed, souvenirs, shoeshine and sexual 'services'.

Tourists on ordinary package holidays are also subject to pressure from tour operators to avoid buying anything from locally owned businesses and entrepreneurs who operate beyond the tour operators' sphere of control. Though companies like the British-owned Thompsons, and German-owned LTI market 'developing world' destinations as 'exotic' and 'different', they also wish to ensure that each tourist is provided with a standardized experience that conforms to accepted Western norms of comfort, convenience and safety. In-flight videos, information packs provided to tourists on arrival and on-site tour representatives all therefore play on tourists' fears, racisms and xenophobia to discourage them from engagement with the local economy – 'don't buy drinks from street sellers or local cafes, the ice in them may be made from impure water'; 'don't use local transport, it doesn't conform to Western safety standards and it's quite a crush'; 'buy your boat trips/jet skiing/scuba diving from us, not from beach touts, they don't have proper insurance'.

Individual Dominicans' opportunities for small-scale, entrepreneurial activity in the tourist economy are thus increasingly restricted to various forms of beach vending. However, because Western tourists do not like to be 'hustled' by an endless stream of economically desperate individuals, the Dominican Tourist Authority has encouraged the enacting of by-laws which make it compulsory for beach vendors to purchase a licence to work the beaches. The numbers for whom beach vending is a viable option are thus increasingly restricted (see Pattullo, 1996). The one form of tourist 'hustling' which, in

1995, remained largely unaffected by such developments was prostitution, and children as well as adults were involved in tourist-related prostitution. Gender and economic oppression combine to make girl children especially vulnerable to prostitution. A UNICEF report on child prostitution in the Dominican Republic concludes that poverty, lack of alternative earning opportunities and the lack of a stable family unit are the factors usually associated with prostitution in girls (Silvestre *et al.*, 1994). Girl children are denied access to the kind of informal work that boy children often undertake (such as shoeshine, bottle collecting, sweet selling). The report states that 30 per cent of child prostitutes aged between 12 and 15 were illiterate, and that girls in particular had not been encouraged to stay on at school. In some areas, up to 60 per cent of the children working as prostitutes had given birth to one or more children by the age of 18, and some of these babies were fathered by clients.

Racism also plays a crucial role in shaping tourist-related prostitution. On the one hand, the demand for prostitution is highly 'racialized', and sex tourists choose the Dominican Republic because they wish to live out racist sexual fantasies about Black and Hispanic 'Others' (see O'Connell Davidson and Sanchez Taylor, 1998). On the other hand, as an ex-slave society, racism is heavily institutionalized in the Dominican Republic and racist ideologies (in particular, the legacy of a colonial 'pigmentocracy', see James, 1993, and a profound anti-Haitianism, see Fennema and Loewenthal, 1987) continue to oppress and marginalize darker-skinned Dominicans. Thus, while white Dominicans are to be found in managerial positions in the tourist industry, they are not present in tourist-related prostitution.

All of this helps to make sense of the scene described above. 'Dad', whose shipping business benefited from the tax exemptions offered to foreign investors, favourable market conditions engendered by export promotion policies, and cheap labour made cheaper still by structural adjustment measures, was in a position to buy a holiday home in Boca Chica, install Lola as his domestic servant-cum-mistress, and support his economically inactive 19-year-old son. Alan told us that Lola was a 32-year-old Black woman who came from the nearby town of San Pedro, and that his father gave her 1,200 pesos a month for 'taking care of the house and the guests', as well as providing her with food, accommodation and clothing. In a country where many people struggle to pay subsistence costs on the same monthly income, this is clearly a relatively attractive 'employment' package, and Lola's situation compares favourably with that of other Dominican women working in factories in the nearby free trade zone or in brothel prostitution serving local clients. Also relevant to understanding Lola's situation is the fact that migration to affluent countries is another common household strategy in response to structural adjustment (Betances and Spalding, 1997).

We did not interview Lola, but on the basis of interview work with women in a situation similar to hers, it seems likely that she may also have hoped that her relationship with 'Dad', a US citizen, might lead to marriage, which would place her in a better position to migrate in the future. Certainly, many women and girls who work in the informal tourist-related prostitution sector do so not simply because it represents the best available means of subsistence in the short term, but also because it is believed to hold out long-term prospects as a migration strategy. There is demand for Dominican prostitutes in the sex industries of European, North American and other Caribbean countries (see Kempadoo, 1998), but some women hope that tourist-related prostitution will lead to migration-through-marriage. The reality for those who achieve this ambition is often a nightmare. One of the young women sitting with the German tourists at 'Dad' and Alan's table was a case in point. She was 23. At 15, she had had a baby fathered by a Dominican man, and at 17, she had had another child fathered by a German tourist who subsequently married her and took her and her two children back to Germany. She had lived there for eighteen months in complete isolation, suffered racism from local people and violence from her husband, and had finally returned to the Dominican Republic with nothing but a suitcase of clothing. She returned to prostitution as it was the only means through which she could support her two children.

Working in Boca Chica's informal prostitution sector represented the best possible means of subsistence available to the other girl at the table, who was only 15. There is no welfare system in the Dominican Republic to safeguard those who are excluded from the formal economy, and this child worked as a prostitute in order to support herself, her unemployed father and her nine-month-old baby. The previous night, the German package holiday maker had paid her 500 pesos to spend the night with him (he had also paid a bribe of 300 pesos to the security guard at the all-inclusive hotel to let him take her into the hotel). Prostitutes in Boca Chica generally manage to negotiate a fee of somewhere between 300 and 1,000 pesos per client and though they cannot always solicit more than two or three clients per week, earnings from one week in prostitution are normally therefore higher than earnings from one month's work in a free trade zone.

Sex Tourism, the State and International Responses

The state, to quote Miles (1987, p. 181), is an institutional complex (government, courts, army, administration, etc.) 'which organizes social relations within a social formation to ensure the reproduction of a particular mode, or articulation of modes, of production'. As such an institutional complex, the state can be said to organize relations between prostitutes and clients, as well as between producers and non-producers, and the most obvious and direct way in which states regulate prostitution is through the criminal law and the criminal justice system. In the Dominican Republic, prostitution is not illegal *per se*, nor are the activities associated with it, such as soliciting and brothel-keeping. However, procuring, pimping and any other form of involvement in the prostitution of a person under the age of 18 is criminal under the legal code governing the treatment of minors, and there are a number of public decency laws which can be applied against adult prostitutes who solicit in public spaces rather than working from licensed, tax-paying brothels. This legal framework leaves the police, and to a lesser extent the judiciary, with a great deal of discretion as regards the treatment of prostitutes, and given that police officers in the Dominican Republic earn well below subsistence wages, it is unsurprising to find that many police officers use such discretion corruptly. When we were conducting research in 1995, for example, corrupt police in sex tourist resorts would, in exchange for bribes, informally 'license' bar owners to allow women and children to solicit on their premises, and we were told by prostitute women and girls who solicited on streets, beaches and in bars and discos that police officers frequently extorted money from them (and also sometimes raped them), but rarely arrested or prosecuted them.

As well as direct involvement in the regulation of prostitution through the criminal law (also often through the civic treatment of prostitutes as a separate class of persons, see Edwards, 1987; Walkowitz, 1980; Alexander, 1991; O'Connell Davidson, 1998), state apparatuses which are designed to regulate relations of *reproduction* (welfare systems, systems of family law, etc.), as well as broader economic policies are critical to shaping the prostitution 'labour market' in any given country. These apparatuses invariably institutionalize highly gendered patterns of inequality, which in turn make women and children especially vulnerable to economic marginalization and so to prostitution. As Davis (1993, p. 8) observes, discriminatory social practices which are upheld by laws have a significant impact on the prostitution 'labour market', so that 'Prostitution is merely one part of the larger picture of systematic gender injustice.'

The prostitution labour market in the Dominican Republic has been powerfully shaped by gender discriminatory social policies, and the Dominican government can also be said to benefit from prostitution in the sense that it operates as a kind of alternative 'welfare' system (just as it does in most countries of the world). Prostitution thus reduces the level of state expenditure necessary to ensure the reproduction of labour and also provides a means by which to supplement below-subsistence wages. However, the prostitution labour market in the Dominican Republic has also been very much affected by national and international economic planning geared towards tourist development and foreign exchange earning to service the country's international debts. Indeed, there are certain parallels between the Dominican Republic and Thailand in this respect. Bishop and Robinson (1998, p. 99) note that Thailand is the fifth largest borrower from the World Bank, yet:

> Thailand has not been reduced to the debt peonage characteristic of so many other oil-importing nations that have no stable source of foreign exchange. Thailand has been able to meet the interest if not the principal on its deficit . . . even as the proportion of foreign debt to GNP (Gross National Product) has more than trebled . . . This enormous increase is precisely coeval with the accession of tourism to the status of top earner of foreign exchange, which means that Thailand's ability to maintain growth while meeting its responsibilities as a debtor nation has been achieved on the back of its female service workers – a significant proportion of whom are working on *their* backs.

Prostitutes may play just as important a role in tourist development as other service workers, but where states will often intervene directly to mediate and regulate conflict between capital and labour, hypocrisy and denial of the ends served by prostitution mean that they do not typically take on such a role as regards clients and prostitutes, or take steps to protect the prostitute as the less powerful party to an economic transaction. So far as 'ordinary' forms of labour are concerned, it is widely recognized that, if people are economically desperate enough, they will 'consent' to enter into contracts which may or will harm them, and this is why labour movements and human rights activists have struggled, with some success, to get governments to outlaw systems of debt-bondage and indentured labour, to legally compel employers to observe health and safety procedures, to ban the use of toxic substances in production processes, in short, to criminalize those who invite others to consent to contracts which will harm them.

Now it is true that, in those countries where brothel prostitution is legal, relationships between third-party organizers of prostitution and prostitutes are subject to state regulation (though this does not always imply protection for the prostitute), but *clients* are almost invariably wholly unconstrained in terms of the kind of contracts they can invite prostitutes to enter into. In fact, far from acting to constrain clients (or indeed third-party employers), states are more likely to use the criminal law to harass and control prostitutes as sexual and moral outlaws and this often remains the case even where the relationship between tourism and prostitution is tacitly or explicitly recognized by government. Because the state's interest in the economic arrangements between prostitutes and clients is not acknowledged, and because the criminal law is rarely if ever used to control clients, these arrangements take on the character of a clients' 'free for all'. Among other things, this makes it extremely difficult for states to respond to the problem of child prostitution. Take the Dominican Republic's reaction to increasing international pressure to end the commercial sexual exploitation of children, for example.

When we conducted fieldwork in the Dominican Republic in 1995, we observed that, as immensely economically powerful 'buyers' in a totally unregulated 'market', sex tourists were free to forge the contracts of their choice on the terms of their choice, even if that involved the technically illegal act of contracting for sex with a child. When we returned to the Dominican Republic in 1998, we found that the Government had adopted a two-pronged response to international concern about child prostitution, one long term, one short term. Very much in line with the Congress Declaration's emphasis on the prevention of CSEC, ministers state that they are committed to a long-term strategy of improving women and children's economic position and promoting education and training for girls so that they are faced with real alternatives to prostitution. Given the huge economic problems the country is currently facing, this is likely to be a long-term strategy indeed. The short-term response has simply been to intensify police control of tourist-related prostitution in general. A handful of third-party organizers of child prostitution – expatriate bar owners – have been deported, but the prime target of police activity is, as ever, female prostitutes. More than 170 women and teenagers were rounded up by the police on a single night in one tourist resort in February 1998, and in another resort, upwards of 50 women and teenage girls a week are now appearing in court on charges involving public decency offences. Every time a prostitute is arrested, it costs her at least 600 to 700 pesos in costs for legal representation and fines, and bribes to corrupt police to avoid arrest are set at a similar level – between 500 and 1,000 pesos. This kind of harassment increases the prostitute's vulnerability to exploitation and abuse by clients and third parties, as well as locking her into prostitution as a means of economic survival. It does absolutely nothing to constrain the powers enjoyed by clients or to prevent them from contracting for the sexual 'services' of children.

There is a sense in which these developments simply express the kind of misogynist, anti-prostitute sentiment that informs the regulation of prostitution the world over (Alexander, 1997). But the close links between indebtedness and tourist development, tourist development and sex tourism, and sex tourism and child sex tourism, and the country's position in the world economic and political order, would make it very difficult for the Dominican Government to switch the focus of policing onto the clients of child prostitutes, even if it wanted to. Since the problem of child sex tourism is not confined to the activities of a small, discrete sub-group of individuals who seek out prepubertal children to abuse, such a switch in focus would raise two questions. First, what effect would it have on tourism if the police were to raid ordinary tourist hotels, bars and discos, round up tourists as well as locals, and, showing the same disregard for civil rights and the due process of law that is currently shown in relation to prostitute women, arrest foreign nationals found in the company of a child under the age of 18, then hold them in prison for several days before prosecuting them for sexual offences against minors? And second, if a country like the Dominican Republic were to do this, how much support and co-operation would it receive from the Western governments whose citizens languished in a 'Third World' jail for offences that, if committed at home, they would probably never even be prosecuted for (in Britain, for example, the use of under-age prostitutes is rarely treated as a child sex offence)?

Governments of both affluent, sex-tourist-sending countries and 'developing', sex-tourist-receiving countries signed the Declaration of the World Congress Against the Commercial Sexual Exploitation of Children. To the extent that governments of sending countries have subsequently been more inclined to co-operate with international efforts to police and prosecute those who sexually exploit very young children, they might be said to be honouring this commitment. However, CSEC is not simply an international problem because those who exploit children cross national borders in order to do so. It is also an international problem because the factors which precipitate children's entry into prostitution and increase their vulnerability within it are global, as well as national and local. On their own, governments in the 'developing' world are simply not in a position to put in place programmes which can meaningfully reverse these global factors. They cannot, for example, cancel their own international debt and so cannot afford to jeopardize industries which earn foreign exchange, even if those industries are dominated by multinational corporations and carry huge environmental and social costs. Nor can they mount an effective challenge to the popular Western racist and sexist discourses about sexuality, gender, prostitution and travel which help to construct a demand for sex tourism, including child sex tourism. It is governments of the affluent world that are empowered to make these kinds of changes. They must be pressured to do so.

Acknowledgements

The support of ECPAT, which funded research in the Dominican Republic, Cuba, Costa Rica, Venezuela, South Africa, India, and the Economic and Social Research Council which is funding an ongoing research project in the Dominican Republic and Jamaica (award number R000 23 7625), is gratefully acknowledged.

Notes

1. It is important to note that children's clients are by no means always tourists. Indeed, because children's invariably weak economic, political and social status makes them vulnerable to extremes of abuse and exploitation within prostitution (just as child labourers in other sectors are especially vulnerable, see Fyfe, 1989; Sawyer, 1986), they often represent the cheapest segment of the prostitution 'labour market' and probably the majority of them therefore serve demand from the poorest clients rather than prostituting in settings geared to the tourist market.

REFERENCES

ACIRRT (1996) 'Agreements Data Base and Monitor', *Report No. 8*. University of Sydney: Australian Centre for Industrial Relations Research and Training.

ACTU/TDC (1987) *Australia Reconstructed*. Canberra: AGPS.

ACTU (1987) *Future Strategies for the Trade Union Movement*. Melbourne: ACTU.

Aglietta, M. (1979) *A Theory of Capitalist Regulation*. London: Verso.

Alasoini, T., T. Kauppinen and P. Ylöstalo (1994) 'Workplace in Finland – New Forms of Bargaining and Participation' in T. Kauppinen and V. Köykkä (eds), *Workplace Europe – New Forms of Bargaining and Participation*. IIRA 4th European Regional Congress, Helsinki, 24–6 August, Plenary 2.

Albert, M. (1991) *Capitalisme contre capitalisme*. Paris: Seuil.

Albrechts, L., F. Moulart, P. Roberts and E. Swyngedouw (1989) 'New Perspectives for Regional Policy and Development in the 1990s' in L. Albrechts *et al.* (eds), *Regional Policy at the Crossroads*. London: Jessica Kingsley.

Alcock, A. (1971) *History of the International Labour Organisation*. London: Macmillan.

Alexander, J. (1991) 'Redrafting Morality. The Postcolonial State and the Sexual Offences Bill of Trinidad and Tobago' in C. Mohanty, A. Russo and L. Torres (eds), *Third World Women and the Politics of Feminism*. Bloomington and Indianapolis: Indiana University Press.

Alexander, P. (1997) 'Feminism, Sex Workers and Human Rights' in J. Nagel (ed.), *Whores and Other Feminists*. London: Routledge.

Ali-Yrkkö, J. and P. Ylä-Antilla (1997) *Yritykset kansainvälistyvät – katoavatko työpaikat?* ETLA B, 130, Helsinki: Taloustieto.

Allen Consulting Group (1994) *Successful Reform: Competitive Skills for Australians and Australian Enterprises*. Report to the Australian National Training Authority.

ALP/ACTU (1983) *Statement of Accord by the Australian Labor Party and the Australian Council of Trade Unions Regarding Economic Policy*. February, National Economic Summit Conference 11–14 April, Documents and Proceedings, Government Documents, pp. 407–26. Canberra: AGPS.

Altvater, E. and B. Mahnkopf (1993) *Gewerkschaften vor der europäischen Herausforderung. Tarifpolitik nach Mauer und Maastricht*. Münster: Westfälisches Dampfboot.

Åmark, K. (1992) 'Social Democracy and the Trade Union Movement: Solidarity and the Politics of Self-Interest' in K. Misgeld, K. Molin and K. Åmark (eds) (1992), *Creating Social Democracy. A Century of the Social Democratic Party in Sweden*. Pennsylvania State University Press.

Amin, A. and N. Thrift (eds) (1994) *Globalisation, Institutions, and Regional Development in Europe*. Oxford: OUP.

Amin, A. and N. Thrift (1995) 'Institutional Issues for the European Regions: From Markets and Plans to Socioeconomics and Powers of Association', *Economy and Society*, **24**, 1, 41–66.

AMWU (1988) *Award Restructuring: Guidelines for Organisers*. Melbourne: AMWU.

Anderson, B. (1983) *Imagined Communities. Reflections on the Origin and Spread of Nationalism*. London: Verso.

Angwin, M. and P. McLaughlin (1990) 'Current Debate: Enterprise Bargaining. The Business Council's Reform Agenda', *Labour and Industry*, **3**, 1, 10–20.

Antonius-Smits, C. and the Maxi Linder Association (1998) 'Gold and Commercial Sex: Exploring the link between small-scale gold mining and commercial sex in the rainforest of Suriname'. Unpublished contribution to the Conference on The Working Sex: Caribbean Development, Tourism, Sex and Work, Kingston, Jamaica, 16 and 17 July.

Appelqvist, Ö. (1996) 'Stabilitet eller expansion? Perspektivskillnader mellan Ernst Wigforss och Gunnar Myrdal i den ekonomiska efterkrigsplaneringen 1944–1945', *Arbetarhistoria*, **1**, 2.

Archer, R. (1992) 'The Unexpected Emergence of Australian Corporatism' in J. Pekkarinen, M. Pohjola and B. Rowthorn (eds), *Social Corporatism*. Oxford: Clarendon.

Archer, R. (1995) *Economic Democracy*. Oxford: Clarendon.

Aris, R. (1998) *Trade Unions and the Management of Industrial Conflict*. London: Macmillan.

Aronsson, P. (1995) 'Vem får vara med – och hur? Om delaktighet i historien' in L. Trägårdh (ed.), *Civilt samhälle kontra offentlig sektor*. Stockholm: SNS Förlag.

Baglioni, G. and C. Crouch (eds) (1990) *European Industrial Relations: the Challenge of Flexibility*. London: Sage.

Bain, G. and R. Price (1983) 'Union Growth' in G. Bain, (ed.) *Industrial Relations in Britain*. Oxford: Basil Blackwell.

Bamber, G. and R. Lansbury (eds) (1987) *International and Comparative Industrial Relations*, 1st edn. Sydney: Allen and Unwin.

Bamber, G. and R. Lansbury (eds) (1993) *International and Comparative Industrial Relations*, 2nd edn. Sydney: Allen and Unwin.

Bardach, E. (1993) *Improving the Productivity of JOBS Programs*. New York: Manpower Demonstration Research Corporation.

Barker, C. (1978) 'A Note on the Theory of Capitalist States', *Capital and Class*, 4, 118–26.

Barnet, R. and J. Cavanagh (1994) *Global Dreams: Imperial Corporations and the New World Order*. New York: Simon and Schuster.

Bayliss, J. and S. Smith (eds) (1997) *The Globalization of World Politics: an Introduction to International Relations*. Oxford: OUP.

REFERENCES

BCA (1986) 'Industry Policy Approaches', *Business Council Bulletin*, 22, April, 9–13.

BCA (1987a) 'The Investment Response to Devaluation', *Business Council Bulletin*, 37, August/September, 1–9.

BCA (1987b) 'Towards an Enterprise Based Industrial Relations System', *Business Council Bulletin*, 32, March, 6–10.

BCA (1989) *Enterprise Based Bargaining Units: A Better Way of Working*. Melbourne: BCA.

BCA (1990) 'Submission to the Training Costs Review Committee', *Business Council Bulletin*, 70, November, 22–39.

Beatty, C. and S. Fothergill (1994) *Registered and Hidden Unemployment in Areas of Chronic Industrial Decline: The Case of the UK Coalfields*. Sheffield: Sheffield Hallam University.

Beck, N., J. Katz, M. Alvarez, G. Garrett and P. Lange (1993) 'Government Partisanship, Labor Organisation and Macroeconomic Performance: a Corrigendum', *American Political Science Review*, **87**, 4, 945–8.

Beck, U. (1997) *Was ist Globalisierung? Irrtümer des Globalismus – Antworten auf Globalisierung*. Frankfurt am Main: Suhrkamp.

Beck, U., A. Giddens and S. Lash (1994) *Reflexive Modernisation. Politics, Tradition and Aesthetics in the Modern Social Order*. Cambridge: Polity.

Beenken, H. (1995) 'Training as a Means of Promoting the Restructuring of the Coal Regions' in Critcher, Schubert and Waddington (eds) (1995) (q.v.).

Bell, S. (1991) 'Unequal Partner: Trade Unions and Industry Policy under the Hawke Government', *Labour and Industry*, 4, 1, 119–37.

Bell, S. (1993) *Australian Manufacturing and the State: The Politics of Industry Policy in the Post-War Era*. New York: CUP.

Bell, S. (1994) 'State Strength and State Weakness: Manufacturing Industry and the Post-War Australian State' in S. Bell and B. Head (eds), *State Economy and Public Policy in Australia*. Melbourne: Melbourne University Press.

Bell, S. and J. Wanna (eds) (1992) *Business–Government Relations in Australia*. Sydney: Harcourt Brace Jovanovitch.

Benders, J. (1996) 'Leaving Lean? Recent Changes in the Production Organization of some Japanese Car Plants', *Economic and Industrial Democracy*, **17**, 1, 9–38.

Bennett, L. (1994) 'Women and Enterprise Bargaining: the Legal and Institutional Framework', *Journal of Industrial Relations*, **36**, 2, 191–212.

Benson, J. (1998) 'Labour management during recessions: Japanese manufacturing enterprises in the 1990s', *Industrial Relations Journal*, **29**, 3, 207–21.

Berry, P. and D. Kitchener (1989) *Can Unions Survive?*. Melbourne: Building Workers' Industrial Union.

Betances, E. and H. Spalding (1997) 'The Dominican Republic After the *Caudillos*', *NACLA Report on the Americas*, **30**, 5, March, 16–19.

Bhagwati, J. and R. Hudec (1996) *Fair Trade and Harmonization: Pre-requisites for Free Trade*. Cambridge, Mass.: MIT Press.

Bieler, A. (1998) 'Austria's and Sweden's Accession to the EU: a comparative neo-Gramscian case study', Ph.D. Thesis, Department of Politics, University of Warwick.

Bishop, R. and L. Robinson (1998) *Night Market: Sexual Cultures and the Thai Economic Miracle*. London: Routledge.

Black, M. (1995) *In the Twilight Zone: Child Workers in the Hotel, Tourism and Catering Industry*. Geneva: ILO.

Blackburn, R. M., J. Jarman and J. Siltanen (1993). 'The Analysis of Occupational Gender Segregation Over Time and Place: Considerations of Measurement and Some New Evidence', *Work, Employment and Society*, **7**, 3, 335–62.

Blank, R. M. (1997) *It Takes a Nation: A New Agenda for Fighting Poverty*. New York and Princeton, N.J.: Russell Sage Foundation and Princeton University Press.

Block, F. (1977) *The Origins of International Economic Disorder*. London: University of California Press.

Block, F. (1980) 'Beyond Relative Autonomy: State Managers as Historical Subjects', *Socialist Register 1980*, pp. 227–42.

Bonefeld, W. (1993) *The Recomposition of the British State During the 1980s*. Aldershot: Dartmouth.

Bonefeld, W. and P. Burnham (1996) 'Britain and the Politics of the European Exchange Rate Mechanism', *Capital and Class*, 60, 5–38.

Bonefeld, W. and P. Burnham (1998) 'The Politics of Counter-Inflationary Credibility in Britain, 1990–1994', *Review of Radical Political Economics*, **30**, 1, 32–52.

Bonefeld, W., A. Brown and P. Burnham (1995) *A Major Crisis? The Politics of Economic Policy in Britain in the 1990s*. Aldershot: Dartmouth.

Boreham, P. (1990) 'Corporatism' in C. Jennet and R. Stewart (eds) (1990), *Hawke and Australian Public Policy: Consensus and Restructuring*. Melbourne: Macmillan.

Boyer, R. (1994) 'Do Labour Institutions Matter for Economic Development?' in G. Rogers (ed.), *Workers, Institutions and Economic Growth in Asia*. Geneva: International Institute for Labour Studies.

Boyer, R. (1997) 'French Statism at the Crossroads' in C. Crouch and W. Streeck (eds) (1997), *Political Economy of Modern Capitalism. Mapping Convergence and Diversity*. London: Sage.

Bray, M. and P. Walsh (1995) 'Accord and Discord: The Differing Fates of Corporatism Under Labo(u)r Governments in Australia and New Zealand', *Labour and Industry*, **6**, 3, 1–26.

Brenner, R. and M. Glick (1991) 'The Regulation School and the West's Economic Impasse', *New Left Review*, 188, 45–119.

Brown, W. and D. Rea (1995). 'The Changing Nature of the Employment Contract', *Scottish Journal of Political Economy*, **42**, 3, 363–77.

Bruun, N. (1979) *Kollektivavtal och rättsideologi. En rättsvetenskaplig studie av de rättsideologiska premisserna för inlemmandet av kollektivavtal och kollektiva kampåtgärder i finsk rättsordning efter år 1924*. Vammala.

REFERENCES

Bruun, N. (1990) 'Den nordiska modellen för facklig verksamhet' in N. Bruun, B. Flodgren, M. Halvorsen, H. Hydén and R. Nielsen, *Den nordiska modellen. Fackföreningarna och arbetsrätten i Noden – nu och i framtiden*. Lund: Liber.

Bruun, N. (1994) 'The Transformation of Nordic Industrial Relations' in Kauppinen and Köykkä (1994) (q.v.).

Bruun, N. (1995) 'Hur förnya arbetsrätten?', *Arbetsmarknad and Arbetsliv*, 1, 2, (Winter).

Bruun, N. and P. Kettunen (1995) 'Interview at the Finnish Federation of Metalworkers', *P+ European Participation Monitor*, 10, 40–1.

Bruun, N., R. Nielsen and D. Töllborg (1994) 'Corporate Labour Law in a European and Nordic Perspective' in *The Future of the Nordic Model of Labour Relations – Three Reports on Internationalisation and Industrial Relations*, Nord 1993:36. Århus: Nordic Council of Ministers.

Buhr, R. (1995) 'Product development as the new function of business promotion' in Critcher, Schubert and Waddington (1995) (q.v.).

Bukharin, N. (1917/1972) *Imperialism and World Economy*. London: Merlin.

Burawoy, M. (1983) 'Between the Labor Process and the State', *American Sociological Review*, 48, 587–605.

Burnham, P. (1990) *The Political Economy of Postwar Reconstruction*. London: Macmillan.

Burnham, P. (1991) 'Neo-Gramscian Hegemony and the International Order', *Capital and Class*, 45, 73–93.

Burnham, P. (1995) 'Capital, Crisis and the International State System' in W. Bonefeld and J. Holloway (eds), *Global Capital, National State and the Politics of Money*. London: Macmillan.

Burnham, P. (1997) 'Globalisation: States, Markets and Class Relations', *Historical Materialism*, 1, 1, 150–60.

Burns, P. and M. Holden (1995) *Tourism: A New Perspective*. London: Prentice Hall.

Butler, D. and G. Butler (1986) *British Political Facts, 1900–1985*. London: Macmillan.

Butler, H. (1951) *Confident Morning*. London: Faber and Faber.

Butler, S. M. and A. Kondratas (1987) *Out of the Poverty Trap: A Conservative Strategy for Welfare Reform*. New York: Free Press.

CAI (1987a) *Employer Perspectives on the ACTU/TDC Report 'Australia Reconstructed'*. Melbourne: CAI.

CAI (1987b) 'Old Wine in New Bottles: A Critique of "Australia Reconstructed" ', *Industrial Review*, September.

Cairncross, A. (1985) *Years of Recovery*. London: Methuen.

Calhoun, C. (1995) *Critical Social Theory. Culture, History, and the Challenge of Difference*. Oxford: Blackwell.

Calmfors, L. and D. J. Driffill (1988) 'Bargaining Structure, Corporatism and Macroeconomic Performance', *Economic Policy*, 6, 1, 14–61.

Campbell, D. (1994) 'Foreign Investment, Labour Immobility and the Quality of Employment', *International Labour Review*, **133**, 2, 185–204.

Campbell, I. (1994) 'The White Paper: Labour Market Deregulation by the Back Door?', *Just Policy*, 1, November.

Campbell, J. (1981) *Final Report of the Committee of Inquiry Into the Australian Financial System*. Canberra: AGPS.

Capelli, P., L. Bassi, H. Katz, D. Knoke, P. Osterman and M. Useem (1997) *Change at Work*. New York: OUP.

Capling, A. and B. Galligan (1992) *Beyond the Protective State: The Political Economy of Australia's Manufacturing Industry Policy*. New York: CUP.

Carney, S. (1988) *Australia In Accord: Politics and Industrial Relations Under the Hawke Government*. South Melbourne: Sun Books.

Carnoy, M. (1993) 'Multinationals in a Changing World: Whither the Nation State?' in M. Carnoy, M. Castells and S. Cohen (eds), *The New Global Economy in the Information Age*. University Park, PA: Pennsylvania State UP.

Castles, F. (1988) *Australian Public Policy and Economic Vulnerability*. Sydney: Allen and Unwin.

Cerny, P. (ed.) (1993) *Finance and World Politics*. Aldershot: Edward Elgar.

Chadwick, M. J., N. H. Highton and L. Lindman (eds) (1987) *Environmental Impacts of Coal Mining and Utilization*. Oxford: Pergamon.

Chant, S. and C. McIlwaine (1995) *Women of a Lesser Cost: Female Labour, Foreign Exchange and Philippine Development*. London: Pluto.

Chaudhri, D. P. (1996) *Dynamic Profile of Child Labour in India 1951–1991*. New Delhi: CLASP, ILO, June.

Children's Defense Fund (1996) *Selected Features of State Welfare Plans*. Legislative Update 19 November, Washington, DC: Children's Defense Fund.

Clarke, S. (1987) 'Capitalist Crisis and the Rise of Monetarism', *Socialist Register 1987*, pp. 393–427.

Clarke, S. (1988a) 'Overaccumulation, Class Struggle and the Regulation Approach', *Capital and Class*, 36, 59–92.

Clarke, S. (1988b) *Keynesianism, Monetarism and the Crisis of the State*. Aldershot: Edward Elgar.

Clarke, S. (ed.) (1991) *The State Debate*. London: Macmillan.

Clarke, S. (1992) 'What in the Ford's Name is Fordism' in N. Gilbert, R. Burrows and A. Pollert (eds), *Fordism and Flexibility: Divisions and Change*. London: Macmillan.

Clegg, H., A. Fox and H. Thompson (1964) *A History of British Trade Unions Since 1889*. Oxford: Clarendon.

Clement, W. and R. Mahon (eds) (1994) *Swedish Social Democracy: A Model in Transition*. Toronto: Canadian Scholars' Press.

Coalition on Child Prostitution and Tourism (1996) *Coalition Update*. Unit 4, Stableyard, Broomgrove Rd, London, 24 October.

Coates, D. (1975) *The Labour Party and the Struggle for Socialism*. Cambridge: CUP.

REFERENCES

Coates, D. (1980) *Labour in Power*. London: Longman.

Coates, D. (1989) *The Crisis of Labour*. London: Phillip Allan.

Coates, D. (1994) *The Question of UK Decline*. Hemel Hempstead: Harvester Wheatsheaf.

Coates, D. (1998) 'Models of Capitalism in the New World Order: the British Case', paper to ESRC Seminar Series in Labour Studies, May 1998, University of Manchester.

Cole, J. and F. Cole (1993) *The Geography of the European Community*. London: Routledge.

Commission on the Status of Women, UN (1995) *World Study on the Role of Women* (ST/ESA/241). New York: UN.

Cox, R. (1977) 'Labor and Hegemony', *International Organization*, **31**, 3, 385–424.

Cox, R. with T. Sinclair (1996) *Approaches to World Order*. Cambridge: CUP.

Creighton, M. (1996) 'The Internationalisation of Labour Law' in R. Mitchell (ed.), Centre for Employment and Labour Relations Law, Monograph No. 3, University of Melbourne.

Critcher, C., D. Parry and D. Waddington (1995) *Redundancy and After: A Study of Ex-Miners from Thurcroft in the Aftermath of Pit Closure*. Sheffield: Pavic Publications.

Critcher, C., K. Schubert and D. Waddington (eds) (1995) *Regeneration of the Coalfield Areas: Anglo-German Perspectives*. London: Pinter.

Cronin, J. (1991) *The Politics of State Expansion*. London: Routledge.

Crouch, C. (1993) *Industrial Relations and European State Traditions*. Oxford: Clarendon.

Crouch, C. (1995) 'Revised Diversity: from the Neo-liberal Decade to beyond Maastricht' in J. van Ruyssevveldt and J. Visser (eds), *Industrial Relations In Europe: Traditions and Transitions*. London: Sage.

Crummett, M. (1987) 'Rural Women and Migration in Latin America' in C. Deere and M. Leon (eds), *Rural Women and State Policy*. Boston: Westview.

Dabscheck, B. (1995) *The Struggle for Australian Industrial Relations*. Sydney: OUP.

Daly, M. (1993) 'No Economy is an Island' in S. Rees, G. Rodley and F. Stilwell (eds), *Beyond the Market: Alternatives to Economic Rationalism*. Sydney: Pluto.

Danziger, S. H. and P. Gottschalk (1995) *America Unequal*. New York and Cambridge: Russell Sage Foundation and Harvard University Press.

Davidson, R. (1992) 'The Failures of Financial Deregulation in Australia' in Bell and Wanna (1992) (q.v.).

Davies, S. (1993) 'Training and Retraining Policies and Practices', paper to conference on Revitalising the Older Industrial Regions: North Rhine Westphalia and Wales Contrasted, University of Wales College, Cardiff.

Davis, N. (1993) 'Introduction: International Perspectives on Female Prostitution' in N. Davis (ed.), *Prostitution: An International Handbook on Trends, Problems and Policies*. Westport, Connecticut: Greenwood Press.

Deacon, A. (ed.) (1997) *From Welfare to Work: Lessons from America.* Choice in Welfare, No. 39. London: Institute of Economic Affairs.

Dean, M. (1995) 'Governing the Unemployed Self in an Active Society', *Economy and Society,* **24**, 559–83.

Department of Labor (1995) *What's Working (and What's Not): A Summary of Research on the Economic Impacts of Employment and Training Programs.* Washington, DC: United States Department of Labor.

Dertouzos, M., R. Lester and R. Solow (1989) *Made in America – Regaining the Competitive Edge.* Cambridge, Mass.: MIT Press.

Deyo, F. (1989) *Beneath the Miracle: Labour Subordination in the New Asian Industrialism.* Berkeley: University of Berkeley Press.

Dicken, P. (1992) *Global Shift: The Internationalization of Economic Activity.* London: Harper and Row.

Dicken, P. (1998) *Global Shift: Transforming the World Economy.* London: Paul Chapman.

DIR (1995) *Enterprise Bargaining In Australia, Annual Report 1994.* Canberra: DIR.

DIR (1996) *Enterprise Bargaining In Australia, Annual Report 1995.* Canberra: DIR.

Dohse, K., U. Jurgens and T. Malsh (1985) 'From "Fordism" to Toyotism? The Social Organisation of the Labor Process in the Japanese Automobile Industry', *Politics and Society,* **14**, 2, 115–46.

Dølvik, J.-E. (1994) 'Norwegian Trade Unionism at a Crossroad?' in Kauppinen and Köykkä (1994) (q.v.).

Dowrick, S. (1993) 'Wage Bargaining Systems and Productivity Growth in OECD Countries', Economic Planning Advisory Council, Background Paper No. 26. Canberra: AGPS.

Dulebohn, J. H., G. R. Ferris and J. T. Stodd (1995) 'The History and Evolution of Human Resource Management' in G. R. Ferris, S. D. Rosen and D. T. Barnum (eds), *Handbook of Human Resource Management.* Cambridge, Mass.: Blackwell.

Edelman, P. (1997) 'The Worst Thing Bill Clinton Has Done', *Atlantic Monthly,* March, 43–58.

Edwards, J. (1996) *Keating: The Inside Story.* Penguin Books Australia.

Edwards, P. K. (1986) *Conflict at Work: a Materialist Analysis of Workplace Relations.* Oxford: Blackwell.

Edwards, P. K., J. Bélanger and L. Haiven (1994) 'The Workplace and Labor Regulation in Comparative Perspective' in J. Bélanger *et al.* (eds), *Workplace Industrial Relations and the Global Challenge.* Ithaca: ILR Press.

Edwards, P. K., P. Armstrong, P. Marginson and J. Purcell (1996) 'Towards the Transnational Company? The Global Structure and Organisation of Multinational Firms' in R. Crompton *et al.* (eds), *Changing Forms of Employment: Organisations, Skills and Gender.* London: Routledge.

Edwards, S. (1987) 'Prostitutes: Victims of Law, Social Policy and Organised Crime' in P. Carlen and A. Worrall (eds), *Gender, Crime and Justice.* Milton Keynes: OUP.

REFERENCES

Eichengreen, B. (1990) *Elusive Stability*. Cambridge: CUP.

Ekachai, S. (1990) *Behind the Smile: Voices of Thailand*. Bangkok: The Post Publishing.

Elam, M. (1994) 'Puzzling out the Post-Fordist Debate: Technology, Markets and Institutions' in A. Amin (ed.), *Post-Fordism: A Reader*. Oxford: Blackwell.

Elger, T. and C. Smith (eds) (1994) *Global Japanization? The Transnational Transformation of the Labour Process*. London: Routledge.

Esping-Andersen, G. (1990) *The Three Worlds of Welfare Capitalism*. Cambridge: Polity.

Esping-Andersen, G. (1992) 'The Making of a Social Democratic Welfare State' in K. Misgeld, K. Molin and K. Åmark (eds) (1992), *Creating Social Democracy. A Century of the Social Democratic Labor Party in Sweden*. Pennsylvania State University Press.

Esping-Andersen, G. (ed.) (1996) *Welfare States in Transition: National Adaptations in Global Economies*. London: Sage.

Esterman, H. and F. Roxlau-Hennemann (1995) 'The Eastern Ruhr Development Agency: A Public-private Sector Initiative for Structural Change' in Critcher, Schubert and Waddington (1995) (q.v.).

Evans, P. M. (1995) 'Linking welfare to jobs: workfare, Canadian style' in A. Sayeed (ed.), *Workfare: Does it Work? Is it Fair?*, pp. 75–104. Montreal: Institute for Research on Public Policy.

Evatt Foundation (1995) *Unions 2001: A Blueprint for Trade Union Activism*. Sydney: Evatt Foundation.

Ewer, P., W. Higgins and A. Stephens (1987) *The Unions and the Future of Australian Manufacturing*. London: Allen and Unwin.

Ewer, P., I. Hampson, C. Lloyd, J. Rainford, S. Rix and M. Smith (1991) *Politics and the Accord*. Sydney: Pluto.

Fagan, R. and M. Webber (1994) *Global Restructuring: The Australian Experience*. Melbourne: OUP.

Federal Campaign Consultative Panel (1996) Draft Report, Australian Labor Party, New South Wales Branch.

Feinstein, C. (1972) *National Income, Expenditure and Output of the UK 1855–1965*. Cambridge: CUP.

Fennema, M. and T. Loewenthal (1987) *Construccion de Raza y Nacion en Republica Dominicana*. Santo Domingo: Editora Universitaia-UASD, Vol. DLXXIV.

Ferguson, J. (1992) *Dominican Republic: Beyond the Lighthouse*. London: Latin America Bureau.

Ferner, A. and R. Hyman (eds) (1992a) *Industrial Relations in the New Europe*. Oxford: Blackwell.

Ferner, A. and R. Hyman (1992b) 'Industrial Relations in the New Europe: Seventeen Types of Ambiguity' in Ferner and Hyman (eds) (1992a) (q.v.).

Ferner, A. and R. Hyman (eds) (1998) *Changing Industrial Relations in Europe*. Oxford: Blackwell.

Ferner, A., E. Keep and J. Waddington (1997) 'Industrial Restructuring and EU-wide

Social Measures: Broader Lessons of the ECSC Experience', *Journal of European Public Policy*, **4**, 1, 56–72.

Fleming, D. and H. Søborg (1995) 'Interview at the Danish Employers' Confederation', *P+ European Participation Monitor*, 10, 37–9.

Flodgren, B. (1990) 'Företagsdemokrati – medbestämmande' in N. Bruun, B. Flodgren, M. Halvorsen, H. Hydén and R. Nielsen, *Den nordiska modellen. Fackföreningarna och arbetsrätten i Norden – nu och i framtiden*. Lund: Liber.

Fothergill, S. and N. Guy (1994) *An Evaluation of British Coal Enterprise*. Barnsley: Coalfield Communities Campaign.

Frankel, B. (1997) 'Beyond Labourism and Socialism: How the Australian Labor Party Developed the Model of "New Labour" ', *New Left Review*, 221, 2–33.

Fransman, M. (1995) *Japan's Computer and Communications Industry: the Evolution of Industrial Giants and Global Competitiveness*. Oxford: OUP.

Friedlander, D. and G. Burtless (1995) *Five Years After: The Long-Term Effects of Welfare-to-Work Programs*. New York: Russell Sage Foundation.

Frizzell, J. (1992) *Pay Equity and Overaward Payments in the Metal Industry*. Canberra: AGPS.

Fröbel, F., J. Heinrichs and O. Kreye (1980) *The New International Division of Labour*. Cambridge: CUP.

Fulcher, J. (1991) *Labour Movements, Employers and the State*. Oxford: Clarendon.

Fyfe, A. (1989) *Child Labour*. Cambridge: Polity.

Gallie, D. (1985) 'Les lois Auroux: the Reform of French Industrial Relations?' in H. Machin and V. Wright (eds), *Economic Policy and Policy Making Under the Mitterand Presidency 1981–84*. London: Unwin.

Gamble, A. (1988) *The Free Economy and the Strong State: The Politics of Thatcherism*. London: Macmillan.

Gardner, M. (1995) 'Labour Movements and Industrial Restructuring: Australia, New Zealand, and the United States' in K. Wever and L. Turner (eds), *The Comparative Political Economy of Industrial Relations*. Madison: Industrial Relations Research Association.

Giddens, A. (1984) *The Constitution of Society*. Cambridge: Polity.

Gill, F. (1994) 'Overaward Payments: Observed Patterns and their Implications', Industrial Relations Research Series, 14, DIR. Canberra: AGPS.

Gill, S. (1995) 'Globalisation, Market Civilisation and Disciplinary Neoliberalism', *Millennium*, **24**, 3, 399–423.

Gilpin, R. (1987) *The Political Economy of International Relations*. Princeton: Princeton University Press.

Glyn, A. (1995) 'Social Democracy and Full Employment', *New Left Review*, 211, 33–55.

Goldthorpe, J. (1978) 'The Current Inflation' in F. Hirsch and J. Goldthorpe (eds), *The Political Economy of Inflation*. London: Martin Robertson.

Goldthorpe, J. (1984) 'The End of Convergence: Corporatist and Dualist Tendencies in

Modern Western Societies', in J. Goldthorpe (ed.), *Order and Conflict in Contemporary Capitalism*. Oxford: Clarendon Press.

Gough, I. (1979) *The Political Economy of the Welfare State*. London: Macmillan.

Gourevitch, P., A. Martin, G. Ross, S. Bornstein, A. Markovits and C. Allen (eds) (1984) *Unions and Economic Crisis: Britain, West Germany and Sweden*. London: Allen and Unwin.

Grant, W. (1993) *The Politics of Economic Policy*. Hemel Hempstead: Harvester.

Gronning, T. (1995) 'Recent Developments at Toyota Motor Co' in Å. Sandberg (ed.), *Enriching Production*. Aldershot: Avebury.

Gronow, J. (1986) *On the Formation of Marxism, Karl Kautsky's Theory of Capitalism, the Marxism of the Second International and Karl Marx's Critique of Political Economy*. Commentationes Scientiarum Socialium, 33. Helsinki: The Finnish Society of Sciences and Letters.

Gudmundsson, G. (1995) 'The Nordic Model: Definitions and Dimensions', *P+ European Participation Monitor*, 10, 5–11.

Gueron, J. M. (1996) 'A Research Context for Welfare Reform', *Journal of Policy Analysis and Management*, **15**, 547–61.

Gueron, J. M. and E. Pauly (1991) *From Welfare to Work*. New York: Russell Sage Foundation.

Gustavsen, B., B. Hofmaier, M. Ekman Philips and A. Wikman (1995) *Utvecklingslinjer i arbetslivet och Arbetslivsfondens roll*. Stockholm.

Habermas, J. (1981) *Theorie des kommunikativen Handelns*, I–II. Frankfurt am Main: Suhrkamp.

Hampden-Turner, C. and F. Trompenaars (1994) *The Seven Cultures of Capitalism: Value Systems for Creating Wealth in the United States, Britain, Japan, Germany, France, Sweden and the Netherlands*. London: Piatkus.

Handler, J. F. (1995) *The Poverty of Welfare Reform*. New Haven: Yale University Press.

Hansenne, M. (1996) 'Trade and Labour Standards: Can Common Rules be Agreed?', address by Director-General of ILO, 46th Wilton Park Conference, on Liberalising World Trade and Prospects for Singapore Ministerial Meeting, West Sussex, 6 March.

Harman, C. (1996) 'Globalisation: a critique of a new orthodoxy', *International Socialism*, Series 2, 73, Winter, 3–33.

Harrison, B. (1994) *Lean and Mean. The Changing Landscape of Corporate Power in the Age of Flexibility*. New York: Basic Books.

Hawkins, K. (1976) *British Industrial Relations, 1945–1975*. London: Barrie and Jenkins.

Haworth, N. and S. Hughes (1996) 'The Global Regulation of Labour and International Labour Standards: Theoretical and Policy Implications of the Social Clause', paper to Conference on the Globalisation of Production and the Regulation of Labour, University of Warwick, September.

Haworth, N. and S. Hughes (1997) 'Trade and International Labour Standards: Issues and Debates Over the Social Clause', *Journal of Industrial Relations*, **39**, 2, 179–95.

Heath, C. (1971) *A Guide to the Industrial Relations Act 1971*. London: Sweet and Maxwell.

Hessling, M. (1995) 'The Role of Ruhrkohle AG in Germany's Energy and Coal Policy' in Critcher, Schubert and Waddington (eds) (1995) (q.v.).

HF-B/LO/NHO in co-operation with I. Munkeby and M. Malmo (1997) 'Norway's Social Partners' Joint Action Programme for Enterprise Development' in A. L. Tolentino (ed.), *Workers: Stakeholders in productivity in a changing global economic environment*, EMD/18/E, Enterprise and Management Development, ILO, Geneva.

Higgins, W. (1985) 'Political Unionism and the Corporatist Thesis', *Economic and Industrial Democracy*, **6**, 3, 349–81.

Higgins, W. (1987) 'Unions as Bearers of Industrial Regeneration: Reflections on the Australian Case', *Economic and Industrial Democracy*, **8**, 2, 213–36.

Higgins, W. (1994) 'Industry Policy' in J. Brett, J. Gillespie and M. Goot (eds), *Developments in Australian Politics*. Melbourne: Macmillan.

Higgott, R. (1997) 'Globalisation, Regionalisation and Localisation, Putting the 'P'' back in international political economy', unpublished conference paper, University of Birmingham.

Hirdman, Y. (1990) 'Genussystemet', *Demokrati och makt i Sverige. Maktutredningens huvudrapport*, SOU, 44, Stockholm.

Hirdman, Y. (1997) ' "Social Planning Under Rational Control". Social Engineering in Sweden in the 1930s and 1940s' in Kettunen and Eskola (1997) (q.v.).

Hirschman, A. O. (1970) *Exit, Voice and Loyalty*. Cambridge, Mass.: Harvard University Press.

Hirst, P. and G. Thompson (1996) *Globalization in Question: the International Economy and the Possibilities of Governance*. Cambridge: Polity.

Hirst, P. and J. Zeitlin. (1989) 'Flexible Specialisation and the Competitive Failure of UK Manufacturing', *Political Quarterly*, **60**, 2, 164–78.

Hobsbawm, E. (1983) 'Introduction: Inventing Traditions' in E. Hobsbawm and T. Ranger (eds), *The Invention of Traditions*. Cambridge: CUP.

Hollingsworth, J. R. (1997) 'The Institutional Embeddedness of American Capitalism' in C. Crouch and W. Streeck (eds) (1997), *Political Economy of Modern Capitalism: Mapping Convergence and Diversity*. London: Sage.

Holloway, J. (1994) 'Global Capital and the National State', *Capital and Class*, 52, 23–49.

Holloway, J. and S. Picciotto (1977) 'Capital, Crisis and the State', *Capital and Class*, 2, 76–101.

Holtham, G., K. Mayhew and P. Ingram. (1998) *Welfare in Working Order*. London: Institute for Public Policy Research.

REFERENCES

House of Commons, Social Security Committee (1998) *Social Security Reforms: Lessons from the United States of America*, HC 552. London: Stationery Office.

Howell, C. (1992) *Regulating Labor: the State and Industrial Relations in Post-war France*. Princeton: Princeton UP.

Howell, C. (1995/6) 'Turning to the State: Thatcherism and the Crisis of British Trade Unionism', *New Political Science*, 33/34, 13–50.

Howes, C. and A. Singh (1995) 'Long-Term Trends in the World Economy: the Gender Dimension', *World Development*, **23**, 11, 1895–911.

Hu, Y.-S. (1992) 'Global Firms are National Firms with International Operations', *California Management Review*, **37**, 1, 107–26.

Hudson, R. (1992) 'Industrial Restructuring and Spatial Change: Myths and Realities in the Changing Geography of Production in the 1980s', Occasional Paper No. 27, Department of Geography, University of Durham.

Hudson, R. (1994) 'Institutional Change, Cultural Transformation and Economic Regeneration: Myths and Realities from Europe's Old Industrial Areas' in Amin and Thrift (1994) (q.v.).

Hyman, R. (1975) *Industrial Relations: A Marxist Introduction*. London: Macmillan.

IBRD (1993) *East Asian Miracle*. New York: OUP.

ICFTU (1994) 'The Need for International Guarantees of Labour Standards', telex to H E Lee Boon Yang, Minister for Labour of the Republic of Singapore, 27 May.

Ilmonen, K. (1996) 'Is Trade Unionism Heading for a Deadlock?'. Paper to the 4th IIRA European Regional Congress, Helsinki, 23–6 August.

Ilmonen, K. and K. Kevätsalo (1995) *Ay-liikkeen vaikeat valinnat. Sosiologinen näkökulma ammatilliseen järjestäytymiseen Suomessa*, Palkansaajien tutkimuslaitos, Tutkimuksia, 59, Helsinki.

ILO (1994a) 'International Labour Standards and Global Economic Integration', special address by Mr Heribert Maier, Deputy Director-General at a Symposium on International Labour Standards and Global Economic Integration, 25 April 1994, Washington DC.

ILO (1994b) 'The International Labour Office Should Continue the Struggle for Social Justice and Economic Development which Create Jobs', Director-General's opening speech at International Labour Conference, 23 June.

ILO (1997) *World Labour Report 1997–1998. Industrial Relations, Democracy and Social Stability*. Geneva: ILO.

Inquiry into Sex Discrimination in Overaward Payments (1992) *Just Rewards*, Human Rights and Equal Opportunity Commission, Canberra: AGPS.

INSAF (1995) 'The needs of children in Goa: Towards building an adequate response', *Interim Report*. Panjim: INSAF.

International Economic and Energy Consultants (1995) 'Reconversion Experiences in the EU's Coalfields: A Balance Sheet', occasional paper.

Jackson, P. and K. Sisson (1976) 'Employers' Confederations in Sweden and the United

Kingdom and the Significance of Industrial Infrastructure', *British Journal of Industrial Relations*, **14**, 3, 306–23.

James, W. (1993) 'Migration, Racism and Identity Formation: The Caribbean Experience in Britain' in W. James and C. Harris, *Inside Babylon*. London: Verso.

Jay, P. (1994) 'The Economy 1990–1994' in D. Kavanagh and A. Seldon (eds), *The Major Effect*. London: Macmillan.

Jenkins, R. (1984) 'Divisions over the International Division of Labour', *Capital and Class*, 22, 28–57.

Jensen, A. (1995) 'Aftalemodellen som forbillede – rygterne om aftalemodellens snarlige død er øverdrevne', *Arbetsliv i Norden*, **4**.

Jenson, J., E. Hagen and C. Reddy (eds) (1988) *Feminization of the Labour Force: Paradoxes and Promises*. Cambridge: Polity.

Jessop, B. (1993) 'Towards a Schumpeterian Workfare State? Preliminary Remarks on Post-Fordist Political Economy', *Studies in Political Economy*, **40**, 7–39.

Jessop, B. (1994a) 'Post-Fordism and the State' in A. Amin (eds) (1994), *Post-Fordism: A Reader*. Oxford: Blackwell.

Jessop, B. (1994b) 'The Transition to Post-Fordism and the Schumpeterian Workfare State' in R. Burrows and B. Loader (eds), *Towards the Post-Fordist Welfare State*. London: Routledge.

Joenniemi, P. (1994) 'Norden – en europeisk megaregion?' in S. Karlsson (ed.), *Norden är död. Länge leve Norden. En debattbok om de nordiska länderna som en 'megaregion' i Europa*, Nord, 11, Stockholm.

Johnson, B. and B.-E. Lundvall (1991) 'Flexibility and Institutional Learning' in B. Jessop, H. Kastendiek, K. Nielsen and O. K. Petersen (eds), *The Politics of Flexibility: Restructuring State and Industry in Britain, Germany and Scandinavia*. Aldershot: Edward Elgar.

Johnson, C. (1982) *MITI and the Japanese Miracle: The Growth of Industrial Policy 1925–75*. Stanford, California: Stanford University Press.

Jonas, A. E. G. (1996) 'Local Labour Control Regimes: Uneven Development and the Social Regulation of Production', *Regional Studies*, **30**, 323–38.

Jones, R. (1987) *Wages and Employment Policy 1936–1985*. London: Unwin.

Julkunen, R. and L. Rantalaiho (1993) 'Women on Strike – Nonexistent or Silenced?' in P. Kettunen (ed.), *Strike and Social Change*, Turku Provincial Museum Publication Series 7, Turku.

Juyal, N. B. (1993) *Child Labour in the Carpet Industry in Mirzapur-Bhadohi*. New Delhi: ILO.

Kalecki, M. (1943/71) 'Political Implications of Full Employment' in M. Kalecki, *Selected Essays on the Dynamics of the Capitalist Economy 1933–1970*. London: CUP.

Kanter, R. M. (1995) *World Class: Thriving Locally in the Global Economy*. New York: Simon and Schuster.

Katzenstein, P. (1978) *Between Power and Plenty: Foreign Economic Policies of Advanced Industrial Societies*. Madison: University of Wisconsin Press.

REFERENCES

Katzenstein, P. (1985) *Small States in World Markets: Industrial Policy in Europe.* Ithaca and New York: Cornell University Press.

Kauppinen, T. (1994) *The Transformation of Labour Relations in Finland.* Finnish Labour Relations Association, No. 8, Helsinki.

Kauppinen, T. and V. Köykkä (eds) (1994) *Transformation of Nordic Industrial Relations in the European Context.* IIRA 4th European Regional Congress, Helsinki, Finland 24–6 August, Plenary 1.

Kauppinen, T. and V. Köykkä (eds) (1994) *Workplace Europe – New Forms of Bargaining and Participation.* IIRA 4th European Regional Congress, Helsinki, 24–6 August.

Kaus, M. (1986) 'The Work Ethic State', *New Republic,* 7 July, 22–33.

Keating, P. (1994) *Working Nation: Policies and Programs.* Canberra: AGPS.

Keech, W. (1992) 'Rules, Discretion, and Accountability in Macroeconomic Policy-making', *Governance,* **5**, 3, 259–78.

Kelly, L., R. Wingfield, S. Burton and L. Regan (1995) *Splintered Lives: Sexual Exploitation of Children in the Context of Children's Rights and Child Protection.* Ilford: Barnardo's.

Kelly, P. (1994) 2nd edn. *The End of Certainty: Power, Politics and Business in Australia.* Sydney: Allen and Unwin.

Kempadoo, K. (1998) 'COIN and MODEMA in the Dominican Republic' in K. Kempadoo and J. Doezema (eds), *Global Sex Workers.* London: Routledge.

Kern, H. and M. Schumann (1984) 'Work and Social Character: Old and New Contours', *Economic and Industrial Democracy,* **5**, 1, 51–71.

Kettunen, P. (1994) *Suojelu, suoritus, subjekti. Työsuojelu teollistuvan suomen yhteiskunnallisissa ajattelu- ja toimintatavoissa* (with an English summary, 'Protection, performance and subject: Labour protection and the social modes of thought and action in Finland, c. 1880–1950'), Historiallisia tutkimuksia, No. 189, Vammala.

Kettunen, P. (1995) 'Lönarbetet och den nordiska demokratin i Finland' in P. Kettunen and T. Rissanen (eds), *Arbete och nordisk samhällsmodell,* papers on Labour History IV, Tammerfors.

Kettunen, P. (1997) 'The Society of Virtuous Circles' in Kettunen and Eskola (1997) (q.v.).

Kettunen, P. and I. Turunen (1994) 'The Middle Class, Knowledge and the Idea of the Third Factor', *Scandinavian Journal of History,* **19**, 1, 63–86.

Kettunen, P. and H. Eskola (eds) (1997) *Models, Modernity and the Myrdals,* Renvall Institute Publications 8, Renvall Institute for Area and Cultural Studies, University of Helsinki.

Kidner, R. (1979) *Trade Union Law.* London: Stevens.

Kjellberg, A. (1983) *Facklig organisering i tolv länder. Forskningsprojektet 'Sverige under socialdemokratin 1932–76'.* Lund.

Kjellberg, A. (1992) 'Sweden: Can the Model Survive?' in Ferner and Hyman (eds) (1992a) (q.v.).

Kjellberg, A. (1998) 'Sweden: Restoring the Model?' in Ferner and Hyman (eds) (1998).

Kmenta, J. (1971) *Elements of Econometrics.* New York: Macmillan.

Knudsen, H. (1995) *Employee Participation in Europe.* London: Sage.

Kochan, T. A., R. D. Landbury and J. P. MacDuffie (eds) (1997) *After Lean Production: Evolving Employment Practices in the World Auto Industry.* Ithaca: ILR Press.

Korpi, W. (1983) *The Democratic Class Struggle.* London: Routledge and Kegan Paul.

Kosonen, P. (1993) 'The Finnish Model and the Welfare State in Crisis' in P. Kosonen (ed.), *The Nordic Welfare State as an Idea and as Reality.* Renvall Institute Publications 5, Renvall Institute, University of Helsinki.

Köykkä, V. (1994) 'Changing Strategies in Nordic Employer Organisations' in T. Kauppinen and V. Köykkä (eds), *The Changing Structures and Strategies of the Employers' and Employees' Organisations.* IIRA 4th European Regional Congress, Helsinki, Finland 24–6 August, Plenary 3.

Krishna, S. (1996) *Restoring Childhood.* Delhi: Konark Publishers.

Kruhse-Mount Burton, S. (1995) 'Sex Tourism and Traditional Australian Male Identity' in M. Lanfant, J. Allcock, and E. Bruner (eds), *International Tourism: Identity and Change.* London: Sage.

Kydland, F. and E. Prescott (1977) 'Rules Rather Than Discretion', *Journal of Political Economy,* **85**, 3, 473–91.

Kyloh, R. (1989) 'Flexibility and Structural Adjustment Through Consensus: Some Lessons from Australia', *International Labour Review,* **128**, 1, 103–23.

Kyloh, R. (1994) 'Restructuring at the National Level: Labour-led Restructuring and Reform in Australia' in W. Sengenberger and D. Campbell (eds), *Creating Economic Opportunities: The Role of Labour Standards in Industrial Restructuring.* Geneva: International Institute for Labour Studies.

Labour Party (1996) *Getting Welfare to Work: A New Vision for Social Security.* London: Labour Party.

Lane, C. (1989) *Management and Labour In Europe.* Aldershot: Edward Elgar.

Lane, C. (1995) *Industry and Society in Europe: Stability and Change in Britain, Germany and France.* Aldershot: Edward Elgar.

Lange, P., M. Wallerstein and M. Golden (1995) 'The End of Corporatism? Wage Setting in the Nordic and Germanic Countries' in S. M. Jacoby (ed.), *The Workers of Nations: Industrial Relations in a Global Economy.* Oxford: OUP.

Larsson, J. (1994) *Hemmet vi ärvde. Om folkhemmet, identiteten och den gemensamma framtiden.* Stockholm: Arena.

Lash, S. (1985) 'The End of Neo-corporatism? The Breakdown of Centralized Bargaining in Sweden', *British Journal of Industrial Relations,* **23**, 2, 215–39.

Lash, S. (1994) 'Reflexivity and its Doubles' in Beck, Giddens and Lash (1994) (q.v.).

Lash, S. and J. Urry (1987) *The End of Organized Capitalism.* Cambridge: Polity.

Lash, S. and J. Urry (1994) *Economies of Signs and Space: After Organised Capitalism.* London: Sage.

Latinfinance (1995) *Tourism in Latin America.* Latinfinance.

Lea, J. (1988) *Tourism and Development in the Third World.* London: Routledge.

REFERENCES

Lee, W. (1991) 'Prostitution and Tourism in South-East Asia' in N. Redclift and M. Sinclair (eds), *Working Women: International Perspectives on Labour and Gender Ideology*. London: Routledge.

Leggett, C. (1988) 'Industrial Relations and Enterprise Unionism in Singapore', *Labour and Industry*, 1, 2, 242–57.

Leggett, C. (1993) 'Corporatist Trade Unionism in Singapore' in S. Frenkel (ed.), *Organized Labour in the Asia Pacific Region*. Ithaca: ILR Press.

Lehmbruch, G. (1979) 'Consociational Democracy, Class Conflict and the New Corporatism' in P. Schmitter and G. Lehmbruch (eds) (1979), *Trends Towards Corporatist Intermediation*. London: Sage.

Lewis, J.and Åström, G. (1992) 'Equality, Difference and State Welfare: Labour Market and Family Policies in Sweden', *Feminist Studies*, 18, 1, 59–87.

Lewis, R. (1983) 'Collective Labour Law' in G. Bain (ed.), *Industrial Relations in Britain*. Oxford: Basil Blackwell.

Lilja, K. (1992) 'Finland: No Longer the Nordic Exception' in Ferner and Hyman (eds) (1992a) (q.v.).

Lilja, K. (1997) 'Bargaining for the Future: the Changing Habitus of the Shop Steward System in the Pulp and Paper Mills of Finland' in R. Whitley and P. H. Kristensen (eds) (1997), *Governance at Work: The Social Regulation of Economic Relations*. Oxford: OUP.

Lilja, K. (1998) 'Finland: Continuity and Modest Moves towards Company-level Corporatism' in Ferner and Hyman (eds) (1998) (q.v.).

Lipietz, A. (1987) *Mirages and Miracles: The Crises of Global Fordism*. London: New Left Books.

Lister, R. (1997) 'From Fractured Britain to One Nation? The Policy Options for Welfare Reform', *Renewal*, 5, 11–23.

Lloyd, C. (1990) 'Accord in Discord', *Australian Left Review*, July, 11–13.

Locke, R., T. Kochan and M. Piore (1995) 'Reconceptualising Comparative Industrial Relations: Lessons from International Research', *International Labour Review*, 134, 2, 139–61.

McAven, L. (1993) 'There is an Alternative', *Town and Country Planning, Coalfield Communities Special Issue*, 62, 7, 3–7.

McCarthy, W. E. J. and S. Parker (1968) *Shop Stewards and Workshop Relations*. London: HMSO (Donovan Commission Research Paper 10).

McEachern, D. (1991) *Business Mates: The Power and Politics of the Hawke Era*. Sydney: Prentice Hall.

Macintyre, S. (1986) 'Labour, Capital and Arbitration 1890–1920' in B. Head (ed.), *State and Economy in Australia*. Melbourne: OUP.

Macintyre, S. (1990) *The Oxford History of Australia, Vol. 4 1901–1942: The Succeeding Age*. Melbourne: OUP.

Macken, J. (1989) *Award Restructuring*. Sydney: Federation Press.

Mahon, R. (1991) 'From Solidaristic Wages to Solidaristic Work: a Post-Fordist Historic Compromise for Sweden?', *Economic and Industrial Democracy*, **12**, 3, 295–325.

Martin, A. (1987) 'The End of the Swedish Model? Recent Developments in Swedish Industrial Relations', *Bulletin of Comparative Labour Relations*, **16**, 1, 93–128.

Martin, A. (1995) 'The Swedish Model: Demise or Reconfiguration?' in R. Locke, T. Kochan and M. Piore (eds), *Employment Relations in a Changing World Economy.* Cambridge, Mass.: MIT Press.

Martin, H. and H. Schumann (1997) *The Global Trap: Globalization and the Assault on Democracy and Prosperity.* London: Zed.

Martin, R. (1989) 'The New Economics and Politics of Regional Restructuring: The British Experience' in L. Albrechts *et al.* (eds), *Regional Policy at the Crossroads.* London: Jessica Kingsley.

Martin, R. and P. Sunley (1997) 'The post-Keynesian State and the Space-Economy' in R. Lee and J. Wills (eds), *Geographies of Economies*, pp. 278–89. London: Arnold.

Marx, K. (1974) *Capital, Volume One.* London: Lawrence and Wishart.

Mathews, J. (1986) 'The Politics of the Accord' in D. McKnight (ed.), *Moving Left.* Sydney: Pluto.

Mathews, J. (1989) *Tools of Change: New Technology and the Democratisation of Work.* Sydney: Pluto.

Matthews, M. and K. A. Becker (1998) *Making Welfare Work.* London: Adam Smith Institute.

Matthews, R. C. O. (1968) 'Why has Britain Had Full Employment since the War?' *Economic Journal*, **78**, 3, pp. 555–69.

Matthews, T. (1994) 'Employers' Associations, Corporatism and the Accord' in S. Bell and B. Head (eds) (1994), *State, Economy and Public Policy in Australia.* Melbourne: Melbourne University Press.

Maurice, M., F. Sellier and J.-J. Silvestre (1986) *The Social Foundations of Industrial Power: A Comparison of France and Germany.* Cambridge, Mass.: MIT Press.

Mead, L. M. (1992) *The New Politics of Poverty: The Nonworking Poor in America.* New York: Basic Books.

Mead, L. M. (1996) 'Memorandum submitted by Lawrence Mead' in House of Commons, Employment Committee, *The Right to Work/Workfare*, pp. 29–30. Second Report, HC 82. London: HMSO.

Mead, L. M. (1997) 'From Welfare to Work: Lessons from America' in Deacon (ed.) (1997) (q.v.), pp. viii–xi, 1–55.

Miles, R. (1987) *Capitalism and Unfree Labour: Anomaly or Necessity?* London: Tavistock.

Miller, P. and T. O'Leary (1989) 'Hierarchies and American Ideals 1900–1940', *Academy of Management Review*, **14**, 2, 250–65.

Mishel, L. and J. Schmitt (1995) *Cutting Wages by Cutting Welfare: The Impact of Reform on the Low-Wage Labor Market.* Briefing Paper 58, Washington, DC: Economic Policy Institute.

REFERENCES

Mjelva, H. (1995) 'Interview at Kvaerner', *P+ European Participation Monitor*, 10, 28–30.

Mjøset, L. (ed.) (1986) *Norden dagen derpå. De nordiske-økonomisk-politiske modellene og deres problemer på 70- og 80-tallet.* Universitetsforlaget AS.

Moody, K. (1997) 'Towards an International Social-Movement Unionism', *New Left Review*, 225, 52–72.

Moran, J. (1998) 'The Dynamics of Class Politics and National Economies in Globalisation: the Marginalisation of the Unacceptable?', *Capital and Class*, 66, 53–83.

Morehead, A., M. Steele, M. Alexander, K. Stephen and L. Duffin (1997) *Changes at Work: the 1995 Australian Workplace Industrial Relations Survey.* Melbourne: Longman.

Mueller, F. (1996) 'National Stakeholders in the Global Contest for Corporate Investment', *European Journal of Industrial Relations*, 2, 3, 345–68.

Mueller, F. and R. Loveridge (1997) 'Institutional, Sectoral and Corporate Dynamics in the Creation of Global Supply Chains' in Whitley and Kristensen (eds) (1997) (q.v.).

Munck, R. (1988) *The New International Labour Studies: An Introduction.* London: Zed Books.

Murphy, C. N. (1994) *International Organization and Industrial Change: Global Governance since 1850.* Cambridge: Polity.

Myrdal, H.-G. (1995) 'The Nordic Model: Does It Exist?', *P+ European Participation Monitor*, 10, 12–14.

Naschold, F. (1994) *The Politics and Economics of Workplace Development: A Review of National Programmes.* Työpoliittinen tutkimus, No. 64, Helsinki.

Neal, A. C. (1994) 'Cautious Convergence or Catastrophic Collision? Aspects of Transformation for Nordic Industrial Relationships in the European Context' in Kauppinen and Köykkä (1994) (q.v.).

Nguyen, T. (1995) 'The World Trade Organisation. WTO: A New International Legal Response to the Problem of Child Labour?', Honours Degree Thesis, Department of Economics, University of Wollongong.

NLI (1992a) *Child Labour in the Brassware Industry of Moradabad.* Noida: NLI.

NLI (1992b) Special Issue on Child Labour Legislation, *Awards Digest*, 18, 3, March–June.

NLI (1993) *Child Labour in the Match Industry of Sivakasi.* Noida: NLI.

Noël, A. (1995) 'The Politics of Workfare' in A. Sayeed (ed.), *Workfare: Does it Work? Is it Fair?*, pp. 39–74. Montreal: Institute for Research on Public Policy.

Noll, W. (1995) 'The Promotion of Business Activities in the Context of Structural Policy in North Rhine Westphalia' in Critcher, Schubert and Waddington, (1995) (q.v.).

Nordiska Metall (1993) *Nordiska Metalls Policy. Policydokument angående lagar och avtal, industripolitik, miljö och kompetensutveckling samt samarbetsavtal och gemensamma mål för de nordiska fackförbunden inom metallindustrin.*

Nordiska Ministerrådet (1991) *Nordens internationella konkurrenskraft – seminarierapport om framtida industristrategier i Norden*. Nordiske Seminar- og arbejdsrapporter, No. 528, Nordisk Ministerråd.

O'Connell Davidson, J. (1996) *The Sex Exploiter*, background paper to the World Congress Against the Commercial Sexual Exploitation of Children, Stockholm, August.

O'Connell Davidson, J. (1998) *Prostitution, Power and Freedom*. Cambridge: Polity.

O'Connell Davidson, J. and J. Sanchez Taylor (1998) 'Fantasy Islands: Exploring the Demand for Sex Tourism', paper presented to Conference on The Working Sex: Caribbean Development, Tourism, Sex and Work, Kingston, Jamaica, 16 and 17 July.

OECD (1990) *Labour Market Policies for the 1990s*. Paris: OECD.

OECD (1994) 'Labour Standards and Economic Integration' in *Employment Outlook*, July. Paris: OECD.

Offe, C. (1985) *Disorganized Capitalism*. Cambridge: Polity.

Offe, C. and H. Wiesenthal (1985) 'Two Logics of Collective Action' in C. Offe, *Disorganised Capitalism. Contemporary Transformations of Work and Politics*. Cambridge: Polity.

Ogden, M. (1992) 'Union Initiatives to Restructure Industry in Australia' in P. Adler (ed.), *Technology and the Future of Work*. New York: OUP.

Ogden, M. (1993) *Towards Best Practice Unionism: The Future of Unions in Australia*. Sydney: Pluto.

O'Grady, R. (1994) *The Rape of the Innocent*. New Zealand: Pace.

Ohmae, K. (1995) *The End of the Nation State: The Rise of Regional Economies*. New York: Free Press.

Østergård, U. (1997) 'The Geopolitics of Nordic Identity – From Composite States to Nation States' in Sørensen and Stråth (1997a) (q.v.).

Panitch, L. (1981) 'Trade Unions and the Capitalist State', *New Left Review*, 125, 21–44.

Panitch, L. (1994) 'Globalisation and the State', *Socialist Register 1994*, 60–93.

Parker, M. (1994) *The Politics of Coal's Decline: The Industry in Western Europe*. London: Royal Institute of Economic Affairs.

Parker, M. and J. Slaughter (1988) 'Management by Stress', *Technology Review*, **91**, 7, 37–44.

Parry, D. J. (1996) 'Regenerating Local Economies: A Comparative Analysis of Three UK Coal Areas', M.Phil. thesis, Sheffield Hallam University.

Pattullo, P. (1996) *Last Resorts: The Cost of Tourism in the Caribbean*. London: Latin America Bureau.

Pavetti, L. (1993) 'The Dynamics of Welfare and Work: Exploring the Process by which Women Work their Way off Welfare', Ph.D. Thesis, Ann Arbor, MI: UMI Dissertation Services.

PCEK/T (Pappas; Carter; Evans; Koop/Telesis) (1990) *The Global Challenge: Australian Manufacturing in the 1990s*. Melbourne: Australian Manufacturing Council.

Peck, J. (1994) 'Regulating Labour: The Social Regulation and Reproduction of Local Labour Markets' in Amin and Thrift (eds) (1994) (q.v.).

Peck, J. (1996) *Work-Place: The Social Regulation of Labor Markets*. New York: Guilford.

Peck, J. (1998a) 'New Labourers? Making a New Deal for the "Workless Class" ', paper to the Royal Geographical Society Annual Conference, Guildford, 5–8 January.

Peck, J. (1998b) 'Postwelfare Massachusetts', *Economic Geography*, **17**, 5, 535–66.

Peck, J. (1998c) 'Workfare: a geopolitical etymology', *Society and Space*, **16**, 1, 133–61.

Peck, J. (1999) *Workfare States*. New York: Guilford.

Peck, J. and A. Tickell (1992) 'Local Modes of Social Regulation? Regulation Theory, Thatcherism and Uneven Development', *Geoforum*, **23**, 3, 347–63.

Peck, J. and Y. Miyamachi (1994) 'Regulating Japan? Regulation Theory versus the Japanese Experience', *Environment and Planning D: Society and Space*, **12**, 639–74.

Peck, J. and A. Tickell (1994) 'Searching for a New Institutional Fix: The After-Fordist Crisis and the Global-Local Disorder' in A. Amin (ed.) (1994), *Post-Fordism: A Reader*. Oxford: Blackwell.

Pekkarinen, J., M. Pohjola and B. Rowthorn (eds) (1992a) *Social Corporatism: A Superior Economic System?*. Oxford: Clarendon.

Pekkarinen, J., M. Pohjola and B. Rowthorn (1992b) 'Social Corporatism and Economic Performance: Introduction and Conclusions' in Pekkarinen, Pohjola and Rowthorn (eds) (1992a) (q.v.).

Pempel, T. and K. Tsunekawa (1979) 'Corporatism Without Labour? Japanese Anomaly' in P. Schmitter and G. Lehmbruch (eds) (1979), *Trends Towards Corporatist Intermediation*. London: Sage.

Penttinen, R. (1994) 'Summary of the Critique of Porter's Diamond Model. Porter's Diamond Model Modified to Suit the Finnish Paper and Board Machine Industry', ETLA Discussion Papers, No. 42. Helsinki: ETLA.

Pestoff, V. (1991) 'Den svenska modellens nedgång och det organiserade näringslivets uppgång som en betydande politisk aktör' in T. Kauppinen and V. Köykkä, *Arbetsmarknadssystem och det politiska systemwet 2000. Framtid och historia i Finland och Sverige*, Arbetspolitisk forskning 17, Arbetsministeriet, Helsingfors.

Petrella, R. (1995) 'Europe Between Competitive Innovation and a New Social Contract', *International Social Science Journal*, 143, 11–23.

Philpott, J. (1997) 'Lessons from America: Workfare and Labour's New Deal' in Deacon (ed.) (1997) (q.v.), pp. 65–78.

Picciotto, S. (1991) 'The Internationalisation of Capital and the International State System' in S. Clarke (ed.), *The State Debate*. London: Macmillan.

Picciotto, S. (1996) 'The Regulatory Criss-Cross: Interaction between Jurisdictions and the Construction of Global Regulatory Networks' in W. Bratton, J. McCahery, S. Picciotto and C. Scott (eds), *International Regulatory Competition and Co-ordination:*

Perspectives on Economic Regulation in Europe and the United States. Oxford: Clarendon.

Pickering, D. (1995) 'British Coal Enterprise' in Critcher, Schubert and Waddington (eds) (1995) (q.v.).

Piven, F. F. and R. A. Cloward (1993) *Regulating the Poor: The Functions of Public Welfare*. 2nd edn. New York: Vintage.

Plant, R. (1987) *Sugar and Modern Slavery*. London: Zed Books.

Pontusson, J. (1992a) *The Limits of Social Democracy. Investment Politics in Sweden*. Ithaca and New York: Cornell University Press.

Pontusson, J. (1992b) 'At the End of the Third Road: Swedish Social Democracy in Crisis', *Politics and Society*, **20**, 3, 305–32.

Pontusson, J. (1997) 'Between Neo-liberalism and the German Model: Swedish Capitalism in Transition' in C. Crouch and W. Streeck (eds) (1997), *Political Economy of Modern Capitalism: Mapping Convergence and Diversity*. London: Sage.

Porter, M. E. (1990) *The Competitive Advantage of Nations*. London: Macmillan.

Preiss, B. (1993) 'From Centralised to Decentralised Pay Bargaining in the Public Sector: Lessons from the Australian Experience' in OECD, *Pay Flexibility in the Public Sector*. Paris: OECD.

Price, J. (1997) *Japan Works: Power and Paradox in Postwar Industrial Relations*. Ithaca: Cornell UP.

PRO CAB 129/087, 'Wages, Prices and the Pound Sterling', memo from Thorneycroft, 27 April 1957.

PRO CAB 129/105, 'Economic Growth and National Efficiency', 10 July 1961.

PRO T236/3242, 'Setting the Pound Free', memo by Cherwell to Churchill, 18 March 1952.

PRO T267/8, 'The Government and Wages 1945–51'.

PRO T267/9, 'The Government and Wages 1951–55'.

PRO T267/10, 'The Government and Wages 1956–1960'.

PRO T267/12, 'Policy to Control the Level of Demand 1953–58', Treasury Historical Memorandum No. 8, July 1965.

PRO T267/28, 'A Special Study of Government Incomes Policy'.

Proctor, S. (1993) 'Floating Convertibility: The Emergence of the Robot Plan, 1951–52', *Contemporary Record*, **7**, 1, 24–43.

Pusey, M. (1991) *Economic Rationalism in Canberra: A Nation-Building State Changes Its Mind*. Sydney: Cambridge University Press.

Radda Barnen (1996) 'Daughters are Worth a Fortune in the Brothels of Bangladesh', *Barnen Och Vi*, special feature issue. Stockholm: Radda Barnen.

Radice, H. (1997) 'The Question of Globalization', *Competition and Change*, **2**, 2, 247–58.

Ramsay, H. (1997) 'Solidarity at Last? International Trade Unionism Approaching the Millennium', *Economic and Industrial Democracy*, **18**, 4, 503–38.

Ravenhill, J. (1994) 'Australia and the Global Economy' in S. Bell and B. Head (eds)

(1994), *State, Economy and Public Policy in Australia.* Melbourne: Melbourne University Press.

Rawson, D. (1986) 2nd edn. *Unions and Unionists in Australia.* North Sydney: Allen and Unwin.

Rector, R. and P. Butterfield (1987) *Reforming Welfare: The Promises and Limits of Workfare,* Backgrounder, No. 585. Washington, DC: Heritage Foundation.

Regini, M. (1997) 'Still Engaging in Corporatism? Recent Italian Experience in Comparative Perspective', *European Journal of Industrial Relations,* **3**, 3, 259–78.

Rehn, O. (1996) 'Corporatism and Industrial Competitiveness in Small European States: Austria, Finland and Sweden, 1945–95', D.Phil. Thesis, University of Oxford.

Reich, R. (1994) 'International Labour Standards and Global Economic Integration', Keynote address as US Labor Secretary at a symposium on this issue, 25 April, Washington DC.

Riccio, J., D. Friedlander and S. Freedman (1994) *GAIN: Benefits, Costs, and Three-Year Impacts of a Welfare-to-Work Program.* New York: Manpower Demonstration Research Corporation.

Riverside County DPSS (1994) *Transferability Package for High Output Job Placement Results.* Riverside, CA: Riverside County DPSS.

Robertson, R. (1992) *Globalization: Social Theory and Global Culture.* London: Sage.

Robertson, R. (1995) 'Glocalization: Time-space and homogeneity-heterogeneity' in M. Featherstone, S. Lash and R. Roberston (eds), *Global Modernities.* London: Sage.

Rosenberg, J. (1993) *The Empire of Civil Society.* London: Verso.

Rowthorn, R. (1992) 'Centralisation, Employment and Wage Dispersion', *Economic Journal,* **102**, 2, 506–23.

Rozario, R. (1988) *Trafficking in Women and Children in India.* New Dehli: Uppal.

Rubery, J. and C. Fagan (1995) 'Gender Segregation in Societal Context', *Work, Employment and Society,* **9**, 2, 213–40.

Rueschemeyer, D. and P. Evans (1985) 'The State and Economic Transformation: Toward an Analysis of the Conditions Underlying Effective Intervention' in P. Evans, D. Rueschemeyer and T. Skocpol (eds), *Bringing the State Back In.* Cambridge: CUP.

Ruigrok, W. and R. van Tulder (1995) *The Logic of International Restructuring.* London: Routledge.

Rukstad, M. (1989) *Macroeconomic Decision Making in the World Economy.* London: Dryen.

Sabel, C. (1994) 'Flexible Specialisation and the Re-emergence of Regional Economies' in A. Amin (ed.) (1994), *Post-Fordism: A Reader.* Oxford: Blackwell.

Sadler, D. (1992) *The Global Region: Production, State Policies and Uneven Development.* Oxford: Pergamon.

Safa, H. (1997) 'Where the Big Fish eat the Little Fish: Women's Work in the Free-Trade Zones', *NACLA Report on the Americas,* **30**, 5, March, 31–6.

Sako, M. and H. Sato (eds) (1997) *Japanese Labour and Management in Transition.* London: Routledge.

Salt, H. (1995) 'Regenerating the Dearne Valley in South Yorkshire' in Critcher, Schubert and Waddington (eds) (1995) (q.v.).

Sandholtz, W. (1993) 'Choosing Union: Monetary Politics and Maastricht', *International Organisation*, **47**, 1, 1–39.

Sassen, S. (1991) *The Global City: New York, London, Tokyo.* Princeton: Princeton University Press.

Sawyer, R. (1986) *Slavery in the Twentieth Century.* London: Routledge and Kegan Paul.

Scheuer, S. (1992) 'Denmark: Return to Decentralisation' in Ferner and Hyman (eds) (1992a) (q.v.).

Schiller, B. (1988) *Samarbete eller konflikt.* Stockholm: Arbetsmiljöfonden.

Schiller, B. (1989) 'En skandinavisk demokratimodell inför framtiden' in *Saltsjöbadsavtalet 50 år. Forskare och parter begrundar en epok 1938–1988.* Stockhom: Arbetslivscentrum.

Schiller, B. (1994) 'The Future of the Nordic Model of Labour Relations' in *The Future of the Nordic Model of Labour Relations – Three Reports on Internationalisation and Industrial Relations*, Nord 1993:36. Århus: Nordic Council of Ministers.

Schmidt, V. A. (1995) 'The New World Order, Incorporated', *Daedalus*, **124**, 2, 75–106.

Schmitter, P. (1979) 'Still the Century of Corporatism?' in P. Schmitter and G. Lehmbruch (eds) (1979) *Trends Towards Corporatist Intermediation.* London: Sage.

Schram, S. F. (1995) *Words of Welfare: The Poverty of Social Science and the Social Science of Poverty.* Minneapolis: University of Minnesota Press.

Schubert, K. and M. Brautigam (1995) 'Coal Policy in Germany: How Durable is the Model of Consensus?' in Critcher, Schubert and Waddington (eds) (1995) (q.v.).

Sengenberger, W. and F. Wilkinson (1995) 'Globalization and Labour Standards' in J. Michie and J. Grieve Smith (eds), *Managing the Global Economy.* Oxford: OUP.

SERC (1996) *Workplace Relations and Other Legislation Bill (No. 2)*, Report No. 1235 (Tabled to Australian Senate11/12/96).

Shragge, E. (ed.) (1997) *Workfare: Ideology for a New Underclass.* Toronto: Garamond Press.

Sihto, M. (1994) *Aktiivinen työvoimapolitiikka. Kehitys Rehnin-Meidnerin mallista OECD:n strategiaksi.* Tampere University Press.

Silbert, M. and A. Pines (1981) 'Sexual Abuse as an Antecedent to Prostitution', *Child Abuse and Neglect*, **5**, 407–11.

Silvestre, E., J. Rijo and H. Bogaert (1994) *La Neo-prostitucion Infantil en Republica Dominicana.* Santa Domingo: UNICEF.

Singleton, G. (1990) *The Accord and the Australian Labour Movement.* Melbourne: Melbourne University Press.

Sisson, K. (1996) *Closing the Gap, Ideas and Practice. Direct Participation in Organizational Change.* Dublin: EPOC.

Sklair, L. (1995) *Sociology of the Global System*. 2nd edn. Hemel Hempstead: Prentice Hall.

Smith, C. and T. Elger (1997) 'International Competition, Inward Investment and the Restructuring of European Work and Industrial Relations', *European Journal of Industrial Relations*, **3**, 3, 279–304.

Smith, D. (1993) *From Boom to Bust*. London: Penguin.

Snell, D. L. (1997) 'Graziers, Butchers, Boners and the Impact of Globalization on Australian Beef Production', Ph.D. Thesis, University of Warwick.

Social Europe. 1995, 2.

Sørensen Ø. and B. Stråth (eds) (1997a) *The Cultural Construction of Norden*. Oslo: Scandinavian University Press.

Sørensen Ø. and B. Stråth (1997b) 'Introduction: The Cultural Construction of Norden' in Sørensen and Stråth (eds) (1997a) (q.v.).

Soskice, D. (1990) 'Wage Determination: the Changing Role of Institutions in Advanced Industrialized Economies', *Oxford Review of Economic Policy*, **6**, 4, 1–23.

SOU (1992) *Kompetensutveckling – en nationell strategi. Slutbetänkande från kompetensutredningen*, SOU, 1992:7. Stockholm.

Standing, G. (1990) 'The Road to Workfare: Alternative to Welfare or Threat to Occupation?', *International Labour Review*, 129, 677–91.

Standing, G. (1997) 'Globalization, Labour Flexibility and Insecurity: the Era of Market Regulation', *European Journal of Industrial Relations*, **3**, 1, 7–37.

Stegman, T. (1993) 'Aggregate Investment and its Sectoral Composition: The Failure of the Restructuring Policy' in G. Mahoney (ed.), *The Australian Economy under Labour*. Sydney: Allen and Unwin.

Steingraber, W. (1995) 'The Campaign for the Future of Coal Mining Areas' in Critcher, Schubert and Waddington (eds) (1995) (q.v.).

Stenius, H. (1997) 'The Good Life is Life of Conformity: The Impact of Lutheran Tradition on Nordic Political Culture' in Sørensen and Stråth (eds) (1997a) (q.v.).

Stephens, J. (1979) *The Transition from Capitalism to Socialism*. London: Macmillan.

Stewart, R. (1990) 'Industrial Policy' in C. Jennet and R. Stewart (eds) (1990), *Hawke and Australian Public Policy: Consensus and Restructuring*. Melbourne: Macmillan.

Stilwell, F. (1986) *The Accord: And Beyond*. Sydney: Pluto.

Stilwell, F. (1991) 'Wages Policy and the Accord', *Journal of Australian Political Economy*, 28, 27–53.

Stimson, J. (1985) 'Regression in Time and Space: a Statistical Essay', *American Journal of Political Science*, 29, 6, 914–47.

Stone, K. V. W. (1996) 'Labour in the Global Economy: Four Approaches to Transnational Labour Regulation' in W. Bratton, J. McCahery, S. Picciotto and C. Scott (eds), *International Regulatory Competition and Co-ordination: Perspectives on Economic Regulation in Europe and the United States*. Oxford: Clarendon.

Strange, S. (1994) *States and Markets*. London: Pinter.

Strange, S. (1996) *The Retreat of the State.* Cambridge: CUP.

Strange, S. (1997) 'The Future of Global Capitalism; or, Will Divergence Persist for Ever?' in C. Crouch and W. Streeck (eds) (1997), *Political Economy of Modern Capitalism: Mapping Convergence and Diversity.* London: Sage.

Streeck, W. (1984) 'Neo-corporatist Industrial Relations and the Economic Crisis in West Germany' in J. H. Goldthorpe (ed.), *Order and Conflict in Contemporary Capitalism.* Oxford: Clarendon.

Streeck, W. (1992a) *Social Institutions and Economic Performance: Studies in Industrial Relations in Advanced Capitalist Economies.* London: Sage.

Streeck, W. (1992b) 'National Diversity, Regime Competition and Institutional Deadlock: Problems in Forming a European Industrial Relations System', *Journal of Public Policy,* **12**, 4, 301–30.

Streeck, W. (1997) 'German Capitalism: Does it Exist? Can it Survive?' in C. Crouch and W. Streeck (eds) (1997), *Political Economy of Modern Capitalism: Convergence and Diversity.* London: Sage.

Stretton, H. (1986) *Political Essays.* Melbourne, Georgian House.

Strøby Jensen, C., J. Due and J. S. Madsen. (1994) 'The Scandinavian Model in Europe – The Choice of IR-roles for the Labour Market Parties at National and EU Levels' in Kauppinen and Köykkä (eds) (1994) (q.v.).

Strøby Jensen, C., J. S. Madsen and J. Due (1995) 'A Role for a Pan-European Trade Union Movement? – Possibilities in European IR-Regulation', *Industrial Relations Journal,* **26**, 1, 4–18.

Sturdevant, S. and B. Stoltzfus (1992) *Let the Good Times Roll: Prostitution and the US Military in Asia.* New York: The New Press.

Sutton, A. (1994) *Slavery in Brazil.* London: Anti-Slavery International.

Suzuki, A.1998. 'Union Politics in Hard Times: The Restructuring of 'Japanese-style Employment Relations'' and the Internal Politics of the Japanese Labor Movement in the 1990s', International Sociological Association, XIVth World Congress of Sociology. Montreal, July.

Swift, J. (1995) *Wheel of Fortune: Work and Life in an Age of Falling Expectations.* Toronto: Between the Lines.

Sykes, T. (1994) *The Bold Riders: Behind Australia's Corporate Collapses.* Sydney: Allen and Unwin.

Tanner, M. (1996) *The End of Welfare: Fighting Poverty in the Civil Society.* Washington, DC: Cato Institute.

Theodore, N. C. (1998a) 'On Parallel Paths: The Clinton/Blair Agenda and the New Geopolitics of Workfare', paper to the Royal Geographical Society Annual Conference, Guildford, 5–8 January.

Theodore, N. C. (1998b) 'Welfare to What? Job Availability and Welfare Reform in the US', *Working Brief,* February, 18–20.

Therborn, G. (1992) 'Lessons from "Corporatist" Theorizations' in Pekkarinen, Pohjola and Rowthorn (eds) (1992) (q.v.).

REFERENCES

Therborn, G. (1995) *European Modernity and Beyond: The Trajectory of European Societies, 1945–2000*. London: Sage.

Thomas, R. and R. Faist (1992) *Social Consequences of Coal Restructuration in the European Community's Countries*. Paris: Enterprise et Personnel.

Thompson, H. (1995) 'Globalisation, Monetary Autonomy and Central Bank Independence' in J. Lovenduski and P. Stanyer (eds), *Contemporary Political Studies 3*. Exeter: PSA.

Thompson, H. (1996) *The British Conservative Government and the European Exchange Rate Mechanism 1979–1994*. London: Pinter.

Tickell, A. and J. Peck (1995) 'Social Regulation after Fordism: Regulation Theory, Neo-Liberalism and the Global-Local Nexus', *Economy and Society*, **24**, 3, 357–86.

Tiratsoo, N. and J. Tomlinson (1993) *Industrial Efficiency and State Intervention*. London: Routledge.

Tolliday, S. and J. Zeitlin (1986a) 'Introduction: Between Fordism and Flexibility' in S. Tolliday and J. Zeitlin (eds), *The Automobile Industry and its Workers*. Cambridge: Polity.

Tolliday, S. and J. Zeitlin (1986b) 'Shopfloor Bargaining, Contract Unionism and Job Control' in Tolliday and Zeitlin (eds) (1986a) (q.v.).

Tomlinson, J. (1981) 'Why Was There Never a Keynesian Revolution in Economic Policy?', *Economy and Society*, **10**, 1, 72–87.

Tooze, R. (1997) 'International Political Economy in an Age of Globalization' in J. Bayliss and S. Smith (eds), *The Globalization of World Politics*. Oxford: OUP.

Touraine, A. (1995) *Critique of Modernity*. Oxford: Blackwell.

Trägårdh, L. (1997) 'Statist Individualism: On the Culturality of the Nordic' in Sørensen and Stråth (eds) (1997a) (q.v.).

Truong, T. (1990) *Sex, Money and Morality: Prostitution and Tourism in Southeast Asia*. London: Zed Books.

Turner, I. (1978) *In Union is Strength*. Melbourne: Nelson.

Turner, R. (1993) *Regenerating the Coalfields*. Aldershot: Avebury.

US Department of State (1994) 'International Labour Standards and the GATT/WTO', presented to the Committee on External Relations, European Parliament, 29 March.

Valenzuela, J. (1992) 'Labour Movements and Political Systems: Some Variations' in M. Regini (ed.), *The Future of Labour Movements*. London: Sage.

Van Dormael, A. (1997) *The Power of Money*. London: Macmillan.

Van Ruysseveldt, J. and J. Visser (eds) (1996a) *Industrial Relations In Europe: Traditions and Transitions*. London: Sage.

Van Ruysseveldt, J. and J. Visser (1996b) 'Contestation and State Intervention for Ever: Industrial Relations in France' in Van Ruysseveldt and Visser (eds) (1996a) (q.v.).

Vazquez, J. A. and I. Del Rosal (1995) 'The Effects of and Responses to Pit Closure in the

Asturias Region', unpublished report. Communications, Media and Communities Research Centre, Sheffield Hallam University.

Venneslan, K. (1990) 'Industrielt demokrati i Norden. Redogjørelse for det norske delprosjektet' in D. Fleming, *Industriel demokrati i Norden*. Lund.

Venneslan, K. and H. J. Ågotnes. (1994) 'Transnationalisation and Participation' in *The Future of the Nordic Model of Labour Relations – Three Reports on Internationalisation and Industrial Relations*, Nord, 1993:36. Århus: Nordic Council of Ministers.

Vijayagopalan, S. (1993) *Child Labour in the Carpet Industry: A Status Report*. New Delhi: National Council of Applied Economic Research.

Visser, J. (1996) 'Corporatism Beyond Repair? Industrial Relations in Sweden' in Van Ruysseveldt and Visser (eds) (1996a) (q.v.).

Visser, J. (1998) 'Two Cheers for Corporatism, One for the Market: Industrial Relations, Wage Moderation and Job Growth in the Netherlands', *British Journal of Industrial Relations*, **36**, 2, 269–92.

Vosko, L. F. (1998a) 'Regulating Precariousness? The Temporary Employment Relationship Under the NAFTA and the EC Treaty', *Relations Industrielles*, **53**, 1, 123–53.

Vosko, L. F. (1998b) ' "Workfare Temporaries": The Rise of the Temporary Employment Relationship, the Decline of the Standard Employment Relationship and the Feminization of Employment in Canada', paper to the Gender, Work and Organisation Conference, Manchester, 9 January.

Vulliamy, E. (1997) 'Banned Imports Made by Children', *Sydney Morning Herald*, 3 October, p. 13.

Waddington, J. (1999) *Globalization and Labour Resistance*. London: Mansell.

Wade, R. (1996) 'Japan, the World Bank, and the Art of Paradigm Maintenance: *The East Asian Miracle* in Political Perspective', *New Left Review*, 217, 3–36.

Wagner, F. (1995) 'Land Reclamation and Economic Restructuring in North Rhine Westphalia' in Critcher, Schubert and Waddington (eds) (1995) (q.v.).

Walkowitz, C. (1980) *Prostitution and Victorian Society: Women, Class and the State*. Cambridge: CUP.

Waltz, K. (1979) *Theory of International Politics*. Reading, Mass.: Addison Wesley.

Wanna, J. (1992) 'Furthering Business Interests: Business Associations and Political Representation' in Bell and Wanna (eds) (1992) (q.v.).

Warhurst, J. (1982) *Jobs or Dogma*. St Lucia: University of Queensland Press.

Waterman, P. (1998) *Globalization, Social Movements and the New Internationalisms*. London: Mansell.

Weiss, L. (1997) 'Globalization and the Myth of the Powerless State', *New Left Review*, 125, 3–28.

Weiss, L. (1998a) *The Myth of the Powerless State*. Cambridge: Polity.

Weiss, L. (1998b) 'Developmental States in Transition: Adapting, Innovating, Recomposing not "Normalising" ', paper to Conference on 'Beyond Liberalisation:

Making Economic Policy in Europe and the Asia Pacific', Florence, 15–16 October.

Western, B. (1995) 'A Comparative Study of Working Class Disorganisation: Union Decline in Eighteen Advanced Capitalist Democracies', *American Sociological Review*, **60**, 2, 179–201.

Whitehouse, G. (1992) 'Legislation and Labour Market Gender Inequality: an Analysis of OECD Countries', *Work, Employment and Society*, **6**, 1, 65–86.

Whitehouse, G. (1995) 'Employment Equity and Labour Organisation: The Comparative Political Economy of Women and Work', Ph.D. Dissertation, University of Queensland.

Whitley, R. (ed.) (1992a) *European Business Systems: Firms and Markets in their National Contexts*. London: Sage.

Whitley, R. (1992b) *Business Systems in East Asia*. London: Sage.

Wilks, S. (1996) 'Class Compromise and the International Economy: The Rise and Fall of Swedish Social Democracy', *Capital and Class*, 58, 89–111.

Williams, K., C. Haslam and J. Williams (1992) 'Ford versus Fordism; The Beginnings of Mass Production?', *Work, Employment and Society*, **6**, 4, 517–55.

Willis, R. (1988) *Labour Market Reform: The Industrial Relations Agenda*. Budget Papers, No. 9. Canberra: AGPS.

Winner, L. (1995) 'Citizen Virtues in a Technological Order' in A. Feenberg and A. Hannay (eds), *Technology and the Politics of Knowledge*. Indiana University Press.

Witt, S. (1990) *When the Pit Closes*. Barnsley: Coalfield Communities Campaign.

Wolf, M. (1997) 'Far from Powerless', *Financial Times*, 13 May.

Womack, J. R., D. T. Jones and D. Roos (1990) *The Machine that Changed the World*. New York: Rawson.

Wood, A. (1994) *North–South Trade, Employment and Inequality*. Oxford: Clarendon.

INDEX